Lonely Planet

JOURNEY
Orient Express

Simon Richmond, Virginia Maxwell,
Helena Smith, Becki Enright, Kata Fári, Mary Winston Nicklin,
Leonid Ragozin, Monica Suma

Contents

Plan Your Trip

- My Orient Express 4
- Thrilling Destinations 8
- Mountains, Lakes & Seas 12
- Tastes & Toasts 18
- Splendid Architecture 22
- A History of the Orient Express 26
- 6 Ways to do the Orient Express 30

Go to p32 for the full route map

The Ride

CLASSIC ORIENT EXPRESS

- City Guide: Paris 36
- Paris to Munich 46
- City Guide: Munich 62
- Munich to Vienna 70
- City Guide: Vienna 84
- Vienna to Budapest 92
- City Guide: Budapest 106
- Budapest to Bucharest 114
- City Guide: Bucharest 134
- Bucharest to Sofia 142
- City Guide: Sofia 158
- Sofia to İstanbul 164
- City Guide: İstanbul 178

THE SIMPLON ROUTE

- Paris to Venice 192
- City Guide: Venice 206
- Venice to Budapest 214

THE ARLBERG ROUTE

- Paris to Vienna 226

INSIGHT ESSAYS

- Your Orient Express Reading List 60
- The Future of the Orient Express 82
- Europe's Imagined East 130
- Brief Encounters 162
- The Ghosts of the Taurus Express 188

Wien Hauptbahnhof, Vienna (p81)

- Orient Express Revivals 240
- Beyond the Orient Express 246

Toolkit

- First Time 252
- Money 253
- On the Rails 254
- Access, Attitudes & Safety 259
- Where to Stay 260
- Responsible Travel 262
- Language 264

Previous page: SBB train travels through Lavaux Vineyard Terraces (p199)

My Orient Express

Simon Richmond @simonrichmond

My European rail adventures are varied and span decades. However, until I researched this book, I had not travelled entirely by rail from Paris to İstanbul – and what a pleasure it was to achieve that goal! Over 25 days I hopped on and off 26 different trains, including five sleeper trains and a narrow-gauge steam train. There were many memorable experiences en route, but what gave me most pleasure was meeting people and making new friends, including a Korean woman and her dog, a hospitable Hungarian journalist and a pair of idealistic Serbian teenagers on their first overland adventure (p162). *Simon is a guidebook writer who has worked for Lonely Planet for over 25 years. He wrote the first edition of the company's* Trans-Siberian Railway *as well as the one (and only) edition of* İstanbul to Kathmandu.

Simon Richmond with the 0km marker, Gare de l'Est, Paris (p50)

MY JOURNEY HIGHLIGHTS

Gellért Baths
Relaxing in the thermal waters of Budapest's most gorgeous art nouveau bathing halls. p112

Varna
Strolling through this Bulgarian resort's bucolic Primorski Park, then taking a dip in the Black Sea. p150

Priem am Chiemsee
Riding a vintage steam train and sailing to Herreninsel to tour Ludwig II's amazing, unfinished palace. p76

Virginia Maxwell @maxwellvirginia

Having travelled extensively on French and Italian trains, I know how comfortable and efficient they are. When I set out on this research trip, I assumed all of my train journeys would be similar. Silly me. Paris to Trieste was problem-free, but soon a European heatwave hit, causing major hiccups. Service cancellations and delays ensued, and when trains were operating, they were often old, slow and as hot as Hades. Despite this, the trip was marvellous, with so many rich experiences along the way. I can't wait to do it again – but next time, it won't be in high summer!

An enthusiastic train traveller, Virginia has authored multiple editions of Lonely Planet's Italy *and* Türkiye *guidebooks. For this book, she researched and wrote the two Simplon route chapters and the Venice and İstanbul city guides.*

Top: Virginia Maxwell; Below: Helena Smith

MY BEST COFFEE STOPS

Le Train Bleu
Pre-departure coffee in belle époque surrounds. p196

Caffè Florian
Gorgeous Piazza San Marco cafe that opened in Venice in 1720. p212

Trieste
Perennially popular historic cafes. p220

Helena Smith @helenasmithpix

Interrailing was a rite of passage for me as a student: hazy night journeys, emerging dazzled into unknown cities and eating supermarket bread and cheese to eke out a meagre budget. I've continued to travel by train across Europe, and loved exploring this most resonantly named journey: the Orient Express. I covered the Arlberg route from Paris through Switzerland and into Austria, where the Alpine views and dizzy gradients were astonishing. I now can't wait to follow in the train tracks of my fellow authors, and go all the way to İstanbul.

Helena is a writer and photographer specialising in slow and eco travel. She wrote the Arlberg route section of this book. Helena grew up in Scotland and Malawi, which gave her a lifelong love of wild places.

MY BEST WATER EXPERIENCES

Rhine, Basel
Floating downriver with a crowd. p230

Frauenbad, Zürich
Dipping into a women-only bathing house. p233

Zürichsee & Walansee
Travelling along the bright waters on the train. p232

MY ORIENT EXPRESS

Becki Enright @bordersofadventure

Browse Vienna's timeline in the Roman ruins in Michaelerplatz, the medieval alleyways, courtyards and market squares spreading around Stephansdom, the imperial history-cached palatial halls and in the neighbourhood pockets of a modern metropolis woven around it all. Beyond exploring my adopted home city, you'll find me at the train station, setting off for another train trip in Europe.

Becki is a travel writer and guidebook author based in Vienna, where she has lived for over a decade.

Kata Fári @kata.fari

I love train journeys because they offer a rare kind of stillness in motion – you're rushing towards the exciting unexpected, yet completely unhurried. Traversing Europe's landscapes is an especially splendid experience, though after all that sitting, there's nothing more relaxing than soaking your stiff muscles in mineral-rich thermal waters at one of Budapest's elegant bathhouses – lucky you!

Kata Fári is a Budapest-based writer singing the praises of the world's best places.

Mary Winston Nicklin
marywinstonnicklin.com

As a longtime Paris resident, I can't think of a better place to start an epic train journey. The city offers a feast of fun cultural experiences – art! music! food! – not to mention its beautiful architecture and multi-layered history. When it comes to France's fast and efficient rail network, I've sometimes found myself booking a train just for the trip itself.

Mary Winston Nicklin is a Franco-American writer and editor based on the Left Bank of Paris.

Leonid Ragozin @leonidragozin

As an author of the Lonely Planet guide to Bulgaria and Romania, I've spent much time on the Orient Express route in these countries. Getting off the train in Sofia in the morning, taking a tram to the centre and treating myself to a sumptuous breakfast at Fabrika Daga (p160) has become one of my most enjoyable routines.

Leonid has co-authored multiple guidebooks, but is mainly a political journalist. For the last decade he has largely focused on the war in Ukraine.

Monica Suma @monicasuma

Growing up in historic Bucharest, I love playing hide and seek with late 19th-century architectural gems, peeking behind Belle Époque mansions in search of serendipitous garden bars. It's what I most missed while living abroad for almost a decade. Train travel is such a gift, especially arriving into monumental stations like Milano Centrale.

Monica is a regular writer for Lonely Planet and contributor to TIME, National Geographic, *airBaltic and many more.*

Tharik Hussain @tharik_hussain

The Orient Express is a powerful symbol of western Europe's gaze; a space where that gaze also has the potential to become blurred, which is why I love cities like Sofia, where Ottoman-era minarets are as much at home as a Byzantine church, making it clear the 'East' is also very much a part of the 'West'.

Tharik is the author of Muslim Europe: A Journey in Search of a Fourteen Hundred Year History, *which explores the Islamic roots of Europe and was published in 2025 by Penguin Viking.*

Oliver Smith @olismithtravel

I visited the Middle East in 2008, and was enraptured by the old Taurus Express stations at Aleppo and Damascus. My tip: French onion soup at Terminus Nord.

Oliver's book On This Holy Island: A Modern Pilgrimage Across Britain *was published in 2024 by Bloomsbury (UK) and Pegasus (US).*

Jon Worth @jonworth.eu

All of the greatest rail adventures happen in southeast Europe – that's where you get unforgettable stories. Stop off in Bucharest – its Palace of the Parliament is a must-see.

Jon is a railway writer and campaigner, working to find political solutions to improve cross-border train connections Europe-wide. #CrossBorderRail.

James Gulliver Hancock @gulliverhancock

I've completed many iconic journeys including the Trans-Siberian Railway and I always have a sketchbook to hand. My 'How Things Work' series spans a wide range of subjects, from space stations to trains.

James drew the illustrated map at the start of this book.

MY ORIENT EXPRESS

Thrilling Destinations

A journey along the original Orient Express routes is your ticket to some of Europe's most historic urban centres.

The Big Hitters

Paris and İstanbul, the western- and easternmost points of the Classic itinerary, are destinations to be savoured. Contrast the grand Haussmann-designed boulevards of the French capital (p36) with the maze of alleys through İstanbul's Grand Bazaar (p178), the creative treasures of the Louvre with those of Topkapı Palace, and sailing in a riverboat along the Seine with ferry-hopping along the Bosphorus Strait and Haliç. Just to scratch the surface of these cities, schedule at least two days in each.

The midpoint break in the journey depends on the route you take. For the Classic (p34) and Arlberg (p226) routes, Vienna (p84) and Budapest (p106) are the obvious choices – you won't regret spending a night in either of these cities. If you're on the Simplon route (p192) via Italy, then Milan (p202) and Venice (p206) are the cities that will be top of the visit list.

Into Eastern Europe

Slower trains and less frequent connections make city stopovers east of Hungary something of a necessity. Memorable experiences await in cities as varied as compact Bratislava (p98), with its eclectic mix of architecture and restored hilltop castle, and sprawling Bucharest (p134), graced with belle époque architecture that makes you realise why it was once compared with Paris. Sofia (p158), Bulgaria's capital, also presents an alluring mix of Roman ruins, Ottoman legacies and socialist-era relics.

Festivals & Performances

Europe's major cities are host to festivities and events throughout the year – consider timing your Orient Express adventure to coincide with

Hungarian State Opera House, Budapest (p108)
CESARE ANDREA FERRARI/SHUTTERSTOCK

one of them. Try the Venice Art Biennale in even-numbered years in February; İstanbul's Music Festival in June; Zürich's techno Street Parade in August; and Oktoberfest in Munich, which runs from mid-September to the first Sunday in October.

With the exception of July and August, when many performing arts companies take a break, it is possible to attend top-quality classical concerts, opera or ballet performances in grand halls such as the Nationaltheater (p68) in Munich, the State Opera House in Vienna and the beautiful Romanian Athenaeum (p138) in Bucharest. If there are no shows scheduled, look into tours of these stately buildings – the Hungarian State Opera House (p108) in Budapest is a stunner and the tours always conclude with a short performance by opera singers. For something different, attend performances by whirling dervishes at İstanbul's Hodjapasha Cultural Centre (p184).

Smaller-Scale Gems

If big cities are not to your travel tastes or budgets, consider smaller, usually cheaper, alternatives. For example, rather than Munich, explore Ulm (p55) or Augsburg (p55); instead of Bucharest, try Braşov (p124) or Sinaia (p126); or swap Sofia for Veliko Tărnovo (p154). Linz (p80) is an alternative to Vienna or Salzburg, or choose Padua (p204) or Trieste (p218) over Venice. And for Ottoman vibes without the crowds of İstanbul, detour to Edirne (p172).

GRAND HOTELS

When its trains proved a hit, Compagnie Internationale des Wagons-Lits (CIWL) began to invest in grand hotels for their passengers, starting in 1894 with the Pera Palace (p187) in İstanbul. Along the Simplon route passengers could – and can still – stay at the 1861 Beau-Rivage Palace Hotel (p200) in Lausanne; the 1911 Hotel Savoia Excelsior Palace (p222) in Trieste; and the 1925 Esplanade Hotel (p222; pictured above) in Zagreb.

EURO TRAINS ON SCREEN

Murder on the Orient Express (Sidney Lumet, 1974)
Original Orient Express carriages feature in this star-studded adaptation of Agatha Christie's murder mystery.

Before Sunrise (Richard Linklater, 1995)
After a meet-cute on a train from Budapest, Julie Delpy and Ethan Hawke spend a memorable night exploring Vienna.

From Russia with Love (Terence Young, 1963)
007 battles an assassin on a night train through the Balkans in this movie based on Fleming's spy novel.

HIGHLIGHTS

❶ Paris, p36
Rich in historic architecture, magnificent museums and galleries, and amazing places to eat, drink and shop, France's capital is on a cultural high following its hosting of the 2024 Olympics.

❷ Venice, p206
Nicknamed La Serenissima (the Most Serene), this beguiling, labyrinthine city of islands, canals and palaces has a unique, magical atmosphere steeped in its long history as a centre for world trade.

❸ Vienna, p84
Waltz around the one-time nucleus of the Austro-Hungarian empire, experiencing its majestic buildings, world-class art museums and contemporary culture spaces. Take a breather beside the Danube.

❹ Budapest, p106
Hungary's handsome capital is another city on the Orient Express route that straddles the Danube. Pause here to discover an eclectic range of architecture, party with the locals, and rest and revive in thermal baths.

❺ Plovdiv, p170
Evidence of thousands of years of human habitation are marked by the incredible ruins of Bulgaria's second city and cultural capital, including a 2nd-century CE Roman amphitheatre that's still used for performances.

❻ İstanbul, p178
Europe meets Asia in the former capital of the Byzantine and Ottoman empires. Admire the timeless beauty of historic mosques, haggle in the Grand Bazaar, and catch the breeze on ferries across the Bosphorus.

Mountains, Lakes & Seas

Orient Express vistas include snow-capped mountains, poppy-speckled farm fields, the sparkle of sunlight on mirror-like lakes and breeze-rippled seas.

Through the Alps

A compelling reason for travelling the Orient Express routes is the access they provide to some of the world's most beautiful mountain landscapes. Stretching from France through Switzerland, southern Germany, Austria, Italy and Slovenia, the Alps are truly spectacular.

For 19th-century railway engineers, this 200km barrier of altitude-busting peaks sweeping in an 800km curve across Central Europe posed a formidable, but not unsurmountable, barrier. Decades before the Orient Express' initial run – and thanks to glowing reports by high-profile visitors such as the poet Bryon and painter JMW Turner – the Swiss Alps in particular were already established as a tourist draw.

The most extensive vistas are along the Simplon route (p192). Before you hit the Alps proper, the Jura Mountains mark the border between France and Switzerland. The mountain scenery is sublime east of Bourg-en-Bresse, along the single-track Haut-Bugey line to the hamlet of Bellegarde-sur-Valserine. There are wonderful views from here on past Geneva as the tracks hug the northern shore of Lac Léman (Lake Geneva) on their way to Lausanne and the steeply terraced slopes of the Lavaux wine region.

Our contemporary route avoids the Simplon Tunnel, which is undergoing renovation until 2029, curtailing passenger services. Instead, enjoy blissful panoramas of more Swiss lakes, peaks and wildflower-speckled meadows on a highly scenic detour via Neuchâtel and Zürich to the Italian Lakes district via the Gotthard Base Tunnel.

Trains at Innsbruck (p235)
AARONCHENPS2/SHUTTERSTOCK

The Arlberg route (p226) from Paris via Mulhouse and Basel also takes you into the heart of the Alps. While the Uetliberg to the west of Zürichsee (Lake Zürich) is an alpine pimple at 871m, the peaks get progressively higher and more jagged as you head further east, particularly so in the Churfirsten range alongside Walensee. Altitude is gained from here up into the mountains and through the 10km Arlberg Tunnel to Innsbruck, where a funicular and cable car can whisk you to well over 2000m. On clear days you'll be able to see as far as the 3798m Grossglockner.

If you are travelling the Classic Orient Express route (p34), your encounters with the Alps will be brief but beautiful as you close in on southern Bavaria, the idyllic lake Chiemsee (p74) and the mountain resort of Berchtesgaden (p79).

Sunset on the Adriatic

If you're following the Simplon route, the aquatic delights of Venice await. Contemplate shimmering reflections on canals and the Venetian Lagoon as you ride gondolas, *motoscafi* (water taxis) and *vaporetti* (water buses). Continuing eastward, you'll be treated to more gorgeous views of the Adriatic in the final stretches of the approach to Trieste.

Check with locals in Trieste for where the best spot is for the golden hour and views of the sun dissolving in yellows, oranges and purples into the Adriatic. For example, from November to February, stand on the Ponte Rosso bridge to see the sun reflected in the Grand Canal,

THE DANUBE

From its source in Germany's Black Forest, to its delta branching into the Black Sea in Romania, the Danube flows around 2730km, making it Europe's second-longest waterway after the Volga. For close-up encounters with this constant companion, hop off the train in Ulm, Vienna, Bratislava, Budapest (pictured above) and Ruse. And to learn more about the Danube read *Blue River, Black Sea* by Andrew Eames.

ORIENT EXPRESS TRAVELOGUES

Slow Trains to İstanbul (Tom Chesshyre, 2025)
A British travel writer partly follows the original Orient Express route across Europe.

The Great Railway Bazaar (Paul Theroux, 1975)
Theroux kicks off his global rail adventures on the Direct Orient Express, meeting eccentric characters.

Venice (Jan Morris, 1960)
Classic love letter to Venice. Also superbly evocative is Morris' *Trieste and the Meaning of Nowhere* (2001).

Devín Castle, Bratislava (p100)

BEST BOAT JOURNEYS

Zürich (p232)
Cruise on the Zürichsee between April and December. Larger boats host restaurants serving delicious meals.

Bratislava (p98)
From the Slovak capital sail either up the Danube to Devín Castle or downriver to the Danubiana Meulensteen Art Museum.

İstanbul (p178)
Board a ferry across the Sea of Marmara to reach Asia. For a full day trip, sail up to the mouth of the Black Sea and back to Eminönü.

while in the summer months climb high into the hills for a bird's-eye view of the Gulf of Trieste glowing golden.

Karsts & Lake Balaton

The original Simplon route would have proceeded from Trieste through the Balkans, via Belgrade and Niš, to Sofia – a journey stacked with scenic drama. However, Serbia's poor rail infrastructure and lack of international connections necessitates a contemporary route via Slovenia to Hungary and then through Romania.

From Trieste the tracks loop steeply upwards about 300m from sea level to the Italian–Slovenia border and the Karst region pockmarked with limestone caves, including a stunning complex at Postojna. From this plateau the railway then descends via marshlands towards Ljubljana. The scenic delights don't let up on the train ride to Zagreb, as you pass verdant farmlands with chocolate-box wooden chalets and steep-spired churches.

Trains from Zagreb to Budapest travel via the southern flank of 77km-long Lake Balaton – there will be glimpses of Europe's largest freshwater lake from the left side of the train. If you have time, slower trains via the north side of Balaton, via Balatonfüred, provide better lake views.

Danube & Carpathians

If you're approaching Budapest along the Classic Orient Express route via Bratislava (p98), then you'll end up shadowing the northern side of

The 8.55 to Baghdad (Andrew Eames, 2004)
Eames journeys from London to Iraq by train tracing routes travelled by Agatha Christie.

A Time of Gifts (Patrick Leigh Fermor, 1977)
Along with *Between the Woods and the Water* (1986), this book covers the writer's journey on foot across Europe in the 1930s.

Orient Express: The Life and Times of the World's Most Famous Train (EH Cookridge, 1979)
Historical account packed with tales about famous passengers.

the Danube Bend – one of the most picturesque stretches of the river. The best views of the Danube are from vantage points up high such as from the terraces in front of Esztergom Basilica (p102), or Budapest's historic castle district (p110).

There are several routes you can take from Hungary through Romania towards Bucharest. Our main route via Sighișoara and Brașov (p124) traverses Transylvania – it certainly delivers on its spine-tingling reputation with moody Southern Carpathian landscapes coated in dense forests, particularly on the stretch between Brașov and Sinaia. The route via the Apuseni Mountains and Cluj-Napoca (p120) is also delightful.

On Towards Türkiye

The flatlands surrounding Bucharest are visually unexciting and might be a good time to pick up a book, but once you cross the Danube and enter Bulgaria, the landscapes again become more varied and interesting. The slow journey east of Ruse to Varna (p156) is in parts spellbinding, particularly for its sweeping vistas across vast farmlands and the canyon-like Provadiya River valley.

Between Gorna Oryahovitsa and Plovdiv lie the forested Central Balkan Mountains and Rozovata Dolina (the Valley of the Roses), where fragrant blooms have been cultivated for centuries. The flowers will be at their peak in June, so time your travel then and you'll see fields of them from the train.

There's also a floral treat in store if you're travelling during late June and July across East Thrace, the easternmost part of Türkiye. Sometimes stretching to the horizon will be battalions of sunflowers, their yellow-petalled heads soaking up the rays.

Esztergom (p102)

HIGHLIGHTS

❶ Chiemsee, p74
Board a boat to sail across this Bavarian lake to the islands Herreninsel and Fraueninsel and you'll soon realise why so many artists have been inspired by the gorgeous surrounding alpine scenery.

❷ Walensee, p232
Sandwiched between the ragged Churfirsten range and Flumserberg, this stunning, fjord-like lake is a sapphire blue vision between Zürich and Innsbruck. Look out for the Seerenbachfälle waterfall.

❸ Innsbruck, p234
Sheer rock faces press in on the tracks as the train winds gently upwards towards this Austrian ski resort. Once in Innsbruck continue by funicular and cable cars even higher into the Alps.

❹ Lavaux Vineyard Terrace, p199
Stretch your legs and drink in the views of Lac Léman as you follow the trails through these World Heritage–listed vineyards, dating to the 12th century and divided by dry-stone walls.

❺ Braşov to Sinaia, p122
Fine views are guaranteed from trains passing through the Prahova Valley slicing through the Bucegi Mountains. Keep an eye out for the Heroes' Cross on Caraiman Peak atop the jagged ridge line.

❻ Varna, p150
Enjoy the golden sands and coruscating waters of the Black Sea at this Bulgarian resort on the Classic Orient Express route. For greenery and shade, there's a beautifully designed seaside park.

MOUNTAINS, LAKES & SEAS

Tastes & Toasts

Prepare for a pan-European gastronomic adventure, ranging from oysters and Champagne in Paris to mint tea and baklava in İstanbul.

National Cuisines

The original Orient Express trains had luxuriously appointed restaurant cars in which meals accompanied by fine wines and spirits were served by uniformed waiters. Today, unless you are travelling on one of the top-tier revival services, such as Belmond's Venice Simplon-Orient-Express (VSOE; p242), the on-train dining options pale in comparison. Instead, search out dining pleasures at stops along the way.

France's delicious range of cuisine may scupper all attempts to venture further east. Contemporary chefs experiment while staying faithful to signature cooking methods, fresh ingredients and regional variety of phenomenal proportion. If you're on the Simplon route, Italy's equally superb kitchens will also induce raptures.

In Germany, Switzerland, Austria and Hungary, the food is good but traditionally more on the meaty, gut-filling side. In Romania, simple cornmeal mush – *mămăligă* – does a star turn. It's eaten (often in place of potatoes) as a popular side or on its own, with a dollop of sour cream. Bulgarian cooking, with its fresh salads and grills, resembles closely what you'd find in Greece or Türkiye.

Much Turkish cuisine is meat-dominated but if you're craving vegetables, mezes are an array of small dishes and most of them are vegetable-based. In addition to mezes, some establishments serve vegetarian versions of classic dishes like *köfte* (meatballs), *mantı* (ravioli) and pizza.

If you have a sweet tooth, you're also in for a treat – French macarons, Swiss chocolates, Viennese *Sacher Torte (*chocolate cake) and *lokum* (Turkish delight) are a few of the sugary pleasures awaiting on the journey.

Lokum (Turkish delight; p181)
EFIRED/SHUTTERSTOCK

What to Drink

France is the world's largest producer of wine after Italy, and its wildly varied *terroir* (land) assures diverse, exciting and sometimes complex wines – increasingly organic, biodynamic or natural. On the route of the original Orient Express are the wine-growing regions of Champagne and Alsace.

Wine has been made in Germany since Roman times but when it comes to alcoholic beverages, beer reigns supreme here. The drink is pretty much consumed any time of day, as in Munich where it's traditional to down a *Weissbier* (wheat beer) with *Weisswurst* (sausages) for breakfast. Hungary, Romania and Bulgaria have very drinkable and affordable wines.

Elegant coffeehouses are a feature of Vienna and Trieste. In Türkiye, coffee is also popular but drinking *çay* (tea) is the national pastime. The country's cup of choice is made with leaves from the Black Sea region. Sugar cubes are the only accompaniment, added to counter the effects of long brewing, although you can always try asking for your tea *açık* (weaker). Alcohol is also widely available in Türkiye. The classic Turkish alcoholic tipple is *rakı*, a grape spirit infused with aniseed. It's served in long, thin glasses and is drunk neat or with water, which turns the clear liquid chalky white.

SCHNITZEL

You'd be hard pressed on any Orient Express journey not to encounter the Central European dish schnitzel (pictured above) on menus. From the German verb *schnitten*, meaning 'to cut,' in its classic form this dish is a thinly sliced serving of meat (veal or pork but sometimes chicken), pounded flat, coated in breadcrumbs and pan fried in butter or oil to a golden crisp. Austrian law requires *Wiener Schnitzel* to be made with veal.

HIT THE MARKETS

Viktualienmarkt, Munich, p65
Gourmet food market in the heart of the city, held since 1807.

Odprta Kuhna Food Festival, Ljubljana, p221
On Fridays March through October Pogačar Sq hosts this street-food market where you can try Slovenia's famed Carniolan sausage.

Marché Couvert, Metz, p51
Built in the 18th century as a bishop's palace, this neoclassical stone building is one of France's grandest food market halls.

HIGHLIGHTS

❶ Le Train Bleu, Paris, p196
Dig into beef or lamb carved at the table with *gratin dauphinois* on the side at this iconic restaurant in Gare de Lyon – the perfect start or end to an Orient Express journey.

❷ Griechenbeisl, Vienna, p87
Dating from 1447, many famous guests have left their mark (literally) on the walls of this Viennese hostelry's Mark Twain Room. Order the classic veal *Wiener Schnitzel* or beef goulash with dumplings.

❸ New York Café, Budapest, p109
This ostentatious cafe – billed as 'the most beautiful in the world' – dates to 1894. A string band plays Hungarian music as guests devour fishermen soup.

❹ KAIAMO, Bucharest, p137
Book ahead for chef Radu Ionescu's experimental tasting menus at this award-winning, fine-dining restaurant that's leading the way for contemporary Romanian cuisine. Expect dishes such as duck with popcorn and elderflower.

❺ Khadzhidraganovite Izbi, Sofia, p160
Outstanding Bulgarian dishes, including succulent lamb kebabs and flavoursome pork stews, are served at this venue that conjures the atmosphere of an ancient stone wine cellar.

❻ Aheste, İstanbul, p181
Modern Turkish cuisine doesn't come any better than the delicious and inventive dishes, such as Marmara seabass with vanilla onion cream or rice pudding with mushroom ice cream, served at this fine-diner in Beyoğlu.

Splendid Architecture

Roman amphitheatres, magnificent mosques and eye-boggling palaces – ambitious, grand architecture is a highlight of the Orient Express routes.

ROYAL RESIDENCES ARE common along the Orient Express routes, each one seemingly more ostentatious in their decoration and vaulting architectural ambitions than the last. Compare and contrast the extravagant tastes of Bavaria's Wittelsbach dynasty at Munich's Residenz (p67) and, on an island in Chiemsee, Herrenchiemsee (p76), with those of Romania's Carol I at Peleş Castle (p128) in Sinaia and the Ottoman sultans at Topkapı Palace (p182).

Fans of baroque architecture will be thrilled by the State Hall of the Austrian National Library at the Hofburg (p89), while the go-to for rococo is Schloss Schönbrunn (p90) – both are located in Vienna. Budapest is another architectural stunner with its star buildings ranging from the vast neo-Gothic Parliament and Moorish-style Great Synagogue (p111), seating 3000 people and the largest such building in Europe, to the gorgeous art nouveau Gellért Baths (p112).

Public squares, such as Milan's Piazza del Duomo (p202), Venice's fabled Piazza San Marco (p212) and Munich's Marienplatz (p69) with its neo-Gothic Neues Rathaus, and giant Gothic cathedrals, including Paris' Notre Dame (p45), Strasbourg's Cathédrale Notre-Dame (p57) and Vienna's Stephansdom (p88), are all locations in which to admire the architecture and feel the sweep of history.

Ancient & Modern

That history stretches back millennia – in the case of Plovdiv (p170), at least as long as 7000 years. In 342 BCE this Bulgarian city was conquered by Philip II of Macedon, Alexander the Great's father, and named Philippopolis. Some 250 years later the Romans took charge – remains of their many civic buildings, including an agora, amphitheatre and stadium seating 30,000 people, are scattered across the city.

The Roman Empire spanned the extent of the Orient Express route and ruins from its era can be found from Paris to İstanbul. Romans set up forts on prominent defensive positions, including a volcano at Deva (p118) in Romania

TOWERING ACHIEVEMENTS

Eiffel Tower (p43)
Built for the 1889 Exposition Universelle, this 330m wrought-iron lattice tower is a Parisienne icon.

Ulmer Münster (p58)
One of the world's tallest churches, with a tower shooting up 161.53m, this German edifice took over 500 years to complete.

Wiener Riesenrad (p91)
For splendid views of Vienna, ride this famous giant Ferris wheel, a 64.75m feature of the Prater recreational park since 1897.

Left: Ulmer Münster (p58)
Right: 1st-century Roman amphitheatre, Plovdiv (p170)

and Tsarevets Hill (p155) near Veliko Tărnovo in Bulgaria – both sites have evocative remains of fortresses built by subsequent rulers of these lands.

Buildings from the Ottoman Empire are also found along the routes, particularly in İstanbul, but also in Edirne, home to the World Heritage-listed Selimiye Mosque (p173).

If your tastes run more to modern and contemporary architecture, add to your must-see list the Centre Pompidou-Metz (p51), European Quarter in Strasbourg (p56), the Mercedes-Benz Museum in Stuttgart (p55), various striking socialist-era edifices in Bratislava (p98) and the futuristic, Zaha Hadid–designed Hungerburg Funicular Railway in Innsbruck (p234).

Railway Temples

A journey along the Orient Express routes will also bring you into contact with some of Europe's most historical train stations. In Paris, the Gare de l'Est (p50) and Gare de Lyon (p196) are portals to the golden age of steam railways. Milano Centrale (p201) is magnificent, sporting stunning art deco statues, carvings and mosaics.

Switzerland offers superb stations in Basel (p230), Lausanne (p198) and Zürich (p232), while Zagreb's Glavni Kolodvor (p223) and Budapest-Keleti (p105) and Budapest-Nyugati (p105) each feature beautiful facades and halls. The impressive architecture of stations in Ruse (p148) and Varna (p150) are also evidence of their past importance on the Bulgarian rail network.

TRANSPORT MUSEUMS

Contemporary carriages of national European railways are plain Janes compared with their finely handcrafted counterparts from the Orient Express' golden days. To admire these vintage beauties up close, visit Cité du Train (p230) in Mulhouse, the Deutsches Museum – Verkehrszentrum (pictured above; p68) in Munich, the National Museum of Transport and Communications (p148) in Ruse and Lokwelt Freilassing (p78).

MEGA PLACES OF WORSHIP

Great Synagogue (p111)
Seating 3000 people, Europe's largest Jewish house of prayer is a gorgeous, mid-19th-century Moorish Revival building in Budapest.

Blue Mosque, p184
This serenely beautiful İstanbul mosque gets its unofficial name from its huge interior adorned with 21,000 blue İznik tiles.

Esztergom Basilica, p102
Hungary's largest Catholic cathedral with a 72m-tall dome provides awesome views of the Danube.

Gare de l'Est, Paris (p50)
SIMON RICHMOND/LONELY PLANET

A History of the Orient Express

Born during the 19th-century boom years of the railways, the Orient Express was a smash hit from the start. Setting the gold standard for luxurious international train travel, its zenith was in the 1930s. Decades after its demise as a regularly scheduled transcontinental service, the name alone continues to weave magic in collective imaginations.

THE ORIENT EXPRESS was the brainchild of Georges Nagelmackers, founder of Compagnie Internationale des Wagons-Lits (CIWL). Born in Liège, Belgium, in 1845, Nagelmackers, the son of an influential banker, studied civil engineering during the golden age of railway construction. The young man dreamt of a train linking Europe's major cities with İstanbul, then known as Constantinople. The tracks to enable this 2200km journey were almost in place. What was missing was a comfortable means of through transport.

In 1868 Nagelmackers spent 10 months travelling around the US, during which time he made frequent use of sleeping cars on the nation's railways. Released by George Pullman in 1865, these dorms on rails were way more comfortable than any European train carriage of the same era. With a few improvements (such as private sleeping compartments), they could suit very nicely Nagelmackers' vision for high-end Euro-

FOTO: FORTEPAN/SCHOCH FRIGYES, CC BY-SA 3.0 VIA WIKIMEDIA COMM

1876
Nagelmackers registers Compagnie Internationale des Wagons-Lits

1883
Maiden journey of the Paris-to-Constantinople *Train Express d'Orient*

1889
Belgrade-Plovdiv tracks completed

1891
Train Express d'Orient is officially renamed Orient Express

pean train travel. The Belgian took note of other US advances in railway technology, including air brakes, rubber shock absorbers and bogies (two wheels on an axel), all of which would improve the safety and smoothness of his dream train.

Maiden Journey

On 4 October 1883, Nagelmackers was ready to launch what the press had dubbed the 'magic carpet to the Orient'. With much fanfare, the *Train Express d'Orient* set forth at 6.20pm – it had been delayed 20 minutes to allow latecomers to board. Among the invited guests were celebrated journalists and writers. No expense had been spared to ensure their enjoyment, with gourmet foods and cases of fine wines ready for a succession of banquets in the dining car.

Passengers were under the impression that the entire journey to Constantinople would be by single train. But that would not be possible for another six years. Instead, the inaugural *Express* made its way via Strasbourg, Munich, Vienna and Budapest to the Romanian border town of Giurgiu. The *Express* waited there for the return journey, while passengers crossed the Danube by ferry and boarded another train bound for the Black Sea port of Varna. From here the Austrian steamship *Espero* sailed the *Orient Express* passengers to Constantinople. Even with this 15-hour crossing, the entire journey was

WAGON-LIT 2419

Among the thousands of carriages that CIWL built or commissioned, the most famous is No 2419, which became the mobile headquarters of Marshal Ferdinand Foch, supreme commander of the Allied Forces during WWI. It was in No 2419 that the German surrender was signed at 11am on 11 November 1918. Symbolically, Hitler made sure the same carriage was used to dictate surrender terms to the French in 1940. Subsequently transported to Germany, this historic carriage was destroyed in 1945 by the SS to prevent it falling back into Allied hands.

Simplon Express, 1906

1895 Constanța replaces Varna as Black Sea port terminus

1906 Simplon Express connects London with Milan via Paris

1919 Orient Express services reinstated following WWI

1929 Orient Express stranded in snow for a week near Çerkezköy in Türkiye

accomplished in under 82 hours – a remarkable feat given travellers today would be very hard pressed to cover the same distance by train in a similar timeframe.

Interwar Heyday

Underpinning the Orient Express' success was Nagelmackers' gift for negotiating with rival national railway companies to secure permission to run his transcontinental services across their rails. He also harnessed the power of publicity to brilliant effect. By 1889, when passengers could travel from the Seine to the Bosphorus without any change of train or need to undertake a sea journey, the Orient Express was the most prestigious form of transport in Europe. Its passengers included royalty, ambassadors and business tycoons, such as the oil magnate Calouste Gulbenkian and arms dealer Basil Zaharoff.

By the turn of the century, Orient Express trains were running daily between Paris and Budapest and three times a week to Constantinople via Belgrade. There were also connections to the Romanian port of Constanța, and to Salonika (Thessaloniki) and Athens. CIWL had over 1000 wagons-lit serving destinations not just in Europe, but also in North Africa and Asia, with the company supplying carriages to Russia's tsar for the Trans-Siberian Railway. However, Nagelmackers' tireless efforts to expand CIWL's operations eventually took their toll – he suffered a fatal heart attack in 1905, just two weeks after his 60th birthday.

Despite the loss of its founder and the interruption of WWI, CIWL's operations continued to grow. Tunnels through the Alps allowed new routes via Switzerland, Italy and the Balkans to open up. By 1930, when Constantinople was renamed İstanbul, the Orient Express was at its zenith – less than half a century old and already a legend.

WWII & the Iron Curtain

WWII caused significant damage to CIWL's rolling stock, not to mention Europe's railway tracks. Still, within months of German capitulation, truncated routes of the Orient Express were back in service and by 1948 it was possible to reach İstanbul with a change of train in Sofia. The Cold War and – in Winston's Churchill's famous phrase, 'the Iron Curtain' – proved no barrier for the Orient Express. At the same time, the journey took on extra frisson as it passed through Eastern Europe's newly communist regimes and became a conduit for spies and refugees. There was even the spy-novel-reminiscent death of US naval attaché Eugene

Orient Express with old locomotive, 1982

1934
Publication of Agatha Christie's *Murder on the Orient Express*

1945
Arlberg Express makes first post-WWII run from Paris to Innsbruck

1977
Final run of *Direct Orient Express* sleeper carriage on Paris–İstanbul route

1982
Start of VSOE luxury train service from London and Paris to Venice

ORIENT EXPRESS LANDMARKS

Gare de l'Est, Paris, p50
From 1883 until 1977 Orient Express trains departed from this beautifully appointed station. *Venice Simplon-Orient-Express* (VSOE) luxury trains still depart and arrive from here.

Simplon Tunnel, p198
Connecting Brig in Switzerland with Domodossola in Italy, this 19.8km tunnel through the Alps enabled the Simplon Express route to commence from 1906 onwards.

Sirkeci Station, İstanbul, p177
Currently undergoing a transformation into a museum dedicated to Turkish emigration, this grand eastern terminus of the Orient Express made its debut in 1890.

Karpe, who fell (or was pushed) from the train around Salzburg in 1950.

Evocative images of the Orient Express from this time, taken by *Life* magazine photographer Jack Birns, can be viewed at life.com/history/the-orient-express-photos-from-a-legendary-train. However, the Express' days of being an exclusively 1st-class affair were over. Now, while passing through the socialist republics of Hungary and Romania, ordinary seat coaches were hitched to the train.

Decline & Revival

The Orient Express persisted through the murky Cold War years of the 1950s and '60s. But with the rise in commercial aeroplane travel, the electrification of the railways allowing faster speeds within Western Europe, and a consequent drop in demand for overnight sleeper trains, the train's days were numbered. Routes were slashed, restaurant cars retired and the final run of the *Direct Orient Express* sleeping car from Paris to İstanbul was scheduled for 19 May 1977. The Orient Express as a named train would limp on until 2009 when the Strasbourg–Vienna sleeping cars were withdrawn, thus ending its appearance on scheduled timetables.

And yet, such is the Orient Express' romantic allure and mystique that the train has refused to die. Revival services (p240), using restored CIWL rolling stock, were up and running in 1982 and continue to this day. The success of the Eurail/Interrail scheme (p255) and new night train services across Europe, such as the European Sleeper, continue to inspire 21st-century rail passengers to follow the varied tracks of the Orient Express routes to İstanbul.

1993 — France is second country in Europe (after Italy) to launch high-speed trains

2009 — EuroNight *Orient Express* train departs Strasbourg on its final run to Vienna

2013 — Halkalı replaces Sirkeci as international train terminus for İstanbul

2025 — Golden Eagle launch Paris–İstanbul via Belgrade service

Ways to do the Orient Express

6

There's an Orient Express route to suit everyone, including those in a hurry who are happy to bunk down on sleeper trains. The best options are leisurely meanders via some of Europe's most historic and scenic locations.

1 Classic Orient Express
Time *14 days*
Best for *Travellers following the historic route*
Follow the original route at your leisure, breaking up the journey with overnight stops in big cities such as Vienna, Budapest and Bucharest, and shorter visits to places such as Strasbourg or Braşov. In Sinaia, gawp at Carol I's over-the-top Peleş Castle, while in Varna, take a dip in the Black Sea.
Possible overnights Paris, Munich, Vienna, Budapest, Sinaia, Bucharest, Varna, Sofia, İstanbul

2 The Simplon Route
Time *14 days*
Best for *Epicures and romantics*
The magnificently decorated Le Train Bleu restaurant at Paris' Gare de Lyon provides an unforgettable start to this historic route that offers plenty more culinary delights, not least in the cafes, restaurants and bars of Milan, Venice and Trieste. Savour the atmosphere of grand hotels from the Orient Express' heyday and enjoy beautiful vistas of vineyards, mountains, lakes, forests and the shores of the Adriatic.
Possible overnights Lausanne, Milan, Venice, Trieste, Ljubljana, Zagreb, Budapest

Go to p246 for other connections

3 The Arlberg Route
Time *10 days*
Best for *Outdoor pursuits*
Railway enthusiasts will want to visit Cité du Train in Mulhouse and Basel's station decorated with spectacular murals of Alpine scenes. The picturesque landscapes of Switzerland and Austria provide ample opportunities to go hiking, biking, skiing and snowboarding.
Possible overnights Paris, Basel, Zürich, Innsbruck, Salzburg, Vienna

Peleş Castle, Sinaia (p128)

SIMON RICHMOND/LONELY PLANET

Train at Varna station (p150)

WHEN TO GO

March–May
One of the best times to travel. Temperatures are milder and landscapes look lush with fresh greenery and flowers.

June–October
Peak season – seat and hotel reservations are essential. During these months there's also a direct couchette car from Bucharest to İstanbul and vice versa. There are often discounts on Eurail/Interrail tickets purchased for use after 1 September.

November–February
Christmas and New Year can be a busy time on Europe's railways and in cities such as Strasbourg and Vienna, where Christmas markets are a big draw. Book well ahead for seat reservations and hotels.

See p240 for Orient Express revivals

4 Night Train Dash
Time *5–6 days*
Best for *The time pressed*
To travel from Paris to İstanbul within a week you'll need to plan carefully. On Monday, Wednesday and Friday there's an ÖBB Nightjet train from Paris to Vienna. Upon arriving in Vienna you'll have around eight hours to explore the city before boarding the DACIA EuroCity service to Bucharest via Budapest. There's one daily 10½-hour direct train from Bucharest to Sofia, where it's necessary to spend a night before connecting to İstanbul.
Possible overnights Bucharest, Sofia and, if you're not in such a hurry, Budapest

5 Eastern European Explorer
Time *10 days*
Best for *Off the beaten track*
The slower pace of Eastern Europe's railways is perfect for observing the beguiling scenery. Build into your itinerary gems such as Oradea, Cluj-Napoca and Sibiu in Romania and Ruse, Veliko Târnovo and Plovdiv in Bulgaria. These trains are also a chance to engage with locals.
Possible overnights Budapest, Braşov, Bucharest, Sofia, Veliko Târnovo, Plovdiv

6 Go West
Time *14 days*
Best for *Travelling in the opposite direction*
Head from İstanbul to the old Ottoman capital of Edirne. Join the night train here and disembark at Plovdiv or Sofia. Continue west through Romania and Hungary. Travel via the historic towns around the Danube Bend into Slovakia and its capital Bratislava. Detour into the Alps at Berchtesgaden and take the slow route back to Paris via Nancy and Épernay in Champagne.
Possible overnights Edirne, Plovdiv, Sofia, Bucharest, Budapest, Bratislava, Berchtesgaden, Nancy

The Ride

A stage-by-stage, mile-by-mile account of the route. Your journey begins here.

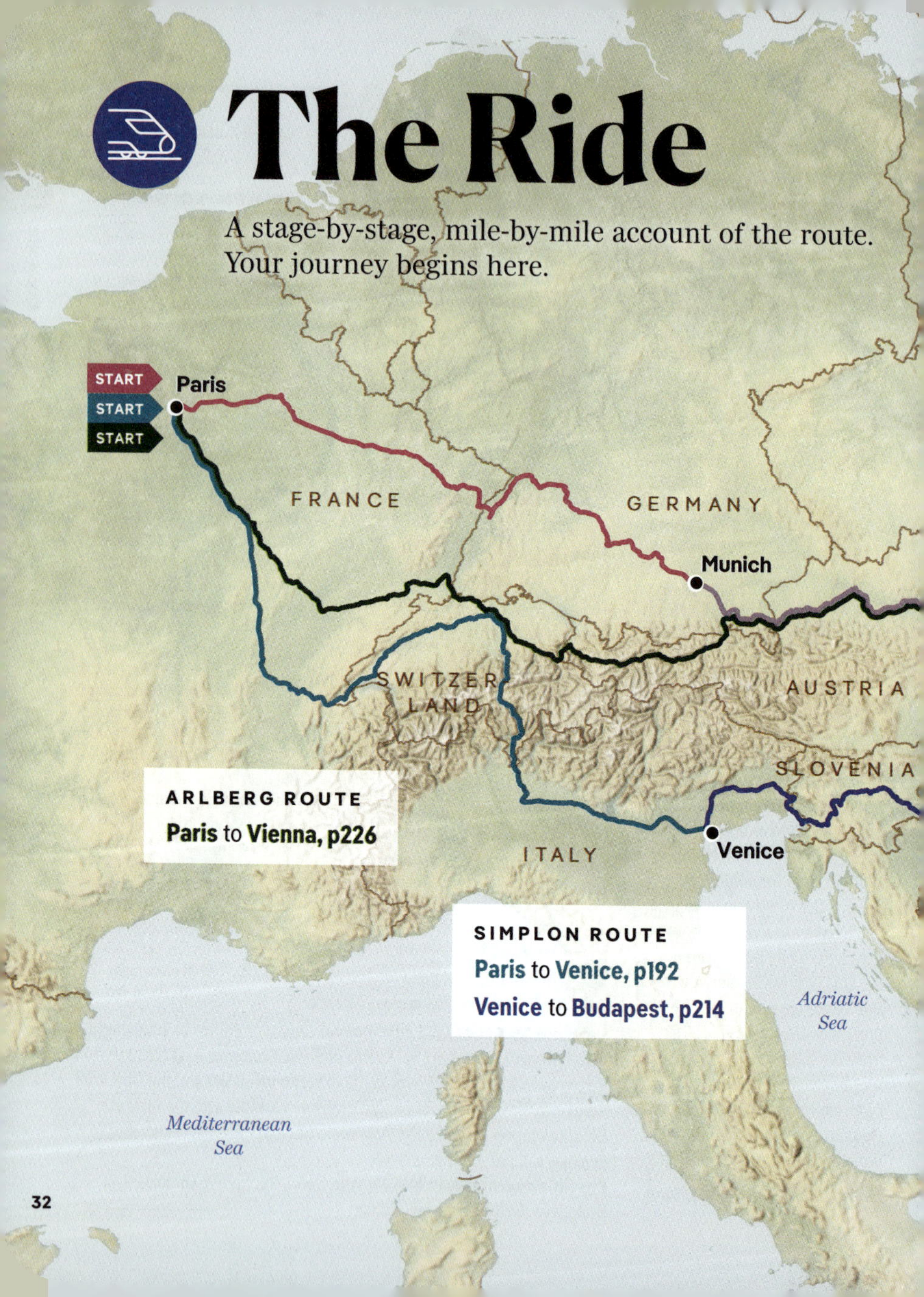

ARLBERG ROUTE
Paris to Vienna, p226

SIMPLON ROUTE
Paris to Venice, p192
Venice to Budapest, p214

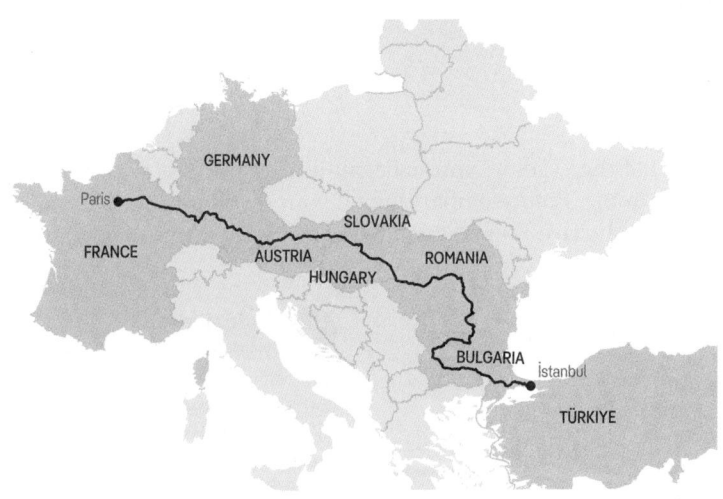

CLASSIC ORIENT EXPRESS

A map of the historic Orient Express routes through Europe looks like a spider's web. But in the beginning there was just one route – Paris to İstanbul, or Constantinople as it was then known. This is the basis for our Classic itinerary from France to Türkiye, via Germany, Austria, Hungary, Romania and Bulgaria. With tickets to a mix of high-speed, regular and sleeper trains, and with stops in places as varied as Munich and Plovdiv, the excitement, fun and romance of an Orient Express trans-European journey is within your grasp.

Train, București Nord station (p127)

CITY GUIDE:
Paris

Terminus Nord

The legend of the Orient Express began in Paris in 1883 with the train's inaugural voyage. Before embarking on your own journey, take time to explore the seductive French capital, packed with instantly recognisable architectural stunners.

WORDS BY
MARY WINSTON NICKLIN
Mary Winston is a Franco-American writer and editor based on the Left Bank.

✈ Arriving

By air Most international airlines fly to **Aéroport Charles de Gaulle** (CDG), 28km northeast of central Paris, or **Orly**, 19km south of central Paris. From CDG, the best way to get to central Paris is the RER B train. From Orly, you can connect to the city via line 14 of the metro, or on the RER B after taking the OrlyVal shuttle. The government mandates fixed prices for taxis to the Right and Left Banks. Note that rideshare services do not have access to Paris' fast taxi lanes, so they're more susceptible to traffic jams.

By train Five major train stations offer international services, including Gare du Nord with Eurostar connections to London, Brussels and Amsterdam.

HOW MUCH FOR A

Glass of wine **from €4**

Two-course bistro menu **from €22**

Louvre ticket **€22**

🍴 Refuelling

Train station fare runs the gamut from fast take-out such as **Paul**, **Monop'Daily** and **Y'a pas de sushi** at Gare de l'Est to full-service brasseries like the art deco–style **Terminus Nord** (1925) across from Gare du Nord. Given Paris' superb culinary reputation, it's worth being picky about your restaurant choice and travelling to get there.

🚶 Getting Around

Easily navigable on foot, the compact city of Paris is a walker's paradise.
Public transport The fastest way to get around is on the convenient Paris metro, while the comprehensive bus system allows you to sightsee while travelling. Download **Bonjour RATP** *(bonjour-ratp.fr/en)*, the app from the Paris metro authority, to get tickets, real-time traffic updates and itinerary options.
Cycling A surge in bike lanes and infrastructure has prompted a cycling revolution. The Vélib' bike-share scheme has over 20,000 bikes, both classic (green) and electric (blue), at nearly 1480 docking stations.
Stay Alert Beware of pickpockets who target busy tourist areas, such as metro lines 1 and 9, and beneath sites such as the Eiffel Tower and Arc de Triomphe.

For schedules and trip planning, download Bonjour RATP:

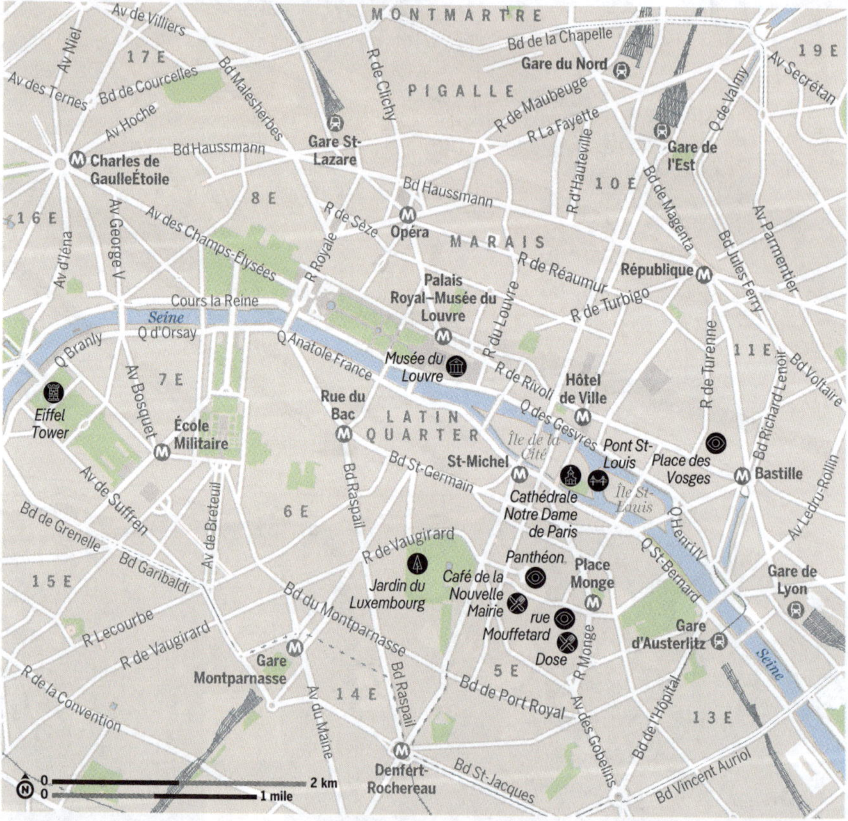

A DAY IN PARIS

 Start your day on the Île de la Cité at **Cathédrale Notre Dame de Paris** (p45), painstakingly restored after the 2019 fire. Cross the **Pont St-Louis**, where buskers play, to stroll the Île St-Louis. Then wander the Marais district to uncover boutiques and treasure-filled museums, such as Victor Hugo's house in **Place des Vosges**.

 Linger for lunch in the Latin Quarter at the **Café de la Nouvelle Mairie** next to the **Panthéon**. For a post-lunch pick-me-up, caffeinate at **Dose** on the medieval market street of **rue Mouffetard**, or laze in the lovely **Jardin du Luxembourg**, the city's most popular park.

 Cross the Seine to immerse yourself in the majesty of the **Musée du Louvre** (p41). You can swoon over the museum's masterpieces until 9pm on Wednesdays and Fridays. Conclude your perfect Paris day with a concert at one of the storied jazz clubs along the **rue des Lombards** (p44).

Where to Stay

Paris has a huge choice of accommodation, from hostels to luxurious *grande dames* such as the Ritz, where fashionable Orient Express passengers once spent the night. Rates for a midrange boutique hotel start at around €160. Favoured neighbourhoods like St-Germain and the Marais have the highest hotel prices. If you look at outlying districts such as the 12e, 14e and 16e *arrondissements* (districts), you'll find cheaper rates while still being able to enjoy the Parisian lifestyle.

BEST PLACES TO STAY

Hôtel des Grandes Écoles €€ Countryside vibes at a three-star hideaway in the Latin Quarter. *hoteldesgrandesecoles.com*

Bloom House €€ Colourful hotel with spa and heated pool near Gare de l'Est. *bloomhouse-hotel.com*

People Marais € Modern, sociable hostel about 1km from Gare de Lyon. *thepeoplehostel.com/en/destinations/paris-marais*

Dandy Hotel €€ Chic four-star hotel at the very heart of Les Halles. *dandyhotelparis.com*

Where to Eat

Eating well is of prime importance to Parisians, and every neighbourhood is peppered with enticing bistros. The trendiest is the 11e, brimming with hip spots run by talented chefs. For a splurge, consider the Michelin-starred institutions in the 8e and 16e. Chinatown in the 13e, and the smaller one in Belleville, are packed with Asian delights. Northern Paris offers a number of *bouillons*, a historic concept, now *en vogue*, serving classics on the cheap.

> ### BOULANGERIE BOUNTY
>
> Few things in Paris are as tantalising as the smell of just-baked baguettes and buttery croissants wafting out of a bakery door. There are roughly 1200 *boulangeries* (bakeries) in Paris and you should absolutely sample their delights. Born in Paris, the baguette (pictured below) is a wand-shaped loaf made with just flour, water, salt and yeast. Its origins are marinated in lore. One legend says Napoléon decreed that bakers create an easily transportable bread for soldiers. Another claims it was a request from Fulgence Bienvenüe, the 'father of the Paris metro', so that his tunnel workers could break their bread without carrying brawl-inducing knives. Whatever the truth, the baguette has become a symbol of France and is classified by UNESCO. An annual Paris competition awards the city's best *boulanger* (baker) with a year-long contract to supply the bread to the Élysée presidential palace.

BEST PLACES TO EAT & DRINK

Bouillon Pigalle € French classics at terrific value. *bouillonlesite.com/en/bouillon-pigalle-2*

La Tour d'Argent €€€ Pressed duck and Notre Dame views since 1582. *tourdargent.com*

Bar Joséphine €€€ Palace hotel bar frequented by Josephine Baker. *mandarinoriental.com*

Little Red Door €€€ Marais speakeasy with talented mixologists. *lrdparis.com*

Le Vaudeville

Celebrate Art Deco

Part of the Palais du Louvre complex, the **Musée des Arts Décoratifs** *(madparis.fr; adult/child €15/free; closed Mon)* is a rich testament to the history of French decorative arts. Dedicated rooms offer an immersion in art deco, the artistic style that was gloriously embodied by Orient Express train carriages in the early 20th century in glam details like marquetry and Lalique glass panels. After you get your fix, lunch at **Le Vaudeville** *(vaudeville paris.com; €€)*, where you can tuck into *oeufs mayo* and *steak au poivre* in a legendary art deco brasserie.

THE TRAIN & IMPRESSIONISM

Two revolutionary inventions changed the art world forever: the advent of the train and new portable tubes of paint allowed 19th-century artists to leave Paris to find inspiration in the countryside. They'd set up their easels *en plein air* in bucolic settings along the Seine such as Giverny, forever linked to Claude Monet's colourful gardens and waterlily pond. Get up close to the *Nymphéas* in Paris at the **Musée de l'Orangerie** *(musee-orangerie.fr; adult/child €12.50/free)* and at the **Musée Marmottan Monet** *(marmottan.fr; adult/child €14/9)*, home to the world's largest Monet collection.

Inaugurated in 1837 as the city's first railway station, **Gare St-Lazare** was particularly important as the portal to Normandy for impressionist painters. The station itself became a subject for these artists, who were fascinated by modernity and the changes wrought to urban life by the Industrial Revolution. Monet captured the steam billowing from locomotives in multiple paintings, while Gustave Caillebotte portrayed the iron rails of the Pont de l'Europe overlooking the station.

Along the Way We Met...

CYRIL GIBON Inaugurated in 1901, Le Train Bleu (p196) is a showcase of French craftsmanship designed to impress travellers: gilding, woodwork, chandeliers and painted ceilings depict the landscapes the train would traverse before reaching the Mediterranean. Among the legends: Salvador Dalí, fascinated by a live lobster on a platter, asked to leave with it...in his bag.

Cyril Gibon is the directeur de salle (dining room manager) at Le Train Bleu, the majestic restaurant inside Gare de Lyon.

CYRIL'S TIP: *Order a signature dish such as the leg of lamb, followed by our famous baba au rhum dessert.*

Wander the Louvre

Once a royal palace, Paris' pièce de résistance displays 35,000 artworks. Glancing at each piece for one minute would take 24 days without sleeping!

HOW TO

Getting here: Take metro line 1 to Louvre-Rivoli or line 7 to Palais Royal–Musee du Louvre.

When to go: The museum is open from 9am to 6pm on Monday, Thursday, Saturday and Sunday, and to 9pm on Wednesday and Friday, but is closed Tuesday.

Cost: Adult/child under 18 €22/free

Tip: Wear comfortable shoes, as you will be walking through 403 halls and nearly 15km of corridors.

More info: louvre.fr/en

Entering the museum for the first time can be intimidating. The key to approaching the vast collections is to consider them from two perspectives: Western art from the Middle Ages to the mid-19th century, and the art and crafts of five ancient civilisations. Simultaneously, admire the stunning architecture forged by multiple sovereigns.

If you're short on time, follow an itinerary highlighting iconic works. Start with the **Great Sphinx of Tanis**, and explore the **Egyptian Antiquities** in the Sully Wing. On Level 1, view the **Seated Scribe** (Room 635), then proceed to the lavishly decorated **Rooms 600–622**, reflecting the 18th-century royal court.

Head to the ground level to admire **Venus de Milo** in Room 345. From here, take the magnificent staircase where the **Winged Victory of Samothrace** holds court. Once on Level 1 again, journey into the Denon Wing to see the golden **Galerie d'Apollon** (Room 705) and the impressive **Great Gallery**, featuring masterpieces by renowned Italian artists, including Leonardo da Vinci. As part of renovation plans, the **Mona Lisa** (currently Room 711) will be moved to its own dedicated exhibition space.

EXPERIENCE ★

Above: Great Sphinx of Tanis
Right: Musée du Louvre

FROM LEFT: LEFTERIS PAPAULAKIS/SHUTTERSTOCK, SAKO3P/SHUTTERSTOCK

Cruise the Seine

Taking to the Seine on a river cruise is an idyllic way to view the city's famous monuments. It's also a firm family favourite among Paris experiences.

HOW TO

Getting here: Many cruises depart from quays near the Eiffel Tower, though the hop-on-hop-off Batobus has nine stops along the Seine.

When to go: Cruises run year-round, regardless of the weather, though boat traffic is stopped during rare river floods.

Cost: Prices vary by operator: Batobus 24hr pass €23, Vedettes de Paris guided cruise €21, Ducasse sur Seine with lunch from €115.

Bateaux Parisiens (bateauxparisiens.com/english.html) runs hour-long circuits with audioguides in 14 languages and themed lunch and dinner cruises. **Vedettes de Paris** (vedettesdeparis.fr/en) offers one-hour cruises from its base at the foot of the Eiffel Tower. **Batobus** (batobus.com) runs glassed-in trimarans that dock every 20 to 25 minutes at nine small piers along the Seine, including one just across the river from Notre Dame. **Green River Cruises** (greenriver-paris.fr/en) has pontoon boats you can privatise for an apéritif with friends or a family birthday party.

Among the gourmet options, there are two standouts. Chef Alain Ducasse oversees the floating restaurant **Ducasse sur Seine** (ducasse-seine.com/en) on a luxurious electric boat, where both lunch and dinner are served. The only Michelin-starred cruise is aboard the **Don Juan II** (donjuan2.yachtsdeparis.fr/en), an art deco–style yacht kitted out with a fireplace, wooden panelling and brass fixtures. The multicourse dinner menu is by chef Frédéric Anton of the Eiffel Tower's Le Jules Verne fame.

Above: Eiffel Tower souvenir
Right: A boat cruises the Seine

CAFE LIFE

For most Parisians living in tiny apartments, cafes have traditionally served as the *salon* they don't have – a place where they can meet with friends over *un verre* (a glass of wine), read for hours over a *café au lait*, debate politics while downing an espresso or swill cocktails during *apéro* (pre-dinner drink). More than a place to refuel, cafes are a cornerstone of daily life. In every neighbourhood, table-packed terraces draw Parisians for drinks and people-watching.

Some of the most storied addresses are in the St-Germain des Prés district. **Les Deux Magots** (lesdeuxmagots.fr), a favourite of Lost Generation writers James Joyce and Ernest Hemingway, is considered to be the birthplace of surrealism. Across the road, **Café de Flore** (cafedeflore.fr) drew existentialist philosophers like Simone de Beauvoir, Jean-Paul Sartre and Albert Camus. Adorned with painters' palettes, **La Palette** (lapalette-paris.com) was also frequented by the 20th-century literati.

And the most legendary of all: **Le Procope** (procope.com), founded in 1686, is the oldest cafe in Paris. A hub for Enlightenment thinkers in the 18th century, it was where Denis Diderot and Jean le Rond d'Alembert wrote the *Encyclopédie* in a coffee-fuelled spree.

Café de Flore

Climb the Eiffel Tower

With its hourly sparkles illuminating the skyline, the **Eiffel Tower** (*toureiffel.paris/en*) is the capital's tallest building. Built for the 1889 Exposition Universelle, it faced opposition from Paris' artistic elite. The 'metal asparagus', as some snidely called it, was slated to be torn down in 1909. It was spared because it proved an ideal platform for transmitting antennas. Now it's Paris' most famous landmark. Book tickets well in advance. Minimise queuing by booking the option to ascend the stairs. A separate lift on the 2nd floor serves the top floor, where you can sip Champagne while drinking in the views.

Le Marché des Enfants Rouges

Oldest Covered Market

Dating to the 17th century, **Le Marché des Enfants Rouges** exudes plenty of charm. It's a vibrant gathering place for both locals and visitors who appreciate the small eateries and food stalls overflowing with fresh fruit, flowers, cheese and charcuterie. Brunch on Sundays has become downright trendy, but you can enjoy lunch every day (except Monday, when it's closed). Among the diverse offerings, you can sample vegetarian delights at **Au Coin Bio** (*aucoinbio-restaurant.fr*), order a Japanese bento at **Chez Taeko** or tuck into Levantine pitas at **Chez Jeanphi** (*instagram.com/chez_jeanphi*).

Viaduc des Arts

Walk the Original High Line

In Paris, old train tracks have been repurposed into greenways. The best starts near Bastille, not far from Gare de Lyon. The **Coulée Verte René-Dumont** (closed at night) is a 4.5km elevated promenade that inspired New York City's High Line. The initial stretch is perched above the **Viaduc des Arts** (leviaducdesarts.com/en), housing galleries and artisanal workshops under the arches. Beautifully landscaped and fragrant with roses, the flower-filled route passes the **Église St-Antoine des Quinze Vingts** and the lovely **Jardin de Reuilly** before reaching the **Bois de Vincennes**.

2000 YEARS OF HISTORY

Spanning more than two millennia, the city's multi-layered history is present at every turn. Construction projects routinely turn up fascinating vestiges, such as the necropolis unearthed during the Port Royal station expansion. Some of the earliest ruins can be found beneath the parvis of Notre Dame. The **Crypte Archéologique** (crypte.paris.fr; adult/child incl exhibition €11/free) displays the 4th-century foundations of the Gallo-Roman town of Lutetia, including quays of the ancient port. A quick walk into the Latin Quarter – on the way, cross the rue St-Jacques; the city's oldest street used to be a Roman road – and you can picnic inside the ancient amphitheatre known as **Les Arènes de Lutèce**. Nearby, the **Musée de Cluny** (musee-moyenage.fr/en; adult/child €12/free), dedicated to the Middle Ages, is built atop a vaulted *frigidarium* from ancient thermal baths.

Speaking of the Middle Ages, the **Tour St-Jacques** (adult/child €12/10) is a less visited monument offering 360-degree views near Châtelet. For a taste of the Renaissance, admire the **Pont Neuf**, the city's oldest bridge, or step into the splendid *hôtel particulier* (mansion) that houses the **Musée Carnavalet** (carnavalet.paris.fr), a museum taking visitors on a journey through Paris' history.

Live music at Duc des Lombards

Storied Jazz Clubs

The Paris jazz scene got its start after WWI, as Black American musicians sought a haven away from US racial segregation, and it's still swinging today. Head to the street that's a place of pilgrimage for jazz enthusiasts to catch a concert. Rue des Lombards is your gateway to an unforgettable night out. There's contemporary and fusion jazz at **Le Baiser Salé** (lebaisersale.com), classical, swing and Latin jazz at **Duc des Lombards** (ducdeslombards.com) and both traditional and improv at **Sunset/Sunside** (sunset-sunside.com), since it's two clubs in one.

Admire Notre Dame

Paris' iconic cathedral is the crowning glory of medieval Gothic architecture. After the catastrophic 2019 fire, thousands of artisans restored it to its original glory.

HOW TO

Getting here: The closest metro/RER station is Cité (line 4) and St-Michel–Notre-Dame (RER B and C).

When to go: Book a free timed ticket on the online ticketing portal – time slots open a few days in advance. The queue is shorter for ticket holders.

Cost: Free

Tip: Catch Notre Dame's soul-soaring Gregorian Mass on Sundays at 10am.

More info: notredamedeparis.fr

The geographic and spiritual heart of the city, **Cathédrale Notre Dame de Paris** has played an outsized role in history – from royal weddings to liberation from Nazi occupation after WWII. Nowadays this Parisian beacon is an actively working church, and also the capital's most visited free sight – more than 29,000 people come daily. In fact, crowds have bustled across the vast square since work first began on the cathedral in the 12th century. Here you'll see a bronze star embedded in the ground that indicates **Point Zéro des Routes de France**, from where distances are measured for all roads in metropolitan France.

Enter the cathedral via the **Portal of the Last Judgement**. You'll follow a clockwise circuit allowing you to gawk at priceless sculptures and paintings as the coloured light from the stained-glass windows reflects on the white limestone walls. Pause to admire the new reliquary, resembling a glowing altarpiece, for the **Crown of Thorns**. The average visit is 35 minutes but it's worth slowing down to appreciate the dazzling restoration sponsored by 340,000 donors from all over the world.

Restored interior, Cathédrale Notre Dame de Paris

Paris

The main route of the Orient Express has always started in the City of Light at Gare de l'Est. TGV trains will whisk you at speeds of around 300km/h from here to Munich, the capital of Bavaria, in under six hours. But take some time to explore several interesting places along the way, including Strasbourg, with its UNESCO-listed historic core, and Ulm, for the first of many encounters with the Danube.

Simon Richmond

Munich

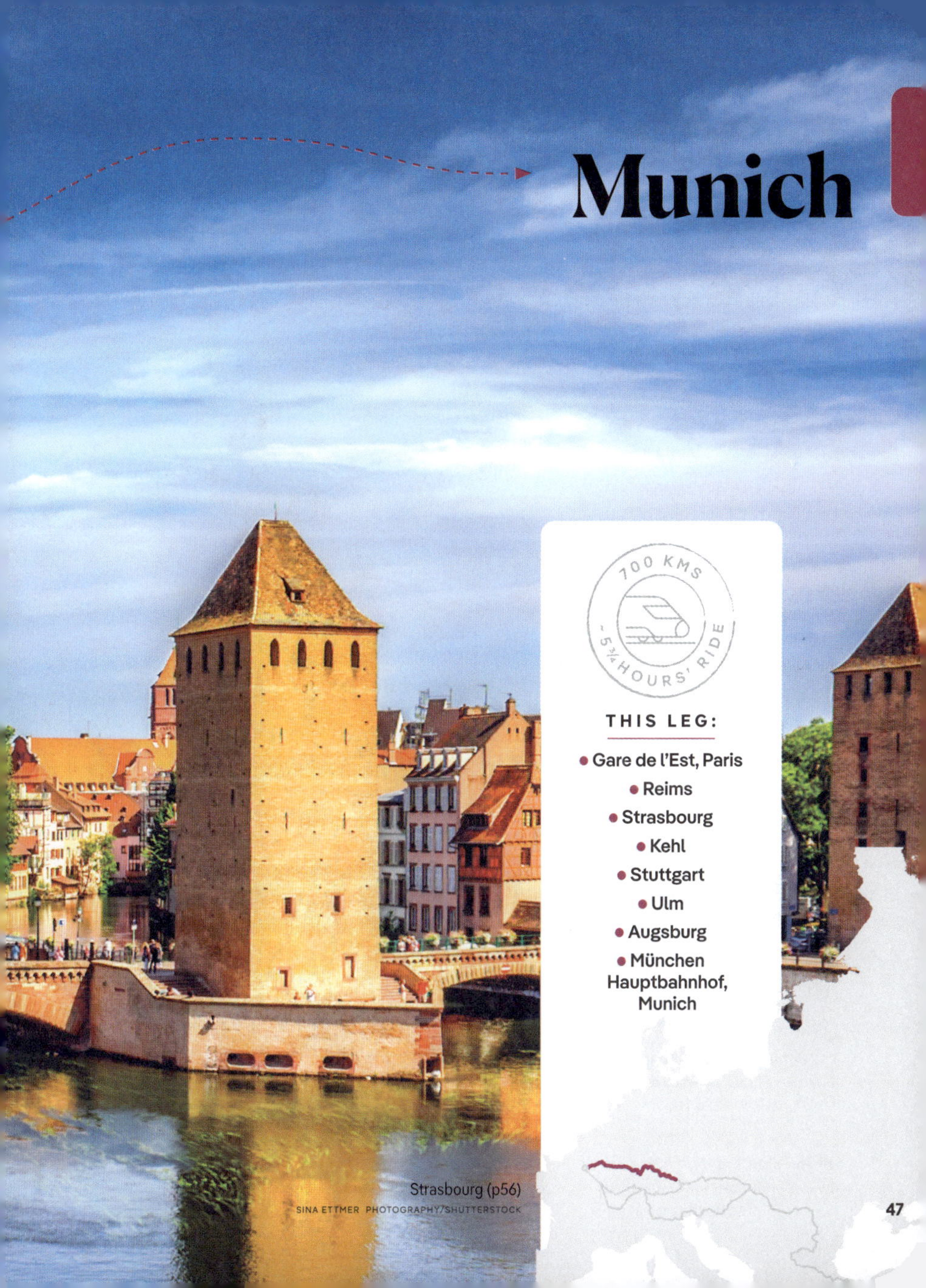

700 KMS - 5¾ HOURS' RIDE

THIS LEG:

- Gare de l'Est, Paris
- Reims
- Strasbourg
- Kehl
- Stuttgart
- Ulm
- Augsburg
- München Hauptbahnhof, Munich

Strasbourg (p56)

Riding Notes

Every Monday, Wednesday and Friday there's an ÖBB Nightjet sleeper service from Gare de l'Est to Vienna (p84) via München Ost station. There's also the daily Deutsche Bahn's ICE 9577 direct daytime service to München Hauptbahnhof – check online for departure times. Otherwise travelling to Munich will involve at least one change of trains, most likely at Stuttgart.

Breaking Your Journey

Less than two hours east of Paris, Strasbourg is the perfect place to break for lunch and sightseeing before continuing your travels. Across the border in Germany, potential stopovers include Stuttgart, Ulm and Augsburg, the latter two being cheaper than Munich.

Simon's Tips

BEST MEAL Sauerkraut dressed with sausage at Le Tire-Bouchon in Strasbourg. (p51)

FAVOURITE VIEW From the tower platform of Ulmer Münster. (p58)

ESSENTIAL STOP Exploring Strasbourg's UNESCO World Heritage-listed island. (p56)

TIP The **UlmCard** *(24hr €23)* covers entry to the Münster tower and many of Ulm's attractions.

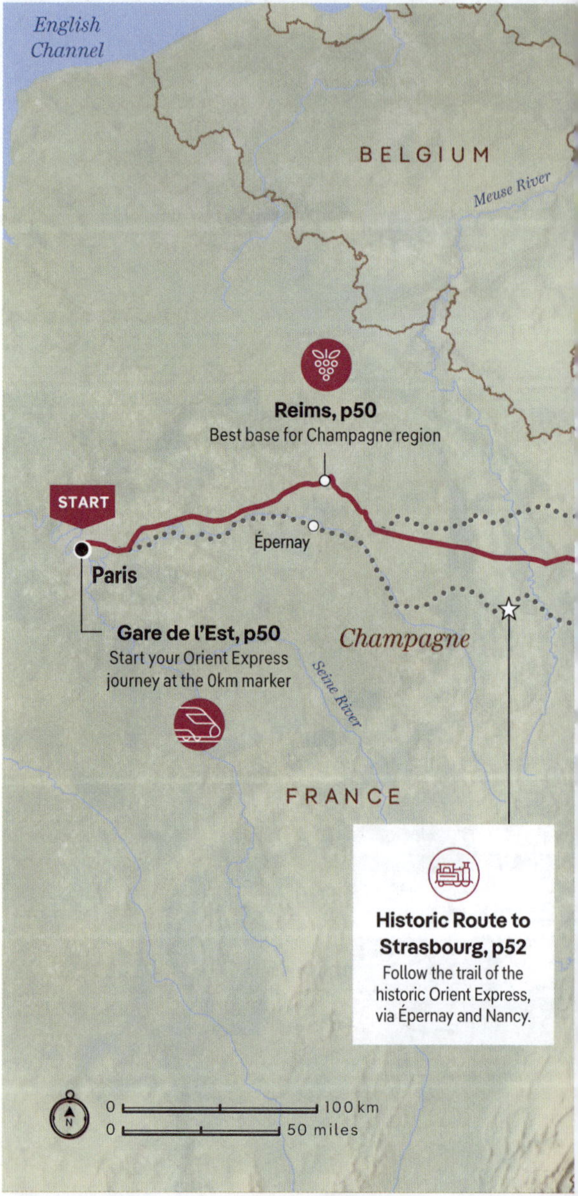
English Channel
BELGIUM
Meuse River
Reims, p50
Best base for Champagne region
START
Épernay
Paris
Gare de l'Est, p50
Start your Orient Express journey at the 0km marker
Champagne
Seine River
FRANCE
Historic Route to Strasbourg, p52
Follow the trail of the historic Orient Express, via Épernay and Nancy.
0 100 km
0 50 miles

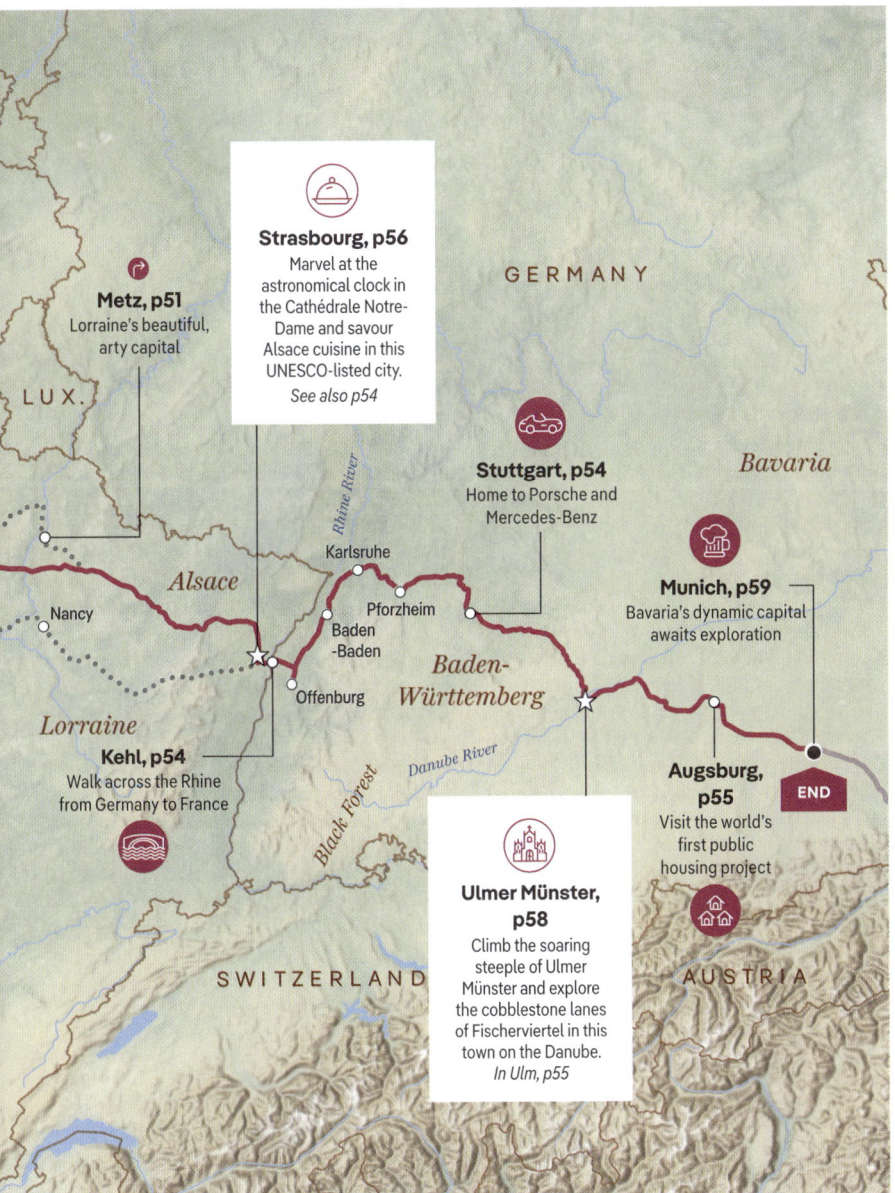

STARTING THE JOURNEY

Gare de l'Est is where our journey along the historic Classic Orient Express route begins. Unless you're following our alternative slow route to Strasbourg (p52), you will board a TGV train here. Gare de l'Est is also the departure station for the luxury VSOE services to Venice (p206) and İstanbul (p178).

If you're travelling on an Interrail/Eurorail ticket (p254) and haven't pre-booked your necessary TGV reservations, or if you need to buy single tickets, the **ticket office** (6am-11.45pm) is in the western Hall d'Alsace.

The **left-luggage office** (*consigne*) is on the lower level. There are many shops and places to eat in the station, including a branch of Italian-style **Roberta Caffe** (roberta-caffe.fr; 6am-9pm Mon-Thu & Sat, to 9.30pm Fri & Sun; €). A one-minute walk west of the station, **Café les Deux Gares** (hoteldeuxgares.com; 9am-midnight Tue-Sat; €) is a pleasant spot to wait for your train.

Gare de l'Est is served by metro lines 4, 5 and 7. If you're transferring from or to nearby Gare du Nord, it's quicker to walk.

Gare de l'Est

One of Paris' six major train terminals, Gare de l'Est opened in 1849 and is the spiritual home of the Orient Express. The station's architecture is graceful, with the east entrance topped by a statue embodying Verdun, and the west entrance, leading to the Hall d'Alsace, by a statue representing Strasbourg.

Set into the floor of the Hall d'Alsace, near the Kusumi Tea outlet, is the **0km marker** from 1849 with a design of the Crampton steam locomotive No 80 – the one that pulled the first *Orient Express*. Gaze towards the ceiling to admire *The Departure of the Poilus, August 1914,* a 12m long **mural** by American artist Albert Herter, of French soldiers leaving Gare de l'Est in 1914. The painting is a memorial to Herter's son, a US Army soldier who died fighting during WWI.

Reims

The full speeds of around 300km/h that TGV trains are renowned for won't be reached until you're well out of the city and heading through the pretty countryside of the Champagne region. Out the window is a blur of rolling fields punctuated by strands of forest and the occasional village.

Around 40 minutes into your journey, you will pass the outskirts of Reims, home to many historic Champagne houses including **Veuve Clicquot** (veuveclicquot.com), **Taittinger** (taittinger.com) and **Maison Ruinart** (ruinart.com). If you're on a TGV train to Reims, the city's most central train station, the 13th-century **Cathédrale Notre-Dame** (cathedrale-reims.fr) is just a 15-minute walk southeast. The baptism of King Clovis on this spot in 496 led to every king of France subsequently being crowned in this magnificent Gothic cathedral. A good place for lunch is the brasserie **Ö Double A** (right).

Reims is served by a second TGV station, **Champagne-Ardenne**, south of the centre and connected to Reims main station by regional TER trains, as well as trams (22 minutes). To continue onto Strasbourg from central Reims, transfer in Champagne-Ardenne.

Gare de l'Est, Paris — *130km* — Reims

Search for the 0km marker on the floor of Gare de l'Est's Hall d'Alsace

Check out the 1910s Wladimir steam locomotive parked beside the platforms

Metz-Ville station

DETOUR: Metz
Via direct train: 45 minutes from Reims

Railway enthusiasts will want to detour to Metz (pronounced 'mess') to admire **Metz-Ville station**, a handsome Romanesque terminus opened in 1908. Lorraine's graceful capital also boasts the Gothic **Cathédrale St-Étienne** *(cathedrale-metz.fr; free)*, with kaleidoscopic stained glass, and a superlative art collection at the **Centre Pompidou-Metz** *(centrepompi dou-metz.fr; adult/child €14/free; closed Tue)*.

A standout place to eat is **Au Cul d'Poule** (right). For supplies for the train, head to the grand **Marché Couvert** *(8am-6pm Tue-Sat)*

Continues on page 54

BEST PLACES TO EAT

Le Tire-Bouchon, Strasbourg €
Arguably Strasbourg's best *choucroute* (dressed sauerkraut) is served at this snug, amiable *winstub* (traditional Alsatian restaurant).
11.30am-9.30pm

Ö Double A, Reims €€
Small corner brasserie on Reims buzzy place du Forum offering top local Champagnes by the glass.
9.30am-9.30pm

Au Cul d'Poule, Metz €€
Top choice for Metz with a light-filled interior, imaginative food and excellent location right near the cathedral.
noon-1.45pm & 7-9.30pm Tue-Sat

Herrenkeller, Ulm €€
Ulm mainstay serving classic German dishes such as schnitzel and *käsespatzle* (cheese pasta). Tables are in cosy timber booths. *11am-10.30pm Mon-Sat*

Detour: Admire Metz' handsome train station, a historic monument

280kms

Travel the Historic Route to Strasbourg

To travel along a more accurate historic Orient Express route out of Paris, opt for the slower trains along the Marne Valley. Stops include Épernay, the self-proclaimed capitale du Champagne, and Nancy, one of the birthplaces of art nouveau.

HOW TO

Getting here: Plenty of trains connect Gare de l'Est in Paris with Épernay and Nancy. For schedules see sncf-connect.com.

Tip: Épernay tourist office has maps and an app detailing bike routes between Champagne producers and through the vineyards.

More info: Épernay's **tourist office** (ot-epernay.fr; 9.30am-1pm & 2pm-6pm) is a seven-minute walk south of the train station. Nancy's **tourist office** (nancy-tourisme.fr; 9am-6.30pm Mon-Sat, 10am-5pm Sun Apr-Oct, shorter hours Nov-Mar) is a 12-minute walk east of the station.

Paris to Épernay

The leisurely train journey from Paris to Épernay (1¼ hours) goes via Château-Thierry and Dormans, past the vineyards of the Marne Valley.

Épernay's famous **avenue de Champagne**, a seven-minute walk south of the station, is bland in an upscale way, but it's what lies underground that's important: over 200 million bottles of Champagne, just waiting to be popped open.

Pay your respects to the statue of 17th-century monk **Dom Pérignon**, who perfected the sparkling method, then choose from tastings and tours at *maisons de Champagne*, including **Gosset** (champagne-gosset.com), **Moët & Chandon** (moet.com) and **Champagne Mercier** (champagnemercier.com), where you ride a train through their 18km of underground cellars. Book in advance as spots can sell out.

Perrier-Jouët (perrier-jouet.com) doesn't offer a tour but its art nouveau mansion and gardens are open for tastings and you can eat at its top-end restaurant. Another favourite with locals is the intimate **Sacre Bistro** (sacrebistro.fr; noon-2pm & 7-10pm Tue-Sat; €€); reservations are advised.

Épernay to Nancy

From Épernay, it's a two-hour ride by a TER train to Nancy, via Toul and the Moselle River valley. Look out for the Marne river as you pass through charming towns such as Châlons-en-Champagne.

TASTING NOTES

From sweetest to driest, Champagnes are labelled: *doux*, *demi-sec*, *sec*, *extra sec*, *brut* and *extra brut*.

A Champagne made from 100% chardonnay, a white grape, is called a *blanc de blancs*, while one made from 100% pinot noir or meunier, both black grapes, is called a *blanc de noirs*.

A 'grower Champagne producer' means that the house grows all its own grapes, which gives it maximum control over its own unique flavour as opposed to those blending grapes from others to produce a set taste.

Place Stanislas, Nancy

Nancy, the former capital of the dukes of Lorraine, catapults you back to the riches of the 18th century. Neoclassical **place Stanislas**, a 15-minute walk east of the station, is named after Polish-born Stanislas Leszczynski, the last Duke of Lorraine. Take in the grand architecture of this UNESCO World Heritage Site over a drink at **Grand Café Foy** (grandcafefoy.com; 7.30am-2am).

Nancy also boasts impressive examples of art nouveau design. **Brasserie L'Excelsior** (excelsior-nancy.fr; 8am-12.30am Tue-Sat, 8am-11pm Sun & Mon; €€), an atmospheric 1911 restaurant, has superb fin-de-siècle decor.

Continued from page 51

across from the cathedral. Once a bishop's palace, it is now a temple to fresh local produce.

To get here, there are a couple of daily direct trains (45 minutes) between Reims and Metz, and even more services between Metz and Strasbourg (50 minutes to 1½ hours).

Strasbourg

Having sped through the forests, green fields and rolling hills of Parc Naturel Regional de Lorraine you'll arrive in Strasbourg. When the *Orient Express* arrived in Strasbourg on its maiden voyage in 1883 the city was part of Germany's territory, and **Gare Centrale** (or Strasbourg-Ville) had not long been completed. The historic station still stands but tacked to its facade is a huge convex glass canopy. Stash your bags in the **left-luggage office** (7am-9pm) off Platform 1 before exploring the city (p56).

Kehl

Back on the train, about five minutes east of Strasbourg you will cross the Rhine into Germany, where some trains pause in the small town of Kehl. Generally, this should be a Schengen 'open border' with no passport checks, but during our research border guards came aboard the train to check travellers' passports, a consequence of the German government's tactics to reduce illegal immigration. Be prepared.

Stuttgart

On the way to Stuttgart, via Karlsruhe, you'll skirt the northern edge of the Black Forest, passing hills and valleys across which lie neat rows of vineyards. Before it became the birthplace of some of the world's most famous automobile marques, Stuttgart was the wine-producing capital of Baden-Württemberg.

Along the Way We Saw...

TWO SHORES GARDEN Inaugurated in 2004, the Two Shores Garden (Jardin des Deux-Rives/Garten der zwei Ufer) flanks the French and German shores of the Rhine. On the Strasbourg side I was charmed by the park's *Alice in Wonderland*–style features, including giant-sized garden furniture, plant pots, crayons sprouting from a hill and a whimsical sculpture of a purple-coloured hare and rose-coloured tortoise. I then walked over the border to Kehl using the 250m-long cable-stayed footbridge, pondering its Euro-harmony symbolism. Tram line D from Strasbourg connects to Kehl town centre, from where you can explore the German side of the garden before walking back to France over the pedestrian bridge.

Simon Richmond

Reims

Strasbourg — 10km

Kehl — 126km

The Rhine River flows past Strasbourg, forming the border between France and Germany

Karlsruhe station is connected by intercity trains to other German cities and Basel, Switzerland

To continue to Munich you may have to transfer at Stuttgart Hauptbahnhof, which poses an opportunity for a stopover. With affordable private rooms and dorms, **a&o Stuttgart City** (aohostels.com; €) is a great budget option. **EmiLu Design Hotel** (emilu-hotel.com; €€€) is a stylish place in the centre, and try **Gasthaus Bären** (noon-midnight Mon-Sat; €€) for Swabian tapas and delicious cocktails.

Motor enthusiasts will want to visit Stuttgart's **Porsche Museum** (porsche.com/germany/aboutporsche/porschemuseum; adult/child €12/6), where almost 100 Porsche vehicles are on display, and **Mercedes-Benz Museum** (mercedes-benz.com/en/art-and-culture/museum; adult/child €16/8), which is located in an architectural marvel.

Augsburg

 ## Ulm

There's some attractive forested and hilly countryside on the route from Stuttgart to Ulm, and coming into Ulm Hauptbahnhof, you won't miss the 161.5m-high steeple of Ulmer Münster (p58), the prime attraction of this picturesque city that's also the birthplace of Albert Einstein.

Ulm spans the Danube – on one side is the Altstadt, partially surrounded by old city walls and with an atmospheric neighbourhood of medieval half-timbered houses, and on the other is the more modern Neu-Ulm. Although 85% of the city centre was destroyed during WWII, the Ulmer Münster and some of the buildings of Fischerviertel survived. Harbouring art galleries, rustic restaurants, courtyards and the crookedest house in the world – as well as one of the narrowest – Fischerviertel's cobbled lanes are ideal for a leisurely saunter. It's also pleasant to watch the Danube flow by.

Ulm's sights are easily walkable from the station. The helpful **Ulm Tourist Office** (tourismus.ulm.de; 9.30am-6pm Mon-Fri, 9.30am-4pm Sat, 11am-3pm Sun) is on Münsterplatz near the cathedral. Places to stay include Ulmer Münster Hotel (p59), also near the cathedral, and historic Hotel Schiefes Haus (p59) in Fischerviertel. For a good meal try Herrenkeller (p51).

Augsburg

Leaving Ulm the tracks cross the Danube – keep an eye out as you'll get brief glimpses of the river again as you speed through Günzburg. Otherwise it's more fields and forests on the way to Augsburg. From the left side of the train, as you pull into the station, look for the church spires marking the medieval core of one of Germany's most ancient cities.

Continues on page 59

Stuttgart Hbf is changing from an above-ground terminus station to a through station with underground lines

Stuttgart

67km

Ulm

67km

Augsburg

Look to the left from the station for Ulmer Münster's spire topping out at 161.53m

CITY GUIDE:
Strasbourg

Alsace's biggest city is a cultural powerhouse serving up historic architecture, gastronomic delights and street art. Piercing the sky like a Gothic stone rocket is the 142m tower of its medieval cathedral. Around its base spreads the picturesque UNESCO World Heritage–listed old town.

HOW TO

Getting here: Trains arrive at Gare Centrale, a 15-minute walk northwest of the historic city centre.

Getting around: Strasbourg is a great place to walk as virtually the whole city centre is pedestrianised. If going beyond the city centre, there are **rental bikes** (velhop. strasbourg.fr) and trams.

Sleeping: There's plenty of accommodation with many options close by the station including Hôtel Tandem (p59) and Graffalgar (p59). More central is Boma (p59). Book well in advance as Strasbourg's hotels can get booked out when the European Parliament is in session, as well as during its famous Christmas markets.

Tip: Away from the historic centre, murals by renowned street artists make casual wandering a pleasure – see strasbourg.streetartmap.eu for details.

More info: The **Main Tourist Office** (visitstrasbourg.fr; 9am-7pm) is opposite the cathedral.

From the station, make a beeline for Grande Île, the UNESCO World Heritage–listed island in the River Ill, where you'll find the cathedral and many other historic treasures. The **Palais Rohan** (musees. strasbourg.eu) is an opulent 18th-century residence, hailed as a 'Versailles in miniature', that's home to a trio of top-notch museums. The antique Alsatian charm continues in La Petite France.

About 2km northeast of the city centre, the European Quarter offers eye-catching, futuristic architecture for key EU institutions including the **Palais des Droits de l'Homme** (European Court of Human Rights; echr.coe.int) and **Palais de l'Europe** (coe.int).

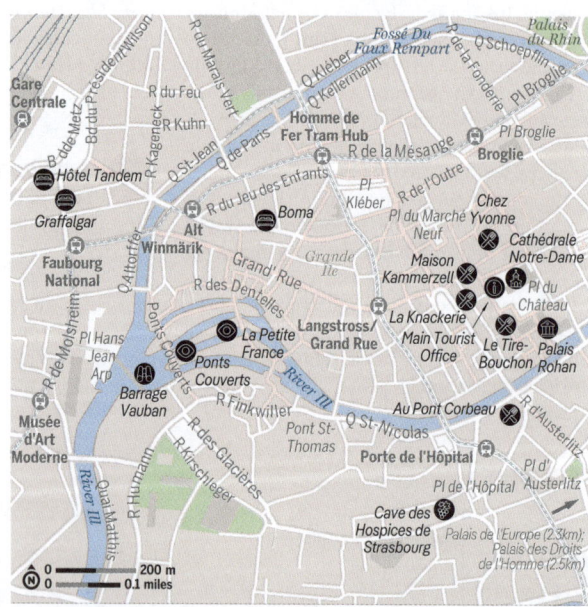

GOURMET CITY

Strasbourg is one of France's top gastronomic destinations, known for its fine Alsace food and wine. Dishes feature the freshest local ingredients, with a French knack for presentation and a German liking for gut-bursting portions.

For the quintessential Strasbourg culinary experience, consider dining at a *winstub* (literally 'wine room'), a traditional Alsatian restaurant renowned for its cosy atmosphere. Specialities include *baeckeoffe* (meat stew), *fleischschnäcke* (minced meat rolls) and *choucroute garnie* (sauerkraut garnished with meat or fish). Vegetarians can opt for *bibelaskäs* (soft white cheese mixed with fresh cream) and *pommes sautées* (sautéed potatoes). **Maison Kammerzell** (maison-kammerzell.com; 8am-10pm; €€), in a 15th-century building with an ornate facade near the cathedral, and Le Tire-Bouchon (p51) are famous for their version of *choucroute garnie*.

To pick up a bottle of Alsatian white wine for your journey, head to **Cave des Hospices de Strasbourg** (vins-des-hospices-de-strasbourg.fr; 8.30am-noon & 1.30-5.30pm Mon-Fri, 9am-12.30pm Sat).

Astronomical clock, Cathédrale Notre-Dame

Medieval Ecclesiastical Marvel

You cannot miss the **Cathédrale Notre-Dame** *(cathedrale-strasbourg.fr; church free, astronomical clock show €4)*, a Gothic masterpiece at the heart of Grande Île. The lace-fine facade carved from dirty pink sandstone lifts the gaze little by little to flying buttresses, leering gargoyles and a single 142m spire. The interior is exquisitely lit by 12th- to 14th-century stained-glass windows. A spiral staircase twists up to the 66m-high viewing platform. Be sure to catch the Gothic-meets-Renaissance astronomical clock that strikes solar noon at 12.30pm.

Meander Around La Petite France

Crisscrossed by narrow lanes, canals and locks, **La Petite France** is a visual treat. The half-timbered houses, bedecked with baskets of scarlet geraniums in summer, and the riverside parks are a tourism magnet, but the area still manages to retain its Alsatian charm. Enjoy views of the River Ill and the **Barrage Vauban** from the **Ponts Couverts**, with its trio of 13th-century towers, or rent a small electric boat (no licence is required) to explore the waterways at your own pace.

BEST PLACES TO EAT & DRINK

Chez Yvonne €€ Excellent Alsatian dishes in a traditionally decorated dining room. *11.45am-2pm & 6.30-10pm Tue-Sat*

Au Pont Corbeau €€ Cosy riverside restaurant serving excellent local specialities. *noon-2pm & 7-9.30pm Mon-Fri, noon-2pm Sun*

La Knackerie € Sample local '*knack*' sausages, with sauces by local Michelin-starred chefs. *11am-9pm*

EXPERIENCE

Scale Ulmer Münster

With its 161.53m tower, Ulmer Münster is one of the world's tallest cathedrals. For unbeatable panoramic views, climb the 768 steps to the highest viewing platform.

HOW TO

Getting here: The cathedral is a 12-minute walk east of Ulm Hauptbahnhof.

When to go: The tower is open 9am to 5pm from April to mid-October and 10am to 4pm the rest of the year.

Cost: Cathedral free; tower adult/child €9/4.50

Tip: At noon Tuesday to Saturday from May to the end of September, there's a free 30-minute organ concert in the cathedral.

More info: ulmer-muenster.de

For centuries, the Ulmer Münster has been the city of Ulm's focus. Started in 1377 and completed in 1890, this Goliath of cathedrals was financed entirely by Ulm's citizens. When more than 80% of Ulm was destroyed in December 1944, the cathedral, miraculously, was barely touched.

Time inevitably does take a toll. In 2026, with the completion of Barcelona's 172m Sagrada Família, Ulm lost its title as the world's tallest church. Restoration work is ongoing at the cathedral, which may mean you cannot climb to the highest viewing platform at 140m. But none of this diminishes the impact of Ulm's Gothic masterpiece as you crane your neck to take it all in from Münsterplatz.

Step inside and admire the stained-glass windows and vaulted ceilings before tackling the narrow spiral steps to the main viewing platform at 101m. From this vantage point on clear days you can see Zugspitze, Germany's highest mountain. Rest on the way up at a gallery displaying sepia-toned images of cathedrals from around the world.

Above: Statue in Ulmer Münster
Right: Ulmer Münster

Continued from page 55

From the station it's a pleasant 20-minute walk east to the heart of the Altstadt and the **Fuggerei** *(fugger.de; adult/concession/child/family €8/7/4/18)*, one of the world's first public housing projects, dating to the 16th century. It's an appealing complex to explore, with its vine-clad homes with Bavarian-style steepled facades. Inside the handsome **Dom Mariä Heimsuchung** *(entry free)*, view some of Bavaria's most magnificent stained-glass windows.

Housed in a renovated, 500-year-old former bishop's guesthouse, some of the rooms at **Dom Hotel** *(domhotel-augsburg.de; €€)* have cathedral views. Dine on light, tasty dishes with a sunny Mediterranean focus at **Perlacht Acht** *(5-11.30pm Tue-Fri, noon-2.30pm & 5-11.30pm Sat & Sun; €€)*.

München Hauptbahnhof

It's only about 30 minutes from Augsburg to Munich (p62) – before you know it, you'll be passing through the Bavarian capital's western suburbs and arriving at München Hauptbahnhof (Munich Central Station; München Hbf). This is one of Germany's busiest transport hubs – some 450,000 passengers pass through daily. It's also a station amid a major reconstruction, scheduled to be completed in 2033.

Munich's first railway station opened in 1839, and the terminus has been rebuilt numerous times. On the *Orient Express*' maiden voyage, the precaution was taken of having a spare restaurant and sleeping car on standby in Munich – a canny move, as the dining car hitched to the train at Paris had developed a serious fault with its axel and needed to be replaced.

BEST PLACES TO SLEEP

Hôtel Tandem, Strasbourg €€
Ecofriendly, characterful hotel across from Strasbourg railway station. *hotel-tandem.fr*

Graffalgar, Strasbourg €
Fun, street art-decorated rooms, plus co-working space cafe near Strasbourg station. *graffalgar-hotel-strasbourg.fr*

Boma, Strasbourg €€
Chic design and congenial atmosphere in central Strasbourg. *boma-hotel.com/en*

Ulmer Münster Hotel, Ulm €€
Appealing modern hotel with splendid views of Ulm's cathedral, a great breakfast and bicycle rental. *en.ulmermuensterhotel.de*

Hotel Schiefes Haus, Ulm €€€
Sleep in the snug, beamed-ceiling rooms of Ulm's crookedest house dating to the 16th century. *hotelschiefeshausulm.de*

München Hauptbahnhof is well connected to other European cities, with most services arriving at Platforms 11 to 26 along the main concourse. At either end of the concourse, head down to a vast lower level for shops, places to eat and entrances to the S-Bahn and U-Bahn tracks.

Augsburg

Clearly visible south of Augsburg station is Hotelturm Augsburg, a 115m tower known locally as the 'corn cob'

50km

München Hauptbahnhof, Munich

Kenneth Branagh and Daisy Ridley in the 2017 film adaptation of *Murder on the Orient Express*
LIFESTYLE PICTURES ALAMY

INSIGHT

Your Orient Express Reading List

From dozing spies and queasy aristocrats to Poirot's omelettes, novelists have used the train as a vehicle for stories of crime, passion and subterfuge.

WORDS BY **HELENA SMITH**
Helena Smith won Vogue's *writing contest; she loves reading on trains.*

Downhill on the Orient Express

Graham Greene likened the arrival of the Orient Express into a city station to the closing moments of an overture, when 'all the rural and urban themes of our long journey were picked up again'. This image comes from Greene's burlesque comic novel *Travels with My Aunt* (1969), where all that's on the menu between Paris and the Turkish border is marijuana and chocolate from the louche woman in the neighbouring couchette, the service having fallen on hard times. Aunt Augusta rhapsodises about caviar and Champagne and an unending party on the Orient Express in times gone by: 'one meal ran into another and night into day'.

The Orient Express likewise gets short shrift in DH Lawrence's *Lady Chatterley's Lover* (1928): travelling to Venice to escape her husband, Constance dislikes 'trains de luxe, the atmosphere of vulgar depravity there is aboard them nowadays'.

Whodunnit?

Vulgar depravity turns to deathly intent with *Murder on the Orient Express* (1934); Agatha Christie's detective Hercule Poirot solves the crime as the train is held up by a snowstorm between Vinkovci and Brod. While the characters of this much-adapted novel are broad-brush and the narrative entirely plot led, there are fascinating insights into the reach and style of the train service: Poirot travels from Syria arriving in İstanbul at 6.55am, crosses the Bosphorus in time to catch the Simplon Express at 9am and consumes omelettes in the restaurant car in between interviews with the suspects.

Uneasy Journeys

If Christie's writing now seems formulaic, Eric Ambler's *The Mask of Dimitrios* (1939) is the prototype of the modern psychological thriller. The protagonist is the diffident and somewhat helpless Latimer, an English novelist tracing the story of the murderous Dimitrios in order to find material for his new crime thriller; the hunter becomes the hunted as Latimer journeys from İstanbul to Paris by train. A sleeping car bound for Sofia sees our non-hero encountering the ornately polite and subtly threatening Peters in a scene that conjures both the comic awkwardness of sharing a confined space with a stranger, and the queasy morality of a world on the edge of wartime chaos. As the novel ends, Latimer speeds away from Paris on the Orient Express.

Orient Express route spotters will enjoy the fact that passengers in Graham Greene's *Stamboul Train* (1932) start their journey in Ostend in Belgium, having taken the Channel Steamer. As it shifts from Ostend to Vienna to Constantinople, the novel's emotional landscape has more in common with *The Mask of Dimitrios* than with Greene's own much later *Travels with My Aunt*. Interspersed with anti-Semitic incidents and threaded with anxiety, *Stamboul Train* anticipates the horrors coming to Europe.

Quick Reads

The train has proved an irresistible setting in popular as well as literary fiction. Spy novel *The Madonna of the Sleeping Cars* by Maurice Dekobra (1927) was a bestseller in its time, as effervescent as an onboard cocktail quaffed by outrageous protagonist Lady Diana Manners.

> The train has proved an irresistible setting in popular as well as literary fiction.

The Simplon Orient Express is the backdrop for the last 100 pages of Ian Fleming's crudely violent and sexist *From Russia, with Love* (1957). But there is some incidental interest in the train's route from İstanbul to Paris via northern Greece, and a rather lovely description of the soothing effect of train travel as Bond struggles to stay awake despite 'the lullaby creak of the woodwork in the little room'.

Veronica Henry hops on board the gravy train with lightweight romance in *A Night on the Orient Express* (2013), while Lindsay Jayne Ashford's *The Woman on the Orient Express* (2016) gets meta, with Agatha Christie herself – escaping a broken marriage – taking a trip on the service in the footsteps of Poirot.

But the true heyday of Orient Express novels is the 1930s. And it's hard to imagine a better evocation of the physical sensation of train travel than that in *Stamboul Train*: 'In the rushing reverberating express, noise was so regular that it was the equivalent of silence, movement was so continuous that after a while the mind accepted it as stillness.'

CITY GUIDE:
Munich

Panoramic view of Munich's Altstadt (p69)

Nowhere else in Germany serves up such a dynamic blend of past and present than Munich. Come here for an attractive Altstadt, traditional Bavarian oompah culture, contemporary arts, lush parks and a delicious food scene. Take your pick from some 50 museums and galleries, including the eye-boggling interior design of the Residenz.

WORDS BY SIMON RICHMOND
Simon is a long-established guidebook writer for Lonely Planet.

Arriving
München Hauptbahnhof
During its reconstruction, the main exits/entrances to München Hauptbahnhof are from Arnulfstrasse to the north, and Bayerstrasse to the south. Apart from being a building site, the area immediately around the station is safe, if not the most attractive part of Munich. However, you are less than a 20-minute walk from the Altstadt and are close by the main location for the Oktoberfest. **Information and ticket offices** *(7am-9pm Mon-Fri, 8am-8pm Sat & Sun)* are to the right of the main concourse; to the left is a section of old terminus building housing **luggage storage lockers**.

Transfers München Hauptbahnhof is a big station with 32 above-ground platforms. DB has a poor reputation for punctuality – keep this in mind when arranging onward connections. Most trains for Austria depart from Platforms 5 to 10 in the Holzkirchner Bahnhof (Holzkirchen wing station), about a seven-minute walk from the main concourse.

Refuelling
There are a few kiosks for takeaway food and drinks on the main concourse; the range of places to eat on the station's underground floor is much wider. If you have a couple of hours to kill between trains, then the leafy Bavarian beer garden Augustiner Keller (p55) is an eight-minute walk from the Arnulfstrasse exit.

Getting Around
Central Munich is easily explored on foot.
Public transport Munich's public transport system includes trams, the U-Bahn and the S-Bahn. For Marienplatz in the Altstadt, ride S-Bahn S1 (five minutes). Download the **MVV app** *(mvv-muenchen.de)* for route planning and to buy tickets. Otherwise buy tickets from machines at the stations and bus/tram stops.

HOW MUCH FOR A

Beer €5

Two Weisswurst €7.20

Residenz admission €20

For schedules and trip planning, download the MVV app:

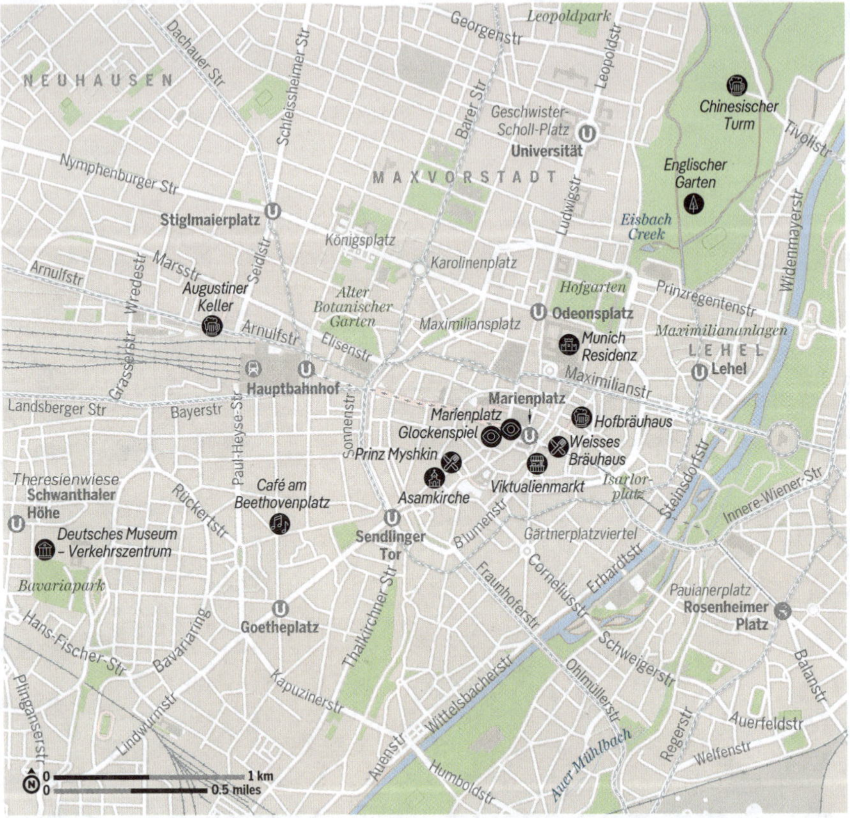

A DAY IN MUNICH

 Tuck into the classic Munich breakfast of plump *Weisswurst* with a pretzel, sweet mustard and a glass of wheat beer at **Weisses Bräuhaus** (right). Check out the cool transport exhibits, including vintage trains, at the **Deutsches Museum – Verkehrszentrum** (p69), then return to the Altstadt's **Marienplatz** (p69) for the noon striking of the **Glockenspiel**.

 Graze the superior food stalls of the **Viktualienmarkt** (right) or have a vegetarian lunch at **Prinz Myshkin** (right). Walk it all off exploring the many dazzling halls and corridors of the former royal palace, the **Munich Residenz** (p67). Alternatively, check out the religious art and architecture in the Altstadt's premier churches, including the baroque **Asamkirche** (p66).

 In summer, an early evening stroll through the **Englischer Garten** (p66) can be magic, especially if you can bag a seat in the beer garden at **Chinesischer Turm** (p66). A short walk from München Hauptbahnhof, choose between **Augustiner Keller** (right), another top beer garden, or the atmospheric **Café am Beethovenplatz** (right) for dinner.

Where to Stay

There are plenty of hostels, midrange places and short-term rental apartments clustered near München Hauptbahnhof. The Altstadt is also within walking distance of the station and near all the sights and best restaurants – this is where you'll find most of the city's high-end hotels.

Room rates across Munich skyrocket during the Oktoberfest, which runs from mid-September to the first Sunday in October. If your train trip is at this time, consider visiting for the day and staying elsewhere.

BEST PLACES TO STAY

Hotel Blauer Bock €€ Near the Viktualienmarkt, this simple hotel is a great deal. *hotelblauerbock.de*

Flushing Meadows €€ Minimalist design hotel in hip Glockenbachviertel. *flushingmeadowshotel.com*

Hotel Mariandl €€ Character-packed, old-tourism hotel with *Jugendstil* period rooms. *mariandl.com*

Wombat's City Hostel Munich Hauptbahnhof € Ensuite privates and dorms not far from the station. *wombats-hostels.com*

Where to Eat

Munich's cultural and economic diversity is reflected in the range of places where you can get a bite to eat – everything from grab-and-go sausage and pretzel stands, to Vietnamese cafes and Michelin-starred dining rooms. The Altstadt has the best range of places, including the gourmet **Viktualienmarkt** *(viktualienmarkt-muenchen.de; 8am-8pm Mon-Sat)*; also check out restaurants in fashionable Schwabing.

LOCAL SPECIALITIES

Bavarian cuisine is hearty and filling. Menus are packed with pork, sausages, veal and river fish, and many dishes are accompanied by dumplings, thick sauces and sauerkraut. Look for restaurants that have been awarded the quality seal **Ausgezeichnete Genuss-Küche** *(bayerischekueche.de)* for the most authentic local cooking.

The most iconic Munich dish is *Weisswurst*, a veal sausage, traditionally eaten for breakfast with a pretzel and a jug of wheat beer – do like locals do and remove the sausage's skin before eating. Meat lovers will also want to try *Schweinshaxe* (pork knuckle) and *Schweinenbraten* (roast pork), usually served with a dark beer sauce.

Munich's food scene is cosmopolitan – Bavarians are bonkers about Italian food, and all kinds of Asian cuisines are also popular. Several Afghan restaurants serve the local Afghani population, and vegetarians and vegans are well catered for in specialist restaurants.

BEST PLACES TO EAT & DRINK

Augustiner Keller €€ Leafy 5000-seat beer garden serving hearty food and beers. *10am-midnight*

Weisses Bräuhaus €€ Altstadt institution for *Weisswurst*, pretzels and beer. *9am-11.30pm*

Prinz Myshkin €€ Munich's premier meat-free restaurant creates culinary magic. *11am-11pm Tue-Sat*

Café am Beethovenplatz €€ Channel vintage Orient Express vibes at this music cafe. *10am-1am*

Asamkirche

☼ Stroll the English Garden

One of the loveliest and largest of urban parks along the Orient Express route is Munich's leafy **Englischer Garten**. Join locals to discover a tranquil world of woodland, birdsong and students swotting up in the sun.

Stretching north from Prinzregentenstrasse for about 5km, the park was commissioned by Elector Karl Theodor in 1789 and designed by Benjamin Thompson, an American-born scientist working as an adviser to the Bavarian government. Two pieces of folly architecture dominate the park's middle: the Greek temple **Monopteros** (1838) and the **Chinesischer Turm** (Chinese Tower), the unlikely setting for a classic Munich beer garden.

MUNICH'S ECLECTIC ARCHITECTURE

The Bavarian capital's architecture is a mixed bag of stone, brick and glass, with everything ranging from 15th-century churches to ultra-modern stadiums. Some of the grandest buildings, like the **Schloss Nymphenburg** palace, 5km northwest of the Altstadt, were commissioned by the city's rulers, from medieval dukes to Adolf Hitler.

A superb example of the late-baroque style is **Asamkirche**, completed in 1746. Every inch of this chapel is swathed with gilt garlands, cherubs, false marble and oversized barley-twist columns.

Jugendstil is the local term for the art nouveau style of the late 19th century and first decades of the 20th century. **Schwabing** is the place to go to see the style in bricks and mortar; the streets in the north of the district are lined with magnificent decorative villas.

The architectural highlight of the economic miracle period of the 1960s and '70s is **Olympiapark**, fashioned out of spare land north of Schwabing for the 1972 Summer Games. The two most striking Olympic structures are the **Olympiastadion**, with its undulating Plexiglas roof, and the 291m-tall **Olympiaturm**.

Along the Way We Met...

DANIEL HOLDER Our most popular day tour is to Dachau Memorial Site. Otherwise, all the cool stuff that people associate with Germany – beer, pretzels, traditional outfits – originated in Bavaria.

Daniel is Head of Operations for Radius Tours (radiustours.com).

DANIEL'S TIP: *Drink some of our beer and go for a relaxed walk around the Altstadt with a slight buzz in your head to experience* gemütlichkeit *(a cosy, easy-going feeling).*

Admire the Residenz

The sprawling palace of the Wittelsbach dynasty from 1508 until WWI, the Residenz is Munich's top attraction, offering a dazzling parade of architectural styles and over-the-top interior design.

Getting here: The palace is a 20-minute walk from München Hauptbahnhof. The closest U-bahn stop is Odeonsplatz.

Opening hours: 9am to 6pm April to mid-October, 10am to 5pm the rest of the year

Cost: All attractions adult/concession €20/16

Tip: If you're pressed for time, follow the shorter route around the palace.

More info: residenz-muenchen.de

Though much of the palace had to be reconstructed after WWII, there's quite a lot of original interior design on display, including a triple whammy of rooms at the very start. The gilded, rococo **Ahnengallery** (Ancestors Gallery) showcases 121 portraits of Bavarian rulers in chronological order. Next comes the **Grottenhof** (Grotto Court), home of the wonderful **Perseusbrunnen** (Perseus Fountain) decorated with tens of thousands of shells. Perhaps most impressive is the **Antiquarium**, a barrel-vaulted hall of frescoes, created by Duke Albrecht V between 1568 and 1571 to house the vast royal collection of Greek and Roman sculptures.

Follow the long route for **Ludwig I's Royal Palace**, a no-holds-barred series of neoclassical quarters including the king's throne room with its entirely gold walls, Roman stucco and huge red velvet canopy.

After your tour of the main palace, the **Schatzkammer der Residenz** contains the Wittelsbachs' collections of jewel-encrusted yesteryear bling, while the sumptuously baroque **Cuvilliés-Theater** sports four levels of balconies, each one plastered in gilt and red stucco.

Above: Crown of the kings of Bavaria, Schatzkammer der Residenz
Right: Interior, Residenz

Trains at Deutsches Museum – Verkehrszentrum

🚆 Visit the Transport Museum

The fascinating **Deutsches Museum – Verkehrszentrum** *(Transport Museum; deutsches-museum.de/verkehrszentrum; adult/child €8/5)* explores the ingenious ways we transport things and ourselves. From skis and bicycles to racing cars and high-speed ICE trains, the collection is a trip through transport history. The exhibition is spread over three halls, each with its own theme – Public Transportation, Travel, and Mobility and Technology. In the railway section, look for detailed models of historic Orient Express trains and a plush 1930s Pullman carriage that ran between Chur and St Moritz.

Nationaltheater

🎭 Tour Munich's Grandest Stage

One of many grand opera houses along the Orient Express route, Munich's **Nationaltheater** *(staatsoper.de; tours adult/child €10/5)* offers a spectacular neoclassical facade and one of the world's largest stages (a whopping 2500 sq metres). Opened in 1818, and rebuilt several times since, it's home to the Bavarian State Opera, one of the world's top opera companies, and the Bavarian State Ballet. Wagner's *Tristan und Isolde* and *Die Walküre* premiered here. If you can't get to a performance, tours of the theatre run between 10am and 6pm weekdays.

BEER CITY

Downing a *mass* (1L tankard) of lager in a traditional beer hall or garden is the quintessential Munich experience. Countless beer gardens; Oktoberfest (and several other minor beer festivals); famous breweries, such as **Paulaner** and **Augustiner**; myriad beers in all shades and strengths; and, of course, the famous **Hofbräuhaus**, the mothership of all beer halls, all form part of the city's famous hop-based culture.

Oktoberfest dates to October 1810, when the future king Bavarian Crown Prince Ludwig I married Princess Therese and the newlyweds threw an enormous party at the city gates, complete with a horse race. The next year Ludwig's fun-loving subjects came back for more. The festival was extended and, to fend off autumn, was moved forward to September. The racehorses were dropped and, today, this 16-day extravaganza draws more than six million visitors, making it the world's biggest collective booze-up.

A special dark, strong beer *(Wies'nbier)* is brewed for the occasion. On the **Theresienwiese** fairground, a temporary city of beer tents, amusements and rides is erected – admission is free and Müncheners dress up in traditional Bavarian costumes to attend.

Explore the Altstadt

Laid out in medieval times, Munich's Altstadt remains the city's heart and soul. Bustling Marienplatz, its central piazza, is where crowds gather to watch the Glockenspiel.

HOW TO

Getting here: Marienplatz is a five-minute ride on S1 S-Bahn from München Hauptbahnhof.

When to go: The Glockenspiel springs into action daily at 11am and noon (and at 5pm from March to October).

Tip: St Peterskirche's tower provides a bird's-eye view of the Glockenspiel.

More info: Munich's **tourist office** *(muenchen.de; 9am-7pm Mon-Fri, to 4pm Sat, 10am-2pm Sun)* is on Marienplatz.

All that remains of the Altstadt's medieval walls are three of its gates: **Isartor** guarding the east, the **Sendlinger Tor** to the south and the **Karlstor** to the west.

No building in the Altstadt can stand taller than the twin 99m, onion dome–topped towers of **Frauenkirche** *(muenchner-dom.de; south tower adult/child €7.50/5.50)*. Like much of Munich, the 15th-century church was severely damaged during WWII. The rebuild created a rather spartan interior illuminated by impossibly elongated stained-glass windows.

Dominating the northern side of **Marienplatz** is the neo-Gothic **Neues Rathaus** *(muenchen.travel; tower adult/child €7/3)*. Its 85m tower is the location of the solar-powered **Glockenspiel**. The charming mechanism's top half depicts a jousting tournament held in 1568 to celebrate the marriage of Duke Wilhelm V to Renata of Lothringen, while the bottom half displays the *Schäfflertanz* (cooper's dance).

Off the southern side of the Marienplatz rises the impressive **St Peterskirche** *(adult/child €5/3; tower 9am-6pm Mon-Fri, from 10am Sat & Sun)*, dating to 1150. Climb the 306 steps of its 56m tower for panoramic views.

Above: Clock face, Glockenspiel
Right: Marienplatz

Munich

With an early start, you could hop off the train at either lake Chiemsee in Bavaria or go in search of *The Sound of Music* in Salzburg and still be in Vienna by nightfall. Vintage train enthusiasts will not want to miss the charming narrow-gauge steam engine railway at Prien am Chiemsee. The scenery becomes more spectacular as you approach the snow-capped Alps straddling the German–Austrian border, and the Danube puts in another appearance near Vienna.

Simon Richmond

Chiemsee (p76)
MATTEO PATETTA/SHUTTERSTOCK

Vienna

464 KMS — 4 HOURS' RIDE

THIS LEG:

- Rosenheim
- Prien am Chiemsee
- Traunstein
- Freilassing
- Salzburg Hauptbahnhof
- Vöcklabruck
- Linz
- Melk
- St Pölten
- Wien Hauptbahnhof, Vienna

Riding Notes

Trains connect Munich and Vienna, either directly or via a transfer at Salzburg, at least hourly. Hop off at Prien am Chiemsee to ride the steam train along the Chiemsee-Bahn. If you end up on one of the trains of Austrian operator Westbahn, note they terminate at Wien Westbahnhof rather than Wien Hauptbahnhof.

Breaking Your Journey

There are plenty of nice places to stay around Chiemsee, including on the island Fraueninsel (p77). If you detour to Berchtesgaden (p79), it's worth spending a night up in the mountains. The wealth of things to do and see in Salzburg (p79) make this another likely overnight stop. Also consider Linz (p80) as an Austrian base.

Simon's Tips

BEST MEAL Hearty Bavarian cuisine at Schlosswirtschaft Herrenchiemsee. (p75)

FAVOURITE VIEW The Chiemgau Alps as you approach the German-Austrian border. (p78)

ESSENTIAL STOP Ludwig II's lavish Herrenchiemsee. (p76)

TIP Book well ahead for tickets to performances during the annual **Salzburg Festival** *(salzburgerfestspiele.at)*.

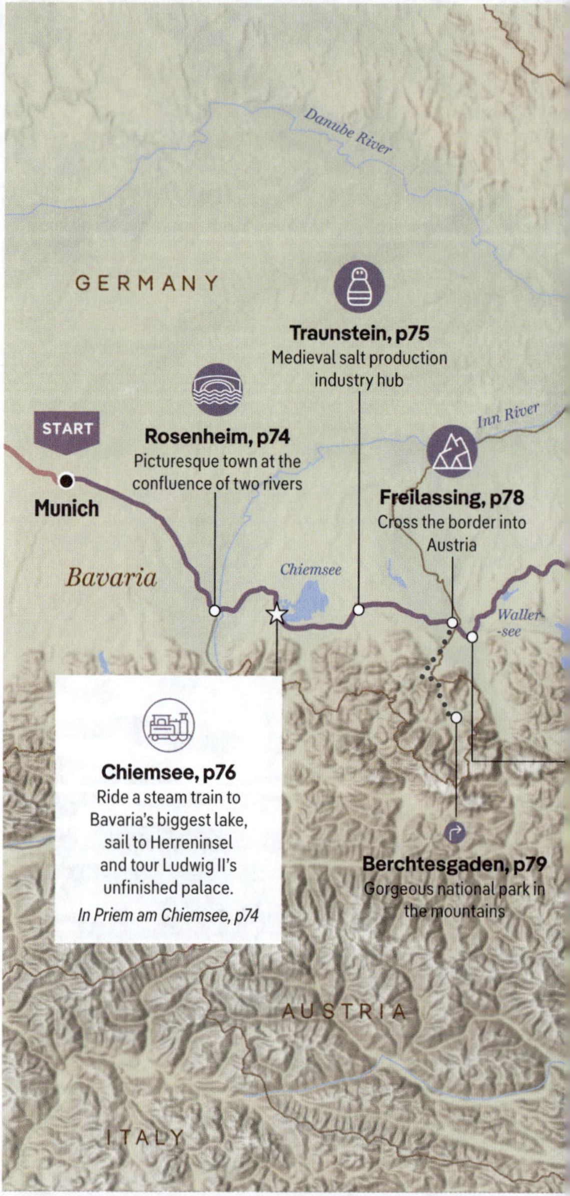
Danube River
GERMANY
Traunstein, p75
Medieval salt production industry hub
Rosenheim, p74
Picturesque town at the confluence of two rivers
START
Munich
Inn River
Freilassing, p78
Cross the border into Austria
Bavaria
Chiemsee
Waller-see
Chiemsee, p76
Ride a steam train to Bavaria's biggest lake, sail to Herreninsel and tour Ludwig II's unfinished palace.
In Priem am Chiemsee, p74
Berchtesgaden, p79
Gorgeous national park in the mountains
AUSTRIA
ITALY

> **ONWARD TRAVEL**
>
> Moving on towards Austria there's a choice of trains. If heading directly to Salzburg, the fastest option is **ÖBB's Railjet** (RJX or RJ; oebb.at; 1½ hours) trains. Services by the Austrian rail operator **Westbahn** (westbahn.at) and Germany's **DB** (int.bahn.de) are only a few minutes slower. Seat reservations are optional, but recommended, particularly at busy times of the year.
>
> You could also take the hourly **Bayerische Regiobahn** (BRB; brb.de) trains, which stop at more stations along the way, including Prien am Chiemsee. Reservation are not needed for these trains.
>
> Most departures will be from Platforms 5 to 10 in the **Holzkirchner Bahnhof** (Holzkirchen wing station) on the Bayerstrasse (south) side of München Hauptbahnhof. These platforms are around a seven-minute walk from the main concourse.

Rosenheim

Leaving Munich, trains usually make a brief stop at **München Ost** before continuing southeast out of the city towards the Bavarian Alps. Neatly tended fields, farmhouses and the distant foothills of the Alps are part of the scenery on the way to Rosenheim, which lies at the confluence of the differently coloured Inn and Mangfall rivers. The heart of town is cobblestoned **Max-Josefs-Platz**, a handsome piazza surrounded by cafes, about a 15-minute walk northeast of the station. From the piazza it's another 15-minute walk to the riverside park.

Prien am Chiemsee

The foothills of the Chiemgau Alps appear on the approach to Prien am Chiemsee and there's a foretaste of the region's lakes as the tracks skirt 470m-long **Simssee**. Shortly after the train pulls into Prien. There are lockers on the train platform to store your bags before you set off for the lake.

Most visitors will want to ride the **Chiemsee-Bahn** (p76) to Stock harbour – this late-19th-century steam train railway was constructed shortly after the opening of Herrenchiemsee to the public to cope with the sharp increase in visitor traffic. Pulled by one of the world's oldest operational steam locomotives, the nine-carriage train includes a plush lounge car that was used by visiting VIPs.

Prien am Chiemsee

München Hauptbahnhof, Munich	München Ost	Rosenheim
4km	55km	

You'll cross the Isar river on the way from München Hauptbahnhof to München Ost

Max-Josefs-Platz, Rosenheim

Prien is an attractive place with a small **local history museum** *(1-5pm Tue-Sun)* behind Mariä Himmelfahrt church. A nice spot for refreshments is **Cafe Heider** (right). Places to stay include **Luitpold am See** (p78) at Stock and lakeside **Panorama Camping Harras** (p78).

Traunstein

As the train rounds the south side of Chiemsee you'll get closer views of the Chiemgau Alps. There's a pause at Traunstein, the region's hub. A centre of the local salt production industry since the Middle Ages, Traunstein lays claim to the world's first pipeline (made of wood), which

Continues on page 78

BEST PLACES TO EAT

Schlosswirtschaft Herrenchiemsee, Herreninsel €€
Beside the Augustinian Monastery on Herreninsel, offering panoramic lake views. Dishes include pork schnitzel and fried pike perch. *11am-4.30pm*

Schloss-Café Herrenchiemsee, Herreninsel €
Ducks waddle around the outdoor tables at this pleasant self-serve cafe in the Royal Palace on Herreninsel. *9am-4.45pm*

Cafe Heider, Prien am Chiemsee €
Cute bakery-cafe beside the market in the centre of Prien am Chiemsee. *8am-6pm Tue-Sat, 8.30am-6pm Sun*

Gaststätte St Bartholomä, Königssee €€
Bavarian restaurant serving hearty meat and fish dishes and HB lager on Königssee, reachable only by boat. *10am-5pm*

Ride the steam railway from Prien to the harbour at Stock

Great views of the Chiemgau Alps around here

17km — Prien am Chiemsee
14km — Traunstein

Ride a Steam Train to Chiemsee

Nicknamed the Bavarian Sea, Chiemsee is Bavaria's largest lake at 80 sq km. Since 1887 a steam train has been transporting visitors to the lake shore, where boats sail to the islands of Herreninsel and Fraueninsel, the former the location of Ludwig II's lavish Schloss Herrenchiemsee.

HOW TO

Getting here: Hourly trains link Munich and Salzburg with Prien am Chiemsee – the journey in either direction takes just under an hour.

Getting around: See chiemsee-schifffahrt.de for the Chiemsee-Bahn steam train schedule and for boats around the lake and to the islands.

When to go: Avoid weekends when Herreninsel can get very busy.

Sleeping: Options include Luitpold am See (p78) and Panorama Camping Harras (p78).

Eating & Drinking: Schloss-Café Herrenchiemsee (p75) or Schlosswirtschaft Herrenchiemsee (p75) on Herreninsel.

More info: Prien am Chimsee's **Tourist Information Centre** (tourismus.prien.de; 8.30am-6pm Mon-Fri, 8.30am-12.30pm Sat)

Full Steam Ahead

One of only a handful of regularly operating steam railways in the world, the **Chiemsee-Bahn** (chiemsee-schifffahrt.de; adult/child return €4.60/2.30) chugs between Prien and Stock harbour. The 19th-century steam engine and nine carriages are in pristine condition and the 1.8km journey is a delight. Use the underpass from Prien am Chiemsee station to reach the departure platform.

At Stock, Chiemsee-Schifffahrt operates 14 passenger boats including the handsome *Ludwig Fessler* paddle steamer from 1926. You can cruise to either island or make a tour of the lake.

Palace on Herreninsel

Herreninsel is home to Ludwig II's **Herrenchiemsee** (herrenchiemsee.de; 9am-6pm Apr-Oct, 10am-4.45pm Nov-Mar; tour €14). It's a lovely walk of around 20 minutes from the boat pier to the palace.

Even though only a dozen or so of its planned 50 rooms were finished, the palace's opulent interiors will blow you away. The early 100m-long Great Hall of Mirrors is hung with 52 candelabras and 33 great glass chandeliers. The Golden State Bedroom dazzles with gilding and the Porcelain Room is dominated by the largest Meissen chandelier ever produced. The palace also hosts excellent art exhibitions from the collection of Munich's Pinakothek der Moderne.

Overlooking the boat pier is the former **Augustinian Monastery**.

LUDWIG'S PRIVATE PALACE

Bavaria's king from 1864 until his death at age 40 in 1886, Ludwig II was partial to architectural flights of fancy, the most famous being Schloss Neuschwanstein. More money was spent on Herrenchiemsee than on Neuschwanstein and his Schloss Linderhof put together – the project nearly bankrupted the royal coffers. A theatrical stage rather than a functioning palace, Herrenchiemsee was Ludwig's private domain – no guests were invited and even the servants had to stay out of sight. He only spent 10 nights here before his death.

Left: Chiemsee-Bahn
Below: Fraueninsel

Ludwig stayed here during the construction of Herrenchiemsee and had the Imperial Hall decorated to his lavish tastes. Other parts of the monastery house an art gallery featuring impressionistic landscapes of the lake and Alps by Julius Exter.

Escape to Fraueninsel

The lake's smaller island, Fraueninsel, is home to **Frauenwörth Abbey** (frauenwoerth.de; tours €6), established in the late 8th century. The 10th-century church has a free-standing 11th-century bell tower.

Gasthaus & Hotel 'Zur Linde' (p78) is a historic place to stay.

BEST PLACES TO SLEEP

Luitpold am See, Stock €€
Pleasant, family-run hotel in an art nouveau villa next to the harbour at Stock/Prien am Chiemsee. Also has a good restaurant. *luitpold-am-see.de*

Gasthaus & Hotel 'Zur Linde', Fraueninsel €€
There are beautiful lake views from this guesthouse in a listed historic monument on Fraueninsel in Chiemsee. *linde-frauenchiemsee.de*

Panorama Camping Harras, Chiemsee €
Camping ground scenically located on a peninsula 3km south of Prien with its own private beach. *camping-harras.de*

Hotel Reikartz Vier Jahreszeiten, Berchtesgaden €€
Traditional lodge where Bavarian royalty once crumpled the sheets. Facilities include a swimming pool and sauna. *hotel-vierjahreszeiten-berchtesgaden.de*

Continued from page 75

transported brine from Reichenhall, some 30km southeast. You can learn all about this at the **Salinenpark open-air museum** (around a 15-minute walk southeast of the train station), which includes a reconstruction of the Reiffenstuel water wheel.

Freilassing

Beautiful mountain vistas (on the right side of the train) will keep you glued to the window as the railway continues towards the Austrian border at Freilassing. Border guards may check passports here, so ensure you have them handy.

Train enthusiasts should consider hopping off the train at Freilassing to visit **Lokwelt Freilassing** (*lokwelt.freilassing.de*; 10am-5pm Fri-Sun; adult/child €6/4). Located in the 1905 locomotive shed next to the station, this train

Lokwelt Freilassing

museum contains part of Munich's Deutsches Museum – Verkehrszentrum's collection.

If you are detouring to Berchtesgaden, Freilassing is where you'll need to change trains.

DETOUR: **Berchtesgaden**
50 minutes from Freilassing

This drop-dead-gorgeous corner of Bavaria is home to **Watzmann** (2713m), Germany's second-highest mountain, and the pristine and super-photogenic lake **Königssee**. Much of the area is protected within the **Berchtesgaden National Park** *(nationalpark-berchtesgaden.bayern.de)*, which is also a UNESCO biosphere reserve. The village of Berchtesgaden is the obvious base for hiking circuits and explorations in the national park.

The area also has a sinister history – Hitler's mountaintop lodge, **Eagle's Nest** *(kehlsteinhaus.de)*, is now a major dark-tourism destination,

while the **Dokumentation Obersalzberg** *(obersalzberg.de)* chronicles the region's Nazi past.

Berchtesgaden Tourist Office *(berchtesgaden.com; 9am-5pm)* has information on the region. A worthy place to stay is **Hotel Reikartz Vier Jahreszeiten** (p78). Make sure you take the boat across the Königssee to eat at **Gaststätte St Bartholomä** (p75).

Salzburg Hauptbahnhof

As the train crosses the Salzach river, there's a picture-postcard view (on the right side) of Festung Hohensalzburg, Salzburg's iconic 900-year-old clifftop fortress. Moments later you are pulling into western Austria's most important rail transportation hub. You may have to transfer here for onward trains to Vienna. Salzburg is also where the historic Orient Express route and the Arlberg route (p226) join up.

For more about Salzburg, see p236.

Along the Way We Met...

CAROLINE The most important part of my job is ensuring passenger safety, particularly if the train has an unscheduled stop and we have to disembark everyone – I've only had to do that once in 19 years of working for ÖBB. After six hours conductors have to take a break – I started my shift at Vienna this morning at 7am, took my break in Innsbruck and will clock off when I get back to Vienna at 7.30pm.

Caroline is a conductor on ÖBB, Austria's national railway.

CAROLINE'S TIP: *Make a seat reservation if you're travelling on a weekend or during peak holiday season as this is when the trains are at their busiest.*

Traunstein — 16km — Freilassing — 6km — Salzburg

Detour: It's 34km up into the mountains from Freilassing to Berchtesgaden

Vöcklabruck

Trains depart Salzburg heading north-east towards Linz. From the right side of the train you'll catch a glimpse of **Wallersee**, the largest lake in the Salzburg Seenlandes region, a habitat for endangered water birds, pheasants and beavers.

About 45 minutes further east is Vöcklabruck, the northern gateway to the Salzkammergut region and **Attersee**, a favourite summer retreat of Gustav Klimt. Transfer at Vöcklabruck for the 15-minute train ride to the lakeside station Kammer/Attersee-Schörfling close by the **Gustav Klimt Center** *(klimt-zentrum.at; 11am-5pm Wed-Fri, 10am-5pm Sat & Sun; €7)*, where you can learn about the founding member of the Vienna Secession movement.

Linz

Feeling peckish? Then you might want to hop off the train at Linz to sample *Linzer Torte* in the town of its invention. Otherwise keep an eye out on the left side of the station for the 134m spire of Linz' Gothic cathedral **Mariendom**. For more about Linz, see p235.

Melk

After Linz the railway tracks swing south shadowing the Danube, which is sadly mostly out of view. However, unmissable atop a granite outcrop as you pass through Melk is the **Stift Melk** *(stiftmelk.at)*. This Benedictine abbey, part of the World Heritage–listed Wachau Cultural Landscape, is one of Europe's finest ensembles of baroque architecture.

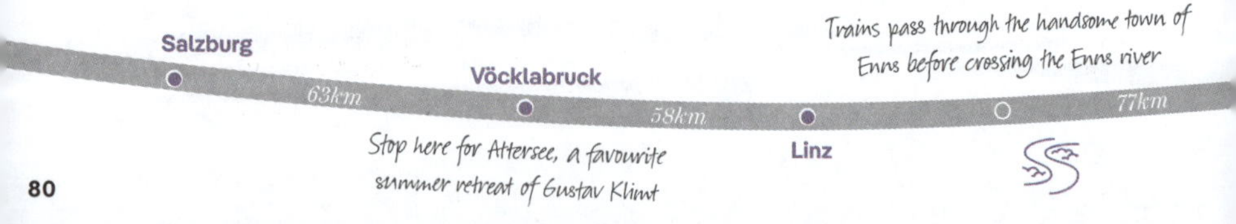

Stop here for Attersee, a favourite summer retreat of Gustav Klimt

Trains pass through the handsome town of Enns before crossing the Enns river

Salzburg — 63km — Vöcklabruck — 58km — Linz — 77km

Stift Melk

St Pölten

As you pass through St Pölten, Lower Austria's capital, look right out of the train window for the spire of the city's **cathedral**, designed by Jakob Prandtauer, one of the most prominent architects of the baroque era.

Shortly before you arrive at Wien Hauptbahnhof your train will likely pause at Wien Meidling.

Wien Hauptbahnhof

Over a quarter of a million travellers pass through Wien Hauptbahnhof, Vienna's busy main train station, every day. This big, modern complex has lots of shops and a fantastic range of places to eat and drink. Upstairs, off the main concourse, there's an **ÖBB Lounge** (for 1st-class and sleeper-train ticket holders). One floor down from ground level are lockers and access to the U1 line of Vienna's U-Bahn.

The current station replaced old Wien Südbahnhof in 2015. A decorative fragment from that original 1869 south station is the winged lion of St Mark (based on the famous ones in Venice) – it's mounted on a plinth outside the ÖBB ticket and information office on the main concourse.

The historic Orient Express never stopped here – it used Wien Westbahnhof terminus and that's where the VSOE luxury train now stops when it pulls into Vienna (p84).

Melk — 99km — **St Pölten** — 55km — **Wien Hauptbahnhof, Vienna**

The baroque monastery complex Stift Melk is an impressive sight as you pass through Melk

High-speed train, Austria
SIMLINGER/SHUTTERSTOCK

INSIGHT

The Future of the Orient Express

The early days of the Orient Express can look like a golden age to modern travellers, who need patience and a sense of adventure to cross Europe by rail today. But, the climate crisis and EU enthusiasm could put grand rail projects back on the agenda.

WORDS BY **JON WORTH**
Jon is an independent consultant and railway campaigner.

THE ERA IN which Georges Nagelmackers founded the Compagnie Internationale des Wagons-Lits (CIWL; 1872), and ran the first Orient Express train (1883), was completely different to the transport era of today. Steamships and steam trains, the dominant modes of long-distance transport back then, were used by a very small proportion of the population. Widespread use of the internal combustion engine and aviation were decades away.

But those were not the only differences. The railway environment in which CIWL could operate was one of opportunity and expansion, in which only in Austria-Hungary were there unitary publicly owned railways. Railways were less of a national preoccupation in Nagelmackers' time and the state-owned behemoths of European rail – such as SNCF, Renfe, Ferrovie dello Stato, Deutsche Reichsbahn – were a 20th-century development. Fast forward to today's luxe Orient Express revival services (p240), and the concept is not dissimilar to the role the original played – long and slow travel in considerable comfort for those with the deep pockets able to travel in luxury.

Today's independent travellers making a Paris to İstanbul trip by rail will have a much less luxurious experience.

Opportunity Awaits

The retrenchment of Europe's railways following WWII, due to competition from cars and planes and a shift in terms of thinking nationally rather than cross-border, pushed the Orient Express as a regular service towards extinction. Despite this, two modern interlinked developments – a renewed focus on railways within the political institutions of the European Union and a strong demand for sustainable travel in light of the climate crisis – mean there are opportunities for 21st-century Nagelmackers enterprising enough to take them.

Anyone exploring Europe by train today soon enough comes up against a constraint. Modern high-speed daytime trains might be adequate for a journey of a few hundred kilometres, but a trip like Madrid–Paris or Rome–Berlin is too far to do in a daytime train, however fast it might be.

Venture further into Central or southeastern Europe along the lines used by the Orient Express and the need for modern and regular overnight services is even more apparent. Anyone bold enough to try travelling from Paris to İstanbul using regular night trains currently has to battle with poor levels of comfort and reliability, while passengers wanting modern standards of privacy are going to have to pay a premium, too.

Calling All Nagelmackers

One country has begun to solve this conundrum – China, with its fleet of modern 350km/h sleeper trains. But these operate within a single state with coordination powers far exceeding those of the EU with its quarrelling members and their conservative, nationally thinking railway companies.

Austria's ÖBB, the only European state-owned railway investing in sleeper services, describes its night trains as 'niche', and none of Europe's bigger state-owned players, like DB or SNCF, are interested in night trains at all. So, it will have to fall to a modern-day Nagelmackers to shake up this European market and navigate the legal framework the EU has put in place to allow companies to bid for paths to operate trains across borders.

Paris-based startup Midnight Trains promised modern hotels on wheels, but folded in 2024 without putting a single train on the tracks. Dutch company European Sleeper fared a little better, managing to run from Brussels to Prague via Amsterdam and Berlin three times a week with a motley collection of carriages more than 50 years old. But perhaps most interesting is Berlin startup Nox, which promises a radical re-think of the sleeper train – 16 carriage trains with one- and two-person compartments for privacy, better able to meet the needs of today's travellers. It hopes to be up and running by 2030.

But remember, it took Nagelmackers 11 years to turn his vision into reality, so a solution for today's night-train conundrum is not right around the corner...but the potential is there.

> Two modern interlinked developments – a renewed focus on railways within the political institutions of the European Union and a strong demand for sustainable travel in light of the climate crisis – mean there are opportunities for 21st-century Nagelmackers enterprising enough to take them

CITY GUIDE:
Vienna

Vienna streetscape

A halfway point of classic Orient Express routes, Vienna is a signature disembarkation point where you can wander between centuries-old majestic architecture, world-class art museums and stroll-worthy palatial parks. All fuelled by plate-sized schnitzel and caffeine delights.

WORDS BY BECKI ENRIGHT
Becki is a travel writer and guidebook author living in Vienna.

Arriving
Wien Hauptbahnhof
Vienna's main railway station, Wien Hauptbahnhof, is the hub for ÖBB's Railjet (RJ) and Nightjet (NJ) trains. It's 3km south of the historic centre, though the U1 metro line will get you straight to cathedral-bound Stephansplatz. Station lockers can store luggage for up to 24 hours. Metro tickets can be purchased from machines at station entrances.
Transfers All international trains depart from Platforms 3 to 12, a level above the main concourse (ground floor). Platform access is located behind the departures board.

Refuelling
Wein Hauptbahnhof's ground floor houses Viennese outlets like the **Anker** and **Ströck** bakeries, **Oberlaa** patisserie and open-sandwich institution, **Trzesniewski**.

HOW MUCH FOR A

Coffee €6

Schnitzel €20

Museum admission €20

Within a 10-minute walk from the station, linger in the art nouveau–style salon of the 1910 Viennese coffeehouse, **Café Goldegg**.

Getting Around
Walking Vienna's historic Innere Stadt (1st district) is walkable; it's less than 20 minutes between the Hofburg and the Danube Canal, and 30 minutes from the Rathaus (City Hall) to Stadtpark. It takes an hour to walk the centre's surrounding architectural belt road, the Ringstrasse.
Metro Vienna's five (soon to be six) metro lines (U-Bahn) run from 5am to midnight on weekdays and 24 hours on Friday and Saturday. Use Stephansplatz (U1, U3) for the historic centre; Karlsplatz (U1, U2, U4) for Karlskirche, Staatsoper and Naschmarkt; Praterstern (U1, U2) for the Wurstelprater amusement park; Museumsquartier (U2) for the MuseumsQuartier cultural hub and the duo-behemoth Kunsthistorisches and Naturhistorische Museums; Schönbrunn (U4) for the palace and gardens; and Südtiroler Platz (U1) for Schloss Belvedere.
Tram Vienna's trams take a slower, though more scenic route, especially trams 1 and 2 that follow the Ringstrasse, and the approach to Schönbrunn on trams 10 or 60 from Westbahnhof station. Buy tickets on board the tram.

For schedules and trip planning, go to Wiener Linien:

A DAY IN VIENNA

Wend through the cobblestoned laneways and grand boulevards of Vienna's historical core, starting at **Stephansdom** (p88). Take your pick of museums at the **Hofburg** (p89) – from the Imperial Apartments to the Spanish Riding School – or muse the art collected by the Habsburgs at the **Kunsthistorisches Museum Vienna** (p88).

Break for coffee and cake in the 1786 rococo-regency salon, **Demel**. Continue the Habsburg trail, touring the gilded rooms of the imperial family's summer residence, **Schloss Schönbrunn** (p90) and its opulent folly gardens. Or visit the palace-turned-museum of masterpieces, the **Belvedere** (p91), to gaze upon Klimt's *Der Kuss* (The Kiss).

Dine in **Griechenbeisl** (right), the city's oldest restaurant, catch a performance at the **Wiener Staatsoper** (Vienna State Opera; wiener-staatsoper.at) then drink in design in the 1908 art deco **Loos American Bar**. Alternatively, eat at restaurant-packed **Naschmarkt**, then hit the boat-bars and watering holes along the **Danube Canal**.

Where to Stay

The 1st district (Innere Stadt) and the Ringstrasse perimeter are chock-full of accommodation options, with modest pensions, heritage hotels and grand palaces on the doorstep of historical sites, but with a price tag to match. The bohemian neighbourhood and nightlife-bound 2nd (Leopoldstadt), 6th (Mariahilf) and 7th (Neubau) districts have a cluster of innovative and boutique hotels (starting from €100 per night). The residential 3rd district (Landstrasse), minutes south of Stadtpark, is the quietest area.

BEST PLACES TO STAY

Hotel Imperial €€€ The most opulent former palace, with the original royal staircase and sumptuous rooms. *imperialhotel.com*

Altstadt Vienna €€€ Art-filled hotel with individually designed rooms, including an Orient Express bunk. *altstadt.at*

Hotel Motto €€ 1920s Paris meets 2020s Vienna, with chic rooms and an art deco restaurant. *hotelmotto.at*

Hotel Lamée €€ Glamorous art deco–styled hotel with rooftop bar minutes from Stephansplatz. *hotel topazzlamee.com*

Where to Eat

The 1st district is the centre for tradition: think coffeehouses, wood-panelled *Beisln* (taverns) and medieval-era cellars. The cuisine cache in the inner districts (2nd to 9th) features modern takes on Viennese classics and *Würstelstand* (sausage stand) bites, vegetarian and vegan fare, and international cuisine from Italian to Indian. Markets are a way of life; find global grub in Naschmarkt (6th), and Balkan and Turkish delicacies in Brunnenmarkt (16th).

VIENNESE CUISINE

Dig into imperial legacy with these classic Viennese dishes, starting with the famed *Wiener Schnitzel* (flattened, breadcrumbed veal cutlet served with potato salad; pictured below left). Try it at **Figlmüller** *(figlmueller.at; €€)*, said to be the original home of the hearty plate-sized dish; **Meissl & Schadn** *(meisslundschadn.at; €€€)*; or in the authentic 1977 tavern, **Gasthaus Reinthaler** *(gasthausreinthaler.at; €€)*.

Emperor Franz Joseph's favourite, *Tafelspitz* (boiled beef with roasted potatoes, vegetables and horseradish sauce) is best dished up at **Plachutta Stammhaus Hietzing** *(plachutta.at/de/hietzing.html; €€€)*.

The legendary late-night favourite *Würstelstand*, is where to sample the signature snack, *Käsekrainer* (sausage filled with tiny cubes of cheese). The imperially beloved 'Emperor's Mess' *Kaiserschmarrn* (shredded fluffy pancake served with a fruit compote; pictured below) and *Apfelstrudel* (flaky pastry with apples and raisins) are timeless coffeehouse staples.

BEST PLACES TO EAT & DRINK

Griechenbeisl €€ Feast in the city's oldest Beisl, dating from 1447. *griechen beisl.at*

Glacis Beisl €€ Mod-classic Viennese cuisine at a city wall site turned tavern. *glacisbeisl.at*

Meierei im Stadtpark €€€ Elegant, park-set cafe of Michelin-starred Steirereck. *steirereck.at/meierei.html*

Würstelstand LEO € This sausage stand has been sizzling *Käsekrainer* since 1928. *wuerstelstandleo.at*

Stephansdom

Soaring Stephansdom

The Gothic **Stephansdom** *(stephanskirche.at; all-inclusive ticket adult/child €25/7)* cathedral is the historic centre's beloved sentinel. Ticketed entry gets you into the central nave with its 16th-century sandstone Pilgramkanzel (pilgrim pulpit) and baroque black marble high altar. Climb the 343 tight, twirling steps up the 136.4m-high **south tower** to its city-window Türmerstube (tower room). An elevator up the half-finished **north tower** opens to a platform for Austria's largest bell, the 21-tonne Pummerin, and a Stephansplatz vista. Venture beneath to the bone-stacked **catacombs** – the ossuary for the more than 10,000 plague victims.

COFFEEHOUSE CULTURE

Vienna's first coffeehouse opened in 1683 and spawned the culture of the 'extended living room'; institutions whose wood-panelled and chandelier-lit interiors, bentwood Thonet chairs, velvet banquette booths and newspaper stacks attracted the creative set. Today, they remain places to linger, continuing a legacy that UNESCO granted Intangible Cultural Heritage status to in 2011.

The coffee menu can be baffling, but a *Wiener Melange* (half coffee, half milk foam) is a classic, still served on a silver platter by waiters in formal attire.

Opulent, though queue-stretchingly popular **Café Central** *(1876; cafecentral.wien)* was the elite meeting place of philosophers and revolutionaries, while artist-hub **Café Sperl** *(1880; cafesperl.at)* was where the Secessionist founders met. The grittier late-night institution **Café Hawelka** *(1939; hawelka.at)* is the bohemian take. The trademarked chocolate and apricot jam torte is 'always in the house' at the sumptuous red-draped **Café Sacher** *(1876; sacher.com)*. From the founding 27 cafes on the Ringstrasse, only art nouveau **Café Prückel** *(1903; prueckel.at)*, Freud's lauded **Café Landtmann** *(1873; landtmann.at)* and the marble-mirrored **Café Schwarzenberg** *(1861; cafe-schwarzenberg.at)* remain.

Kunsthistorisches Museum

Kunsthistorisches Museum Magnificence

The Habsburgs' colossal art collection, amassed over 600 years, is housed in the neo-baroque **Kunsthistorisches Museum** *(khm.at; adult/child €23/free)*. The **Egyptian and Near Eastern Collection** showcases sacred objects; the **Collection of Greek and Roman Antiquities** collates ancient reliefs, mosaics and statues; and the **Kunstkammer Wien** (Cabinet of Art and Curiosities) amasses exotic and fantastical objects. Ascend the grand staircase to the **Picture Gallery** for European masterpieces from the likes of Raphael, Caravaggio and Velázquez, of which Pieter Bruegel the Elder's *The Tower of Babel* is a highlight.

Tour the Imperial Hofburg Palace

The house the Habsburgs built was an imperial stronghold for seven centuries; now, it's a multi-museum complex with 18 wings and 19 courtyards housing art, artefacts, antiquities and the world-famous white Lipizzaner stallions.

HOW TO

Getting here: Take the U-Bahn to Herrengasse (U3) or walk 12 minutes from Stephansplatz.

When to go: The complex is open 24/7. Museums are open 9am to 6pm; some have late-night Thursday admission until 9pm.

Cost: From €18; kids (mostly) free

Tip: Winter Riding School performances are only held on weekends. Training is held on weekday mornings and there are daily guided tours of the Spanish Riding School.

Walk through the life of Empress Elisabeth at the **Sisi Museum** (sisimuseum-hofburg.at; adult/child €20/12), a sensitive display of personal possessions, before stepping into the splendorous **Kaiserappartements** (Imperial Apartments), a stretch of 17 resplendent rooms, all accompanied by a 75-minute audioguide.

View the coveted crown jewels of Austria in the **Kaiserliche Schatzkammer** (Imperial Treasury; kaiserliche-schatzkammer.at; adult/child €18/free), a majestic display of Holy Roman and Habsburg Empire heirlooms.

The Lipizzaners' ballet-like dressage performances in the **Spanische Hofreitschule** (Spanish Riding School; srs.at; adult from €26, children reduced admission) arena continue a classical equestrian art form practised here since 1565.

The 18th-century baroque **Prunksaal der Österreichischen Nationalbibliothek** (State Hall of the Austrian National Library; onb.ac.at/museen/prunksaal; adult/child €11/free) has dark-walnut shelves stacked with 200,000 leather-bound books.

FROM LEFT: JULIA MOUNTAIN PHOTO/SHUTTERSTOCK, ECSTK22/SHUTTERSTOCK

Above: Imperial crown, Kaiserliche Schatzkammer
Right: Hofburg Palace

Saunter Through Schönbrunn Palace

Take a rococo roam inside the Habsburg summer residence, Schloss Schönbrunn, or stroll the splendid horticultural gardens and fountains, mazes and viewpoints of its palace park.

HOW TO

Getting here: Take the U-Bahn to Schönbrunn (U4 line) or the scenic trams 10 or 60 from Westbahnhof to the Schloss Schönbrunn stop.

When to go: 8.30am to 6pm July to August, to 5pm November to March, to 5.30pm the rest of the year

Cost: Classic Pass adult/child €40/31, Palace Ticket adult/child €34/24, Exclusive Gardens at Schönbrunn adult/child €15/10

Tip: Skip the line with pre-booked time-allocated tickets.

More info: schoenbrunn.at

Schloss Schönbrunn is a 1441-chambered mega palace of which 40 rooms are open for a peek into imperial living. The Palace Ticket covers the full sweep of grand salons and reception rooms, Maria Theresa's 18th-century sumptuous State Apartments and the private quarters of the palace's last residents, Franz and Elisabeth. Highlights include the 43m-long mirrored, gilded stucco and frescoed Great Gallery, the Blue Chinese Salon, the black lacquer Vieux Laque Room and the rosewood-panelled Millions Room. The Napoleon Room was the French commander's operational quarters during his dual occupation of Vienna in 1805 and 1809.

Freely roam the **Schönbrunn Gardens**' Great Parterre, Neptune Fountain, Obelisk Fountain, temple effigy Roman Ruins and Rose and Japanese Gardens. The Exclusive Gardens combo ticket includes entrance to the parterre and trellised pergola of the 1700 Privy Garden and Orangery, the reconstructed and interactive maze from 1720, and the archway Gloriette terrace for its viewpoint over Schönbrunn.

Schloss Schönbrunn

GREEN SPACES

Vienna's historically piled metropolis is half-covered in green space. Beyond the corridors of masterpiece-filled museums and imperial abodes, there are plenty of free-to-roam spaces encapsulating the city's gentle pace. There's the folly- and fountain-dotted **Schloss Schönbrunn Gardens**, the landscaped **Belvedere** and the Hofburg's **Burggarten**, and rose-bush fragrant **Volksgarten** lawns. The city's first public park, **Stadtpark**, opened in 1862 and remains a woodland escape on the city's fringes. **Augarten** is the oldest baroque garden, though it's dominated by two 1944 air-raid defence bunkers, Flakturm (Flak towers). Former imperial hunting ground turned largest recreational park **Prater** is better known for the **Wurstelprater** fairground and the iconic Wiener Riesenrad (giant Ferris wheel). Waterside spots include the bar and boat restaurant-lined **Danube Canal**; warmer months are for bathing and boating in the **Alte Donau** and skating, strolling and swimming (with stretches of artificial beach) at the **Donauinsel** (Danube Island). The only European capital to grow wine within its city limits, sip Grüner Veltliner in the vineyards that fold into the circumambient **Vienna Woods**: 14 city hiking trails forge through it all.

Marble Hall, Lower Belvedere

Art-Bound Belvedere Palace

Schloss Belvedere's three-century-long art legacy began with esteemed military general to the Habsburgs and art aficionado Prince Eugene of Savoy filling his 1723 baroque palace with his collections. By 1777 Empress Maria Theresa had turned it into the Imperial Picture Gallery, Vienna's first public museum. Today's two-floor display of Austrian art from the Middle Ages to the present day finds its pride in housing the world's largest collection of Gustav Klimt works: his most famous, *Der Kuss* (The Kiss), never leaves the gallery. **Lower Belvedere**, while hosting a smaller gallery, is a through-the-keyhole look into Prince Eugene's extravagant residential wing.

Along the Way We Saw...

OTTO WAGNER CREATIONS Ornamental facades, a hilltop church, an art nouveau bank hall – the stamps of urban architect Otto Wagner are all over Vienna. Twentieth-century Viennese Modernism melded practicality with aesthetic elements, a style embossed on Wagner's biggest project: the Stadtbahn (Vienna metropolitan railway). Spot his signature green, white and gold *Jugendstil* trademarks at the Pavillon Karlsplatz and its twin portal, and the converted U-Bahn stations, Schönbrunn and Stadtpark (U4), Währinger Straße-Volksoper and Josefstädterstrasse (U6).

Becki Enright

Vienna

Visit three countries in one day on the shortest leg of the classic Orient Express route. Only an hour east of Vienna, Bratislava, Slovakia's historically multi-layered capital, is located on the Danube. Walk around its handsome old town, indulge in its lively food and drink scene, and view an eclectic range of architecture. Heading into Hungary, the train hugs the Danube Bend, a scenic region of peaks and quaint riverside towns including Esztergom, home to a massive basilica.

Simon Richmond

Bratislava (p95)

Budapest

277 KMS
~3½ HOURS' RIDE

THIS LEG:

- Marchegg & Devínska Nová Ves
- Bratislava Hlavna
- Nové Zámky
- Štúrovo
- Nagymaros-Visegrád
- Vác
- Budapest-Nyugati
- Budapest-Keleti

Riding Notes

Hourly Regional Express (REX) trains link Wien Hauptbahnhof with Bratislava Hlavna in 56 minutes. It's another 2½ hours from Bratislava to Budapest-Nyugati (p105) – if you travel on MÁV's EuroCity service *Hungaria* there's a good dining car. If you plan to travel directly between Vienna and Budapest, avoiding Slovakia, see p96.

Breaking Your Journey
Although Bratislava can easily be visited for the day, an overnight stay will allow you more time to explore the city's sights as well as take a cruise along the Danube. To see more of the Danube Bend than the view out the train window, stay the night either in Esztergom or Visegrád.

Simon's Tips

BEST MEAL Experimental cuisine and cocktails at Bratislava's Sky Bar & Restaurant. (p97)

FAVOURITE VIEW The Citadel looming over Visegrád on the Danube. (p103)

ESSENTIAL STOP The compact, picturesque old town of Bratislava. (p98)

TIP The multi-genre festival **Bratislava Cultural Summer** *(bkis.sk)* runs from mid-June to the end of August.

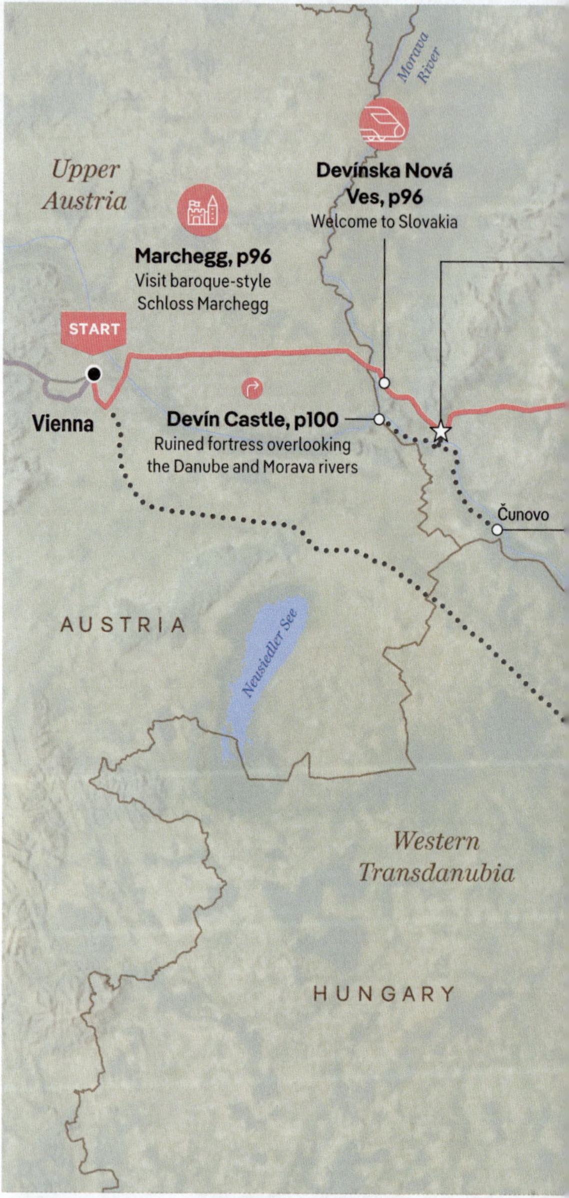

Upper Austria

Marchegg, p96 — Visit baroque-style Schloss Marchegg

START

Vienna

Devínska Nová Ves, p96 — Welcome to Slovakia

Devín Castle, p100 — Ruined fortress overlooking the Danube and Morava rivers

Čunovo

Morava River

Neusiedler See

AUSTRIA

Western Transdanubia

HUNGARY

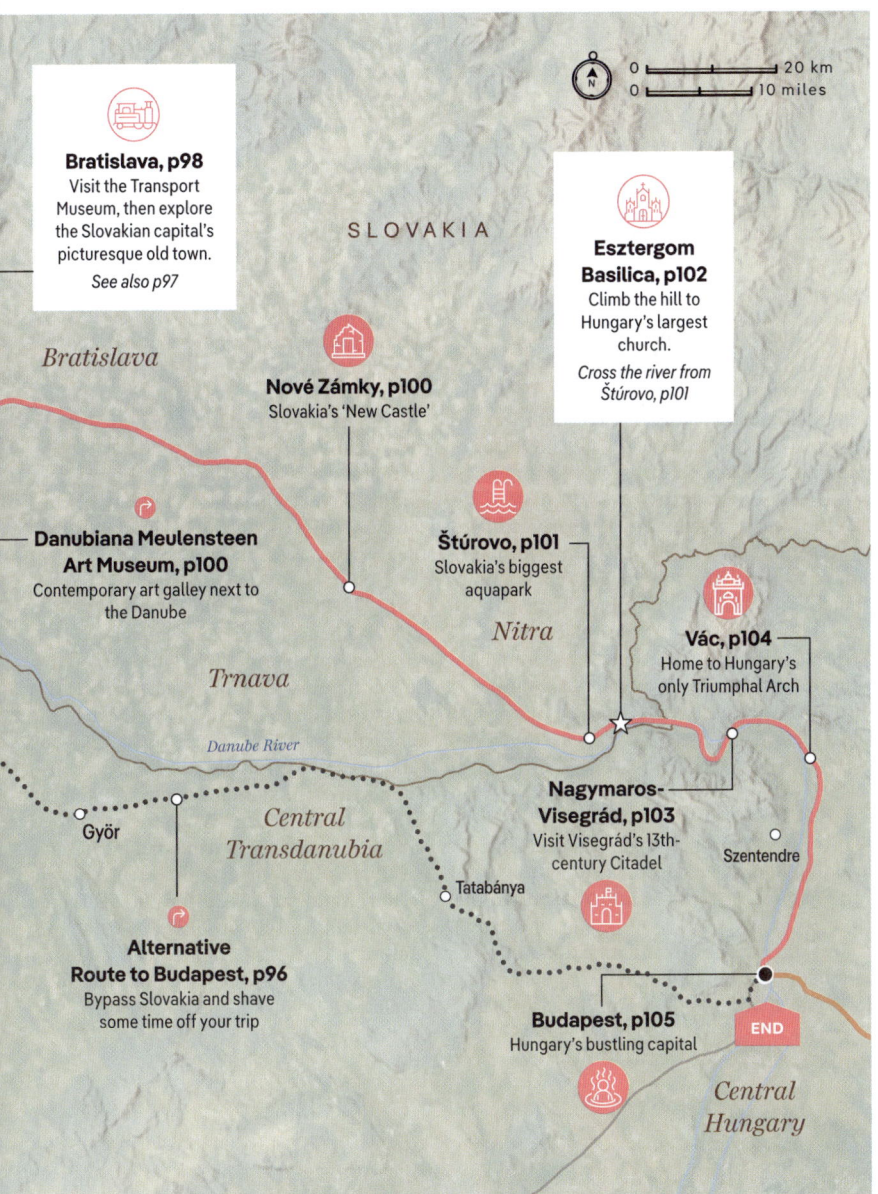

> **ONWARD TRAVEL**
>
> Reservations are not needed for the REX8 train linking Wien Hauptbahnhof with Bratislava Hlavna, the Slovak capital's main station, within walking distance of the old town. The REX6 service terminates at Bratislava Petržalka station, west of Bratislava's city centre across the Danube – if you end up here, bus 80 runs to the old town. A taxi between Petržalka and Bratislava Hlavna costs around €11.
>
> The fastest direct trains between Wien Hauptbahnhof and Budapest-Keleti are around two hours, 40 minutes. Slightly faster services (two hours, 20 minutes) terminate at Budapest-Kelenföld, southwest of the centre on the Buda side of the city. For schedules see **ÖBB** *(oebb.at)* and **MÁV** *(mavcsoport.hu)*. **Regiojet** *(regiojet.co)* trains also connect Wien Hauptbahnhof with Budapest-Kelenföld and Budapest-Déli.

 ### Leaving Vienna

Leaving Wien Hauptbahnhof, the REX8 train swings southeast through the city to stop first at **Wien Simmering** (also the southeastern terminus of U3 of the Vienna U-Bahn) before crossing the Prater park and the Danube to arrive at **Wien Stadlau**.

By the time you reach **Wien Aspern Nord**, the city is behind you and you're travelling through countryside on Austria's longest completely straight railway line (approximately 32.5km).

As you pass through **Siebenbrunn-Leopoldsdorf**, you might notice a sweet aroma. Look to the right side of the train to see the silos of AGRANA Zucker GmbH Leopoldsdorf, a giant sugar factory.

 ### DETOUR: Alternative Routes to Budapest

Many direct trains link Vienna and Budapest avoiding Slovakia altogether. Along the way you'll pass through **Győr** and **Tatabánya** in Hungary.

Most direct trains (two hours, 20 minutes) terminate on the Buda side, either at Budapest-Kelenföld or Budapest-Déli. From either of these stations you can use the city's metro to connect to Budapest-Keleti.

There is also one direct daily train (IC 201 AGRAM InterCity) from Zagreb (p223) to Budapest, usually terminating at Budapest-Déli – check online at jegy.mav.hu or czech-transport.com for current schedules. This service runs along the southern shore of Lake Balaton, with superb views across the water.

Marchegg & Devínska Nová Ves

Approaching the March river, which is the border with Slovakia, you'll travel thorough the fecund fields of Marchfeld. Marchegg is the final station before the river, known as the Morava in Slovakian.

The town of **Marchegg** *(marchegg.at/en)* is 3km north of the station. Here you'll find the baroque-style **Schloss Marchegg** *(schloss marchegg.at)* next to a wetlands nature preserve that's home to one of the largest colonies of tree-breeding white storks in Central Europe. There's also a walking and cycling bridge over the river.

Across the river the train pauses briefly at Devínska Nová Ves, the very first station in Slovakia.

Wien Hauptbahnhof, Vienna

46km

The train line crosses Vienna's famous Prater park and the Danube en route to Wien Stadlau

The track between Wien Aspern Nord and Siebenbrunn-Leopoldsdorf is part of the longest straight railway line in Austria

White stork, Marchegg

🚂 Bratislava Hlavna

The historic Orient Express paused at Bratislava (then called Pozsony in Hungarian and Pressburg in German) on its way to and from İstanbul. Bratislava Hlavna (abbreviated to Bratislava hl), the city's main train station, is a mash-up of a 1905 terminus and a 1960s glass-and-concrete extension, nicknamed the Sklenik (greenhouse). The main booking hall is decorated with a striking Socialist Realist fresco created by František Gajdoš in 1960.

The left-luggage office is in the far-left corner of the booking hall and there are self-service luggage lockers at Platform 1. Take the stairs

Continues on page 100

BEST PLACES TO EAT

Koliba Kamzík, Bratislava €€
Rustic restaurant in Bratislava's old town serving tasty versions of traditional cuisine including *pierogi* (dumplings). *11am-10pm Sun-Thu, 11am-11pm Fri & Sat*

Bratislava Flagship, Bratislava €€
Try *kapustové strapačky* (dumplings with cabbage and bacon) at this huge restaurant inside a former theatre in Bratislava. *11am-10pm Mon-Thu, 11am-11pm Fri, noon-11pm Sat, noon-10pm Sun*

Foodstock, Bratislava €
Contemporary, self-serve canteen in Bratislava's old town with a fully vegetarian menu of Asian favourites including sushi and noodles. *11am-10pm Mon-Fri, 11am-midnight Sat & Sun*

Sky Bar & Restaurant, Bratislava €€€
Beautifully presented fusion cuisine and cocktails with spectacular skyline views of Bratislava from its 8th-floor terrace. *5pm-midnight*

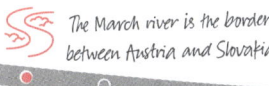

The March river is the border between Austria and Slovakia

Marchegg — 7km — Devínska Nová Ves — 7km — Bratislava ★

CITY GUIDE:
Bratislava

Slovakia's capital since independence in 1993, Bratislava is a compact city with an eclectic range of architecture. A medieval and Gothic old town stands alongside communist-era constructions, while 21st-century designs vie for attention with baroque palaces and a neo-Renaissance castle.

HOW TO

Getting here: Hourly trains link Vienna with Bratislava in under an hour. From Budapest, trains take 2½ hours.

Getting around: You can walk from Bratislava Hlavna to the old town in under 20 minutes, or you can ride tram 1; a 24-hour metro ticket for all public transport is €5.90. The old town is small and best explored on foot. Check imhd.sk/ba for city-wide transport schedules.

Sleeping: Convenient for the station is Clarion Congress Hotel Bratislava (p101); closer to the old town are Loft Hotel Bratislava (p101), Patio Hostel (p101) and Marrol's Boutique Hotel (p101).

Tip: From mid-April through October, **LOD** (lod.sk) operates a range of cruises along the Danube.

More info: Tourist Information Centre (visitbratislava.com; 9am-4.30pm Mon-Fri, 9am-4pm Sat, 10am-4pm Sun)

Hlavné Námestie (Main Sq), the nucleus of Bratislava's old town, is surrounded by architectural finery. On its north side is **Stará Radnica** (Old Town Hall), a complex of attractive 14th- and 15th-century buildings that house the **City History Museum** (muzeumbratislava.sk; 10am-6pm Tue-Sun; adult/child €8/4) and which includes an exhibition on Slovakian wines.

Of Bratislava's original 13th-century walls, **Michael's Gate** (muzeumbratislava.sk; 10am-6pm Wed-Mon; adult/child €6/4) is the last gate standing. Capped with an onion dome, the gate's tower was rebuilt in baroque style in 1758. There are superb old-town views from the top.

BRAVE NEW BRATISLAVA

Slovakia's half-century of communist rule left its mark on Bratislava in the form of several monumental constructions. The most obvious is **Most SNP**, a highway and bridge across the Danube completed in 1972. The asymmetrical cable-stayed bridge has a circular observation deck/restaurant atop its 84.6m pylon – hence its nickname the UFO bridge. A chunk of the old town, including much of the historic Jewish quarter, was demolished to build the bridge.

In the shape of an inverted pyramid, the **Slovak Radio Building** took 16 years to build from 1967. The 80m-tall building houses a 523-seat concert hall with one of the largest organs in Central Europe.

Nearby is **Námestie Slobody** (Freedom Sq), looking splendid after a renovation. The centrepiece is the 12-tonne stainless-steel **Družba Fountain** (1980) in the shape of a lime blossom, symbolising friendship and peace between nations.

Discover more about Bratislava's brutishly beautiful architecture, including the vast concrete socialist housing estate district Petržalka and the **Slavín War Memorial**, on a tour with **Authentic Slovakia** (authenticslovakia.com).

Blue Church

Climb the Hill to Bratislava Castle

Atop a hill overlooking the old town is the fairytale-like **Bratislava Castle** (bratislava-hrad.sk; grounds 8am-10pm, castle 10am-6pm Wed-Mon; grounds free, museum adult/student €14/7). The fortification dates to the 9th century CE, but has been rebuilt many times, most recently in the 1960s. The oldest original feature is the 13th-century Crown Tower; climb it for bird's-eye views. Parts of the castle are used to house the collection of the national history museum. Without a ticket you are free to explore the grounds, including the castle's manicured baroque gardens.

Visit Two Beautiful Churches

The coronations of 19 royals have taken place in 14th-century Gothic **St Martin's Cathedral** (dom.fara.sk/sk/). Bratislava's key place of worship features huge rib vaults and stained-glass windows that lift the gaze in the interior. Also look out for a dramatic horseback statue of St Martin.

A five-minute walk east of the old town is the aptly named **Blue Church** (modrykostol.fara.sk). Painted powder-blue and white, from its undulating arches and ceramic roof tiles to the 36.8m tip of its clock tower, it's a marvel of art nouveau design.

BEST PLACES TO EAT & DRINK

Slovak Pub €€ Rustic tavern serving local beers, *slivovica* (plum brandy) and traditional food. *11am-10pm Mon-Fri, noon-10pm Sat & Sun*

Schokocafe Maximilian Delikateso € Retro cafe in the neo-baroque Palugyayov Palác with views onto Hlavné Námestie. *9am-9pm*

Grand Cru Wine Gallery €€ Serves Slovak and Moravian wines alongside tasty nibbles. *5-10pm Mon-Thu, 5-11pm Fri & Sat*

Continued from page 97

or the escalator down from the station to reach the stop for tram 1, which will take you into the old town (p98).

There are plenty of food and drink stalls in the station, including **Koruna** *(5.30am-7pm Mon-Fri, 8am-6pm Sat & Sun; €)*, which has an appealing selection of takeaway items. Other recommended places to eat in town include Koliba Kamzík (p97), Bratislava Flagship (p97), Sky Bar & Restaurant (p97) and Foodstock (p97).

If you have time to kill before catching an onward train, walk down to the original 1848 station building, 450m south of Bratislava Hlavna. Behind here, in the old rail yard, **Transport Museum Bratislava** *(Múzeum Dopravy Bratislava; muzeumdopravy.com; 10am-5pm Thu-Sun; €8)* has some intriguing local railway memorabilia and rusting locomotives. Photographs and explanation panels provide insight into historic Bratislava.

Display train, Transport Museum Bratislava

DETOUR: Devín Castle & Danubiana Meulensteen Art Museum

Bratislava has nature on its doorstep. The city banks the Danube, while rolling north are the Malé Karpaty (Small Carpathians), their lowlands draped with vineyards. There are several good day trips from the city.

Located atop a high crag, 9km west of Bratislava, are the atmospheric ruins of **Devín Castle** *(Hrad Devín; hraddevin.mmb.sk; 10am-6pm Tue-Sun Apr, May & Sep, 10am-7pm Jun-Aug, 10am-5pm Oct; adult/child €8/4)*. The castle offers a panoramic view of the confluence of the Danube and Morava rivers. If your tastes run to contemporary art, aim for **Danubiana Meulensteen Art Museum** *(danubiana.sk; 10am-6pm Tue-Sun;*

adult/child €10/5) in Čunovo, about 20km south of Bratislava. Surrounded by a sculpture park, this innovative gallery is built on a spit of land jutting into the river.

LOD *(lod.sk)* runs boat trips from Bratislava to both Devín and Čunovo between April and November; see the website for the schedule.

Nové Zámky

Heading east out of Bratislava you'll travel through farmlands that are nothing to write home about. The first major station is Nové Zámky. Meaning 'New Castle', the town dates to the 16th century when a then state-of-the-art star-shaped fortress was built to defend the location against Ottoman armies. Following bombing during WWII, little of the fortress remains.

Esztergom Basilica stands out on a hilltop across the Danube from Štúrovo

Bratislava — 91km — Detour: 9km up the Danube is the ruined Devín Castle — 47km — Nové Zámky — Štúrovo

Štúrovo

This leg of the Orient Express journey begins to get interesting around the spa town of **Štúrovo** *(eng.sturovo.sk)*, which is on the north bank of the Danube. Štúrovo train station is 3km from the city centre and the internationally renowned **Thermal Spa VADAŠ** *(vadasthermal.sk/en; 10am-6pm May & Sep, 9am-7.30pm Jun-Aug; adult/child from €10/7)*, Slovakia's biggest aquapark with a dozen bathing pools, water slides, a fishing lake, sport courts, an adventure park and a hotel.

Whether you decide to linger in Štúrovo itself or not, you cannot fail to notice the Esztergom Basilica (p102), Hungary's largest church, which towers above the historic Danube Bend town of Esztergom and is visible from both the train and station.

Continues on page 103

BEST PLACES TO SLEEP

Clarion Congress Hotel Bratislava, Bratislava €€
This pop-art-decorated business hotel is pleasant and super convenient for Bratislava Hlavna station. *clarioncongresshotelbratislava.com*

Loft Hotel Bratislava, Bratislava €€
Retro industrial-style hotel attached to the Fabrika microbrewery pub and handily located midway between the station and old town. *lofthotel.sk*

Patio Hostel, Bratislava €
A good range of dorms and private rooms with or without ensuite bathrooms at this backpackers' choice. *patiohostel.com*

Marrol's Boutique Hotel, Bratislava €€€
Plushly decorated rooms in soft shades of ivory and gold, with king-sized beds. *hotelmarrols.sk*

Danubiana Meulensteen Art Museum

Climb Up to Esztergom Basilica

Cross the Danube from Štúrovo to Esztergom to visit Catholic Esztergom Basilica, Hungary's biggest church. Perched atop Castle Hill and offering panoramic views of the Danube Bend, its 72m-high dome can be seen for miles around.

HOW TO

Nearest stop: Štúrovo (p101)

Getting here: From Štúrovo, you can walk across the graceful Mária Valéria Bridge and climb up to the basilica in about 30 minutes.

Cost: Basilica free, crypt 700Ft, dome adult/concession 2800/1500Ft, treasury adult/concession 1900/900Ft, combination ticket 4200/3000Ft

Opening hours: Basilica 8am-7pm

More info: bazilika-esztergom.hu

The **Cat's Stairs**, a well-hidden set of steps off Berényi Zsigmond utca, lead up to the basilica. Consecrated in 1856 with a sung Mass composed by Franz Liszt, the church stands on the site of a 12th-century predecessor destroyed by the Ottomans.

Stepping inside, an explosion of frescoes awaits, brightly lit by windows around the dome and high on the walls. The **Treasury**, on the northwest side, is an Aladdin's Cave of vestments and church plates in gold and silver, studded with jewels, the richest ecclesiastical collection in Hungary. The **Panorama Café** and an exhibition about the basilica's renovation are near the Treasury.

Descend 50 steps to the **crypt**, a series of eerie vaults with tombs guarded by monoliths representing Mourning and Eternity.

The pleasant hotel **Szent Kristóf Panzió** (szentkristof panzio.com; €€) is close to the basilica. **BorYou Bistro** (noon-10pm Tue-Thu, noon-midnight Fri & Sat, noon-8pm Sun; €€) serves wine and good food on Esztergom's main square, Széchenyi tér.

Interior of Esztergom Basilica

Visegrád Citadel

Continued from page 101

Nagymaros-Visegrád

The tracks continue hugging the Danube crossing into Hungary at **Szob**. Glimpses of the river and highlands through the trees along this stretch of the journey are fantastic, particularly so as you approach Nagymaros-Visegrád, the train station for Nagymaros.

The town of **Visegrád** *(visitvisegrad.hu)*, on the Danube's southern bank, is watched over by the 13th-century **Citadel** *(parkerdo.hu/turizmus/latnivalok/visegradi-fellegvar)* perched atop a 333m-high hill – it's an unmissable feature on the skyline. Walking along the ramparts of this eyrie provides panoramic views of the Börzsöny Hills and the river. To reach Visegrád from Nagymaros, catch a ferry that departs each hour – the jetty is a five-minute walk from Nagymaros-Visegrád station.

Hotel Silvanus *(hotelsilvanus.hu; €€€)*, on a forested hillside near the Citadel, has great views, an outdoor pool and delightful spa. For something to eat, **Kovács-Kert** *(kovacs-kert etterem.hu; noon-9pm; €€)* serves Hungarian classics not far from the ferry landing in Visegrád.

Štúrovo

Cross the Danube into Hungary at Szob

31km

Visegrád's Citadel is a landmark high above the Danube river

Nagymaros-Visegrád

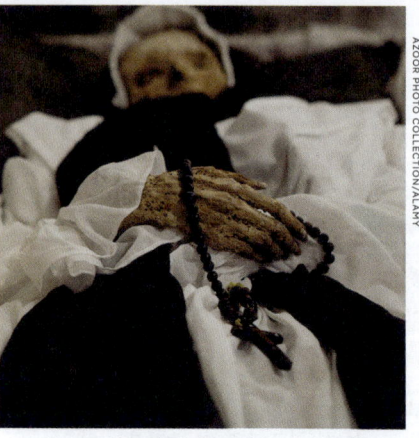

Mummy, Tragor Ignác Museum Memento Mori, Vác

AZOOR PHOTO COLLECTION/ALAMY

Vác

The final stop before Budapest is **Vác** *(visitvac.hu)*, another historic town on the Danube Bend, where the river heads south. This stretch of track, between the capital and Vác, is the oldest in Hungary, dating to 1846.

Vác features the country's only **Triumphal Arch**, built in 1764 for a visit by Empress Maria Theresa. The town's attractive main square is surrounded by baroque architecture and there's a pleasant riverside promenade. For a touch of the macabre, the **Tragor Ignác Museum Memento Mori** *(10am-6pm Tue-Sun)* displays three of the 264 naturally mummified bodies from the mid-18th to the early 19th century discovered in the crypt of Vác's Fehérek Church in 1994.

Along the Way We Met...

ANDRAS NEMETH I live in the Danube Bend town of Szentendre, a 19km train trip north of Budapest on the west bank of the river. I used to come to this artists colony regularly as a child with my mother. The town has a 'Mediterranean' feel and is very popular with day-trippers from Budapest. There are also many Serbian Orthodox churches and some Serbian restaurants, too, a legacy of the Serbs who settled here over the centuries.

Andras is a Hungarian journalist working for the news website hvg.hu.

ANDRAS' TIP: *Passata (passata.hu; 11.30am-9pm Sun-Thu, 11.30am-10pm Fri & Sat; €) is a good place in the centre of town for pizza.*

Nagymaros-Visegrád		Vác			Budapest-Nyugati		Budapest-Keleti
	12km			32km		3km	

On the Buda side of the city are Budapest-Kelenföld and Budapest-Déli train stations

Budapest-Nyugati

Trains from Slovakia arrive at Budapest-Nyugati, an elegant iron-and-glass terminus built in 1877 by the Paris-based Eiffel Company. The former dining hall on the station's south side houses one of the world's fanciest McDonald's.

In 1962, a train crashed through the enormous glass screen on the main facade. Thankfully, staff were quick to issue warnings over the loudspeakers, so only one person was injured.

To connect to Budapest-Keleti, the fastest option is taxi (10 minutes; around 1600Ft); if you take the metro you'll need to transfer at Deák Ferenc between lines M3 and M2.

Budapest-Keleti

Some direct trains from Vienna or other stations in Austria and Germany arrive at Budapest-Keleti, the station you'll need for onward journeys east. Dating to 1884, Budapest-Keleti is an architectural gem that's one of the grandest stations along the Orient Express route. The station's main facade is 40m tall and topped with allegorical sculptures of the gods Neptune and Vulcan and a winged female figure, all symbolising steam locomotion. Beneath this tableaux, look for statues in niches of Scottish inventor and engineer James Watt and the English engineer George Stephenson, the 'father of the railways'.

On the station's north side, off Platform 6, the Lotz Hall is lined with gorgeous murals by renowned Romanticist painters Mór Thán and Károly Lotz.

The station has 13 platforms, all with level access. The MÁV customer centre is on the lower level, where you'll also find the entrance to the metro.

Budapest-Keleti station

CITY GUIDE:
Budapest

A boat on the Danube with the Parliament building

Straddling the Danube, the 'City of Spas' is the perfect place to take a break and melt your muscles in mineral-rich thermal waters. Beyond elegant bathhouses, one of Europe's prettiest capitals charms with breathtaking architecture and buzzes with life at night.

WORDS BY KATA FÁRI
Kata is a writer who sings the praises of the world's best places online and in print.

Arriving
Budapest has three main train stations: Keleti (Eastern), Nyugati (Western) and Déli Pályaudvar.
Budapest-Keleti Since Keleti is the key spot for international train travel, you'll likely be arriving and leaving from there. The majestic building is a true architectural gem blending neo-Renaissance and eclectic styles. Before exiting the station, be sure to visit the Lotz Hall on the north side of the station off Platform 6, where the walls are festooned with murals by renowned Romanticist painters Mór Than and Károly Lotz.

Refuelling
Steps away from the station, **Lakomatív Étterem** 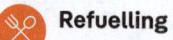 (Restaurant Locomotive) is a hole-in-the-wall restaurant serving decent, inexpensive food. It's an easy win if you have kids, as drinks arrive on a model train. If you don't mind a 15-minute walk, the breathtaking and historic **New York Café** serves dishes and drinks amid gilded and marble surfaces, etched glass, frescoes and live Hungarian music – note that there's almost always a queue, so book ahead.

Getting Around
Public Transport Keleti is well-connected to the centre by metros M2 and M4 and buses that take you pretty much anywhere within the city. Budapest has four colour-coded and numbered underground lines, three of which converge at central Deák Ferenc tér. Buses running on more than 200 lines serve greater Budapest day and night; night buses begin with 9. Trams on three dozen lines are faster and more pleasant than buses. Trolleybuses on 15 lines go along cross streets in central Pest.
BudapestGO The BudapestGO mobile app is all you need to navigate Budapest's public transport network. You can buy and store digital tickets and passes directly through the app – don't forget to validate tickets with QR codes and show passes to the inspectors. It also includes timetables, connections and travel times, as well as updates on schedules, arrivals, potential delays and other relevant information.

HOW MUCH FOR A

Lángos from **1000Ft**

Fröccs from **600Ft**

Széchenyi Baths from **10,000Ft**

For schedules and trip planning, download the BudapestGO app:

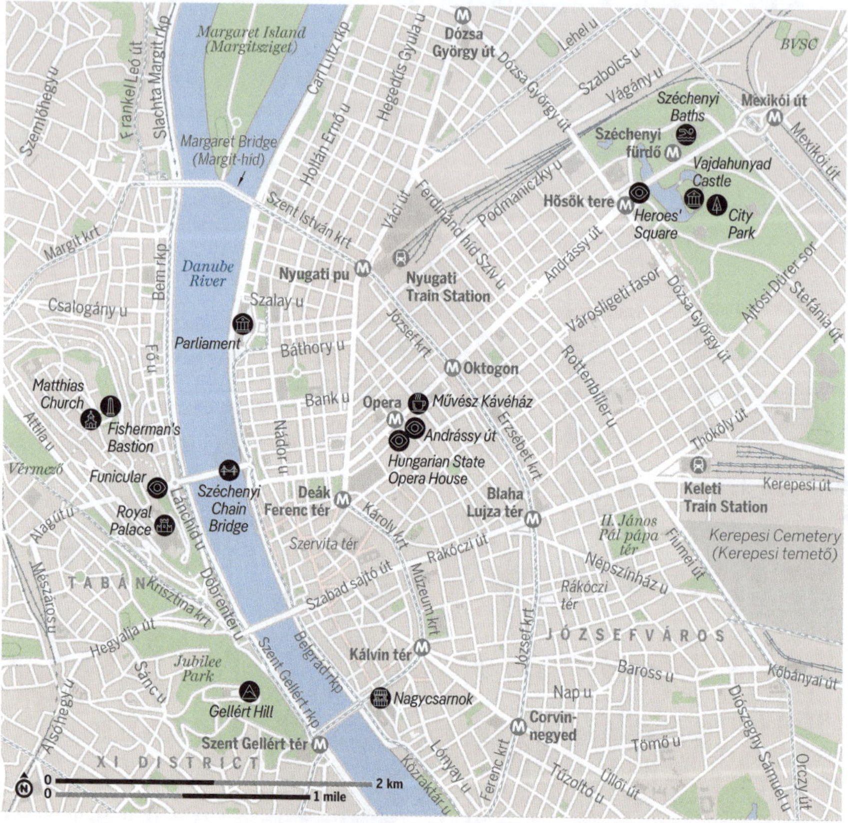

A DAY IN BUDAPEST

Start your day early at the city's biggest market, the **Nagycsarnok** (Great Market Hall) – head upstairs for cooked foods and souvenirs – then walk along the **Danube** riverside to admire the splendid architecture and views across to the iconic Royal Palace, **Gellért Hill**, and the beautiful bridges that span the river.

Cross the **Széchenyi Chain Bridge**, then take the **funicular** (p110) up **Castle Hill** (p110) for a close-up view of the **Royal Palace**. Explore the Castle District to see **Matthias Church** and **Fisherman's Bastion**, providing one of the prettiest views of the Pest skyline and the **Parliament** (p111).

Catch bus 16 to central Deák tér, then stroll along leafy **Andrássy út**, past the **Hungarian State Opera House** and delightful **Művész Kávéház** to majestic **Heroes' Square**. Afterwards, wander around picture-perfect **City Park** to see **Vajdahunyad Castle** and the surrounding lake, then soak at splendid **Széchenyi Baths** (p112).

Where to Stay

District V (Belváros) is the heart of Budapest, close to major attractions like the Parliament, St Stephen's Basilica and the Danube river, and offering a mix of upscale hotels and boutique options. The City Park area is lovely and quiet, and only about 10 minutes away from the centre. Inner District VII (Erzsébetváros) is the happening part of town with boutique hotels and cheap hostels galore. A little pricier but picturesque is the Castle District, home to the Royal Palace and splendid views.

BEST PLACES TO STAY

Four Seasons Hotel €€€ Housed in the gorgeous Gresham Palace decorated with wrought-iron Peacock Gates. fourseasons.com/budapest

Maverick Hostel € Well-run hostel with private doubles and multiple-bed dorms. mavericklodges.com/hostel/budapest-downtown

Hotel Central Basilica €€ Super-central with 47 rooms, 10 of which face St Stephen's Basilica. hotelcentral-basilica.hu

Alice Hotel Budapest €€€ Set in a 19th-century villa, blending historic charm with modern amenities. alicehotel.hu

Where to Eat

When in Budapest, visiting a historic coffeehouse like Centrál Grand Cafe & Bar, Hadik or New York Café, as well as ruin bars such as Szimpla Kert, Csendes Létterem or Púder Bárszínház, is a must. Coffeehouses serve both food and drinks, while ruin bars are better for drinks than a culinary experience. You'll find plenty of street-food spots and restaurants serving Hungarian, international and vegetarian/vegan dishes all around Belváros and District VII.

BUDAPEST'S FAVOURITE FOOD & DRINKS

One of the ways to a Hungarian's heart is knowing how to mix or order a good *fröccs* (wine spritzer). Most often made with white or rosé wine, a *kisfröccs* (small spritzer) is 100mL of wine and the same amount of sparkling water. A *nagyfröccs* (big spritzer) is double the wine and 100mL of water. A *hosszúlépés* (long step) is 100mL of wine and 200mL of water, while a *házmester* (janitor) is 300mL of wine and 200mL of water.

The most famous spirits are fiery *pálinka* (fruit brandy; pictured below) and historic Unikum, a bitter aperitif made according to a top-secret formula. You can order these drinks at any bar or restaurant.

Traditional dishes to taste include *pörkölt*, a meaty stew with a side of *nokedli* (Hungarian egg dumplings) – vegetarians can try it with mushrooms – and *gulyás* soup with meat cubes and vegetables. Try these at **Gettó Gulyás** (reservours.com/gettogulyas; €€).

BEST PLACES TO EAT & DRINK

KIOSK €€ Hungarian favourites – most ingredients come from their own farm. kiosk-budapest.hu

Menza €€ Retro-chic place with a modern take on Hungarian cuisine. menzaetterem.hu

Paprika Vendéglő €€ Rustic Hungarian restaurant – book ahead. paprikavendeglo.hu

Retro Lángos €€ The best place to try *lángos* (deep-fried dough with toppings). retrolangos.hu

Walk the Castle District

One of the best areas for sightseeing in Budapest is the World Heritage–listed Castle District, where a mesmerising monument awaits on practically every corner.

HOW TO

Getting here: For a speedy and fun way to ascend Castle Hill, take the **funicular** *(adult/concession 5000/2000Ft)* from the Buda embankment of the Chain Bridge. Alternatively, hop on bus 16.

When to go: Castle District is always packed with tourists, so visit early in the morning or late afternoon to avoid the crowds.

Hungarian National Gallery: Adult/concession 5400/2700Ft

Castle Museum: Adult/concession 3800/1900Ft

National Széchenyi Library: Day pass 1200Ft

Matthias Church: Adult/student 3100/2500Ft

House of Houdini: Adult/child 5200/3200Ft

Rock Nuclear Bunker Museum: Adult/concession 9500/7000Ft

Tip: Wear comfy shoes for the cobblestone streets.

The historic Castle District is one of Budapest's loveliest neighbourhoods to wander; the charming cobblestone streets, splendid staircases, fascinating museums and stunning viewpoints set the stage for a journey back in time. You'll find many heavyweight sights steps away from each other, such as the emblematic and immediately recognisable **Royal Palace** – home to the **Hungarian National Gallery** *(mng.hu)*, containing an overwhelming collection of thousands of artefacts; the **Castle Museum** *(varmuzeum.hu)*, which tells the story of Budapest; and the **National Széchenyi Library** *(oszk.hu)*.

Lace-like **Matthias Church** *(matyas-templom.hu)* and fairy-tale **Fisherman's Bastion**, as well as great museums like the **House of Houdini** *(houseofhoudinibudapest.com)*, honouring the great illusionist, and the **Hospital in the Rock Nuclear Bunker Museum** *(sziklakorhaz.eu)*, a real underground hospital turned into a nuclear bunker, are also found here. There are plenty of cafes and restaurants around, too. Don't miss taking photos from the Fisherman's Bastion.

South gate, Fisherman's Bastion

Entrance, Great Synagogue

THAT FAMOUS HUNGARIAN WIT

While you've probably heard of legendary illusionist Harry Houdini, you may not know that he was born Erik Weisz in Hungary. But Houdini is just the start: Hungary is the birthplace of many remarkable creations, discoveries and ideas. Dr Ignác Semmelweis was the first person to discover the medical benefits of handwashing – he found that childbed fever was spread by doctors who did not wash their hands between dissections and seeing patients. Pulitzer, the publisher who funded the prestigious journalism prize, was born József in Hungary. Five Hungarian scientists played key roles in the Manhattan Project, which developed nuclear weapons: Tódor Kármán, János Neumann, Leó Szilárd, Ede Teller and Jenő Wigner. Albert Szent-Györgyi, who won the Nobel Prize for discovering vitamin C in 1937, was Hungarian, as was László Bíró, who invented the ballpoint pen. Hungarian architect Ernő Rubik invented the Rubik's cube and Katalin Karikó jointly won the Nobel Prize in 2023 for the development of mRNA vaccines against COVID-19. Hungary boasts a high number of Nobel Prize laureates, and Hungarians are known for their wit, inventiveness and cleverness.

Marvel at Iconic Big Buildings

Despite its modest size, Hungary punches well above its weight when it comes to having some of the world's most impressive architectural giants. The country's biggest building – and the third-largest national assembly in the world – is the stunning neo-Gothic **Parliament** *(parlament.hu)*, stretching for 286m along the Pest riverbank. The city's largest and the most sacred Catholic church in all of Hungary is **St Stephen's Basilica** *(bazilika budapest.hu)* – don't miss the view from the dome. With its crenellated red-and-yellow glazed-brick Moorish facade, the **Great Synagogue** *(jewish tourhungary.com)* is the largest Jewish house of worship in Europe, seating 3000 people. Due to their close proximity, all can be visited in a day.

Along the Way We Saw...

MYKHAILO KOLODKO STATUES Something special and quirky about wandering the streets of Budapest is stumbling upon tiny bronze statues scattered around town by Hungarian-Ukrainian guerrilla artist Mykhailo Kolodko *(kolodkoart.com)*. These miniature masterpieces make great photo ops. The most famous ones are Franz Joseph hanging out in a hammock on Liberty Bridge (north side, near the first pylon), a Rubik's Cube on the Buda embankment opposite the Parliament, and Dracula reading a book by Vajdahunyad Castle in City Park.

Kata Fári

EXPERIENCE

Soak at a Historic Thermal Baths

As Hungary is blessed by naturally heated springs bubbling up from below ground, taking the waters is a way of life here. Budapest boasts famously elegant bathhouses, which are also architectural marvels, portals to the past, sanctuaries of wellness, social hotspots and a quintessential part of the Budapest experience.

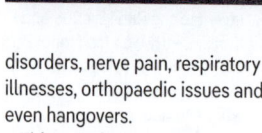

HOW TO

Getting here: The two big-name baths, Gellért and Széchenyi, are easy to reach via public transport, as are Lukács, Rudas and Veli Bej Baths. Use the BudapestGO app to plan your journey.

When to go: Baths operate year-round, but soaking in the warm water in the outdoor pools is most magical on dreary winter days. On weekends and during the winter holiday season, people pack into the pools like sardines, so visit on weekdays or early morning for a more peaceful experience.

Cost: Varies depending on services required.

More info: spasbudapest.com

Know Before You Go

Pack swimwear, a towel and flip-flops as the floor can be quite slippery – or rent or buy them on the spot. Swimming caps must be worn in the lap pools. Showers and hair dryers are available, so bring personal cleaning products. Nudity is not permitted in public areas at any thermal baths; the Turkish bath section at Rudas is the only one that still holds single-sex sessions on weekdays.

Hungarians swear by the healing properties of their thermal waters, and bathing in these pools is not only luxuriously calm but also curative. Bubbling up from a network of underground caves, the warm waters are rich in dissolved minerals and can help to relieve health problems ranging from arthritis and muscle pain to slipped discs, circulatory disorders, nerve pain, respiratory illnesses, orthopaedic issues and even hangovers.

Kids must be over 14 to use the baths (some bathhouses won't even let them enter and pregnant women are also discouraged).

What to Expect

In most Budapest bathhouses, you'll find a series of indoor thermal pools ranging in temperature from lukewarm to piping hot, as well as colder pools for swimming laps. Other amenities include saunas, steam rooms, ice-cold plunge pools and indulgent spa services such as massages. Except for Veli Bej, all

CHOOSE YOUR BATHS

The most beautiful is **Gellért**, an art nouveau wonderland with mosaics, stained-glass windows and marble columns. **Széchenyi** is Europe's largest spa complex in a wedding cake–like building with sunflower-yellow walls and old chaps playing chess in the water. One of Budapest's longest-standing baths is **Lukács**, a true medical mecca. **Rudas**, an original Turkish baths with a contemporary touch, has a rooftop hot tub. **Veli Bej**, another traditional Turkish bath with a modern twist, is never really that busy, and since it's accessible from a hospital, many people come here to heal.

Left: Széchenyi Baths
Below: Gellért Baths

baths have an outdoor section with water fountains, whirlpools and wave machines, while some even offer fun extras like private or night-time bathing or a beer bath. Always specify which services you need when you enter, as admission charges vary.

Some spa etiquette to note is to first take a shower and tie your hair back to avoid being told off. Keep noise to a minimum as it can get quite echoey inside – most people are here to relax or heal, so anything more than quiet chatting is usually frowned upon. Remember to stay hydrated – drinking fountains are generally available.

Budapest

The shift from Western to Eastern Europe that you sense in Budapest intensifies on the way to Bucharest. You'll traverse a wide swathe of Romania on this leg, most likely travelling on a sleeper train. Fewer electrified modern tracks means a slower pace, hence more opportunities to take in the passing landscapes, including the chiselled mountain peaks and densely forested valleys of Transylvania, one of the scenic highlights of the classic Orient Express route.

Simon Richmond

Apuseni Mountains (p120)
SEBASTIAN PLONKA/ALAMY

Bucharest

873 KMS · 17½ HOURS' RIDE

THIS LEG:

- Szolnok
- Curtici
- Arad
- Deva
- Alba Iulia
- Mediaș
- Sighișoara
- Brașov
- Predeal
- Bușteni
- Sinaia
- Ploiești Vest
- București Nord, Bucharest

Riding Notes

Timetables take account of clocks going forward an hour as you cross the border into Romania. Electrification of Romania's railways is ongoing – expect trains to run much slower here than in Western Europe. Eurorail or Interrail passes only cover trains run by CFR Călători and are not valid on any other Romanian train companies.

Breaking Your Journey

Really, the only way to include Bran Castle in your itinerary along our main route is to stay at least one night in Braşov (p124). Sinaia (p126) is another great base, as are Alba Iulia (p119) and Sighişoara (p122). On the alternative route (p120), consider stopping overnight in Cluj-Napoca and Sibiu.

Simon's Tips

BEST MEAL Enjoy traditional Romanian dishes at Ograda while taking in Braşov's Piaţa Sfatului. (p119)

FAVOURITE VIEW The mountainous scenery on the journey between Braşov and Sinaia. (p122)

ESSENTIAL STOP Sinaia for its royal castles and ethereal monastery. (p126)

TIP Book ahead for tickets to Peleş Castle, which is closed Mondays and Tuesdays.

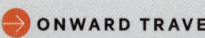 **ONWARD TRAVEL**

Arrive at Budapest-Keleti (p105) well in advance, as the train departure platform can be a fair walk from the main entrance. If you have a 1st-class ticket, there's a comfortable lounge accessed from Platform 9. If you need to buy a ticket or get information, go to the lower level to find the MÁV customer centre – this is also where the entrance to the metro station is.

To stock up on food and drinks for the journey (a good idea, as most trains will not have buffet or restaurant cars), there's a **City SPAR** *(6.30am-9pm Mon-Sat, 8am-7pm Sun)* grocery store immediately north of the station on Thököly út.

Szolnok

Catch up on your reading or diary notes on the initial stretch of the journey – the countryside is flat and mostly treeless. About 1½ hours' journey east of Budapest-Keleti is Szolnok. Located on the Tisza River, one of Central and Eastern Europe's major waterways, this long-established town of around 66,000 is at the heart of the **Great Hungarian Plain**.

Lőkösháza, another 1½ hours down the line, is the last station in Hungary before crossing the border into Romania – be prepared for passport checks on board the train.

Curtici

Arriving at Curtici, the first station in Romania, you'll need to wind your watch ahead an hour. This may appear to be a remote border crossing, but since the advent of Central Europe's railways, Curtici has been an important junction – hence the larger-than-expected station.

In 1934 Patrick Leigh Fermor entered Romania by train at Curtici while journeying from the Hook of Holland to İstanbul – an episode covered in his memoir *Between the Woods and Water*.

Arad

Less than 15 minutes after Curtici, the train pulls into Arad, which has a handsome station dating to 1858. Neoclassical and Secession architecture from the late 19th and early 20th centuries can be enjoyed on a stroll up the city's tree-lined central boulevard, B-dul Revoluţiei. Look out for the impressive **Town Hall**, with its 54m-tall clock tower, and the 1913 **Palace of Culture**, which houses a couple of museums.

Deva

Two hours travel further east into Transylvania, via the picturesque Mureş River valley, is Deva, an industrial city crowned by the remains of the 13th-century **citadel**, which looms from the top of an extinct 300m volcano. It's around a 15-minute walk from the station to the steep steps up to the citadel. Alternatively, ride a **funicular** *(adult/child 30/15 lei; 9am-5pm)* from the foot of the hill. At the top there are stone walls and views of the surrounding hills.

Also at the foot of the fortress hill, and housed in the early-17th-century Renaissance Magna Curia Palace, is the **Museum of Dacian & Roman Civilisation** *(Muzeul Civilizaţiei Dacice*

Clocks go forward one hour as you cross from Hungary into Romania

Corvin Castle, Deva

BUDAPEST TO BUCHAREST

şi Romane; mcdr.ro/index.php/ro; adult/child 20/4 lei; 10am-6pm).

If you have time for a detour, spectacular Gothic **Corvin Castle** (Castelul Corvinilor; castelul corvinilor.ro; adult/child 50/12 lei; noon-8pm Mon, 9am-8pm Tue-Sun) is 19km south of Deva in the city of Hunedoara.

Alba Iulia

You'll be treated to rural views and the rolling hills of the Transylvanian Plateau and the Apuseni Mountains (p120) in the hour or so journey between Deva and **Alba Iulia** (turism. apulum.ro), Romania's 'spiritual capital'. It was

Continues on page 122

BEST PLACES TO EAT

La Ceaun, Braşov €€
Tasty traditional Romanian food at pocket-friendly prices on Braşov's Piaţa Sfatului. *noon-10pm*

Ograda, Braşov €€
Overlooking Braşov's Piaţa Sfatului, this is a relaxed dining spot with a tempting menu of local and international dishes. *noon-9.30pm*

La Teleferic, Sinaia €
This cute, family-run bistro is a fine brunch choice. It's in the B&B next to Sinaia's cable car. *8am-4pm Thu-Mon*

Bruma GastroBar, Sinaia €€
Centrally located restaurant in Sinaia with international dishes, traditional Romanian and very good pizza. *noon-midnight*

Take the scenic route through Oradea, 114km north of Arad, known for its neoclassical and art nouveau architecture

17km — Arad — 127km — Deva — 62km — Alba Iulia

Corvin Castle, one of Romania's most amazing fortresses, is 19km south of Deva

Travel Another Route to Braşov

Take your time to see some more places and gorgeous Romanian landscapes on your way to Braşov from Budapest by following this alternative itinerary.

HOW TO

Nearest stop: From Budapest (p118), head to Püspökladány in Hungary where you can transfer to a train to Oradea. There are also slower connecting trains to Oradea from Arad (p118).

Getting here: See Romania's main train operator **CFR Călători** (cfrcalatori.ro) and private operator **Interregional Călători** (interregional.ro) for schedules.

When to go: Sibiu International Theatre Festival (sibfest.ro) is held in June. **Untold** (untold.com), Romania's largest music festival, is held in Cluj-Napoca in early August over four days.

Tip: Cluj Guided Tours (clujguidedtours.ro) runs by-donation walking tours in English daily at 11am and 6pm, as well as day trips around the region.

Budapest to Oradea
For the most conveniently timed train connections, go from Budapest-Keleti (p105) to **Püspökladány** (2¼ hours), from where there are direct trains to Oradea (1½ hours).

Oradea (visitoradea.com) has scores of art nouveau (Secession) buildings and monuments. While some have fallen into disrepair, others have been restored, such as the **Moskovits Palace** on Calea Republicii. Secession design elements on buildings can be viewed along this pedestrian walkway and across the Crişul Repede river in Piaţa Unirii. A delightful Secession-style building is **Darvas-La Roche House** (oradeaheritage.ro/casa-darvas-la-roche; admission 20 lei; 10am-6pm Tue-Sun).

Oradea to Cluj-Napoca
It takes around four hours to travel by train the 152km to Cluj-Napoca ('Cluj'), passing through the scenic Apuseni Mountains. Around 2.5km south of Cluj's 1870 train station is 14th-century **St Michael's**, Romania's second-largest Gothic church and showpiece of the Old Town's Piaţa Unirii.

Cluj teems with bohemian cafes, art galleries, nightlife and music festivals. During the 19th century, when Hungary governed Transylvania, Cluj served as regional capital. The Hungarian influence is still felt and adds another dimension to city life.

Cluj Napoca to Sibiu
Head south of Cluj via Alba Iulia (p119) to Sibiu (about four hours), one of Transylvania's most

ADVENTURES IN THE APUSENI MOUNTAINS

Cluj-Napoca is a popular centre for organising caving and mountain-biking, with the dramatic Apuseni Mountains offering a wealth of caverns and trails. Some 760 sq km are protected as the **Apuseni Nature Park** *(parcapuseni.ro)*, best accessed from Oradea.

In Cluj, **Retro Hostel** *(retro.ro/retro-tours)* has a travel agency that can organise tours to the Apuseni Mountains, the impressive Turda salt mine and much more. In Oradea, contact responsible tourism company **Apuseni Experience** *(apuseniexperience.ro)* about multiday hiking and biking trips in the mountains.

Left: Moskovits Palace

picturesque and historic towns. The main sights are grouped on three main squares: **Piaţa Mare** (Large Sq), **Piaţa Mică** (Small Sq) and **Piaţa Huet** (Huet Sq). A stairway leads down to the trendy **Lower Town**, home to bars and restaurants, from behind Piaţa Huet. Sibiu also has well-preserved **medieval city walls**, which originally featured 39 towers.

It takes at least three hours to travel the 149km between Sibiu and Braşov, but you'll be glad of the slower pace as the scenery is spectacular with the peaks of the Carpathian Mountains rising majestically in the distance.

Continued from page 119

here on two occasions – in 1600 and 1918 – that the nation announced the union of Transylvania with the traditional Romanian lands of Wallachia and Moldavia. The latter date, 1 December 1918, is celebrated as Romania's National Day.

The crowning jewel is the **Alba Carolina Citadel**, a 25-minute walk north of the station. This magnificent baroque fortress, built in the early 18th century by the ruling Habsburg monarchy, is in a heptagonal star shape, surrounded by moats, with bastions at the points. It's an immense space enclosing grand monuments, museums, archaeological treasures, the 13th-century **St Michael's Cathedral** and the Orthodox **Coronation Cathedral**, completed in 1922 for the crowning of King Ferdinand and Queen Marie. You can stay here at Hotel Medieval (p126).

Mediaș

Bucolic Transylvanian scenery alternates with the dark, industrial ruins around Copșa Mică, on the 45-minute journey from Alba Iulia to Mediaș, an attractive Saxon town. At its heart stands the fortified church of **St Margaret** *(evkm.ro)* – from the left side of the train, the church's soaring spire is clearly visible along with the towers of the fortified walls.

Sighișoara

Continuing east for around 30 minutes, the train pauses at Sighișoara, another splendid Saxon fortified town – you can see its UNESCO-listed **Citadel** from the right side of the train.

Sighișoara's pastel-coloured buildings, stony lanes and medieval towers look like a film set. During the Middle Ages, the centre supported more than a dozen traditional guilds, and towers still honour guilds like 'Tinsmiths' and 'Tailors'. The town is also associated with Vlad Țepeș (p125): the bloodthirsty Wallachian prince was allegedly born here in 1431 at **Casa Vlad Dracul** *(casavladdracul.ro)*, now a restaurant.

There are several ways to access the citadel, which is about a 20-minute walk south of the train station; the main stairway starts north of the main square, Piața Hermann Oberth. Amble around and take in the splendour at your own pace. Alternatively, **Wanderlust Tours** *(wanderlust-tour.ro)* offers guided tours of the citadel.

> **DETOUR: Viscri**
>
> From Sighișoara arrange for a taxi or guided tour to picturesque **Viscri** *(viscri-info.ro)*. Many Romanians will tell you that this Saxon fortified village is a favourite of Charles III – the British king has owned a farmhouse here since 2006 and has done much to revive the village's fortunes.

Brașov

The mountainous Carpathian landscape gets steadily more dramatic as you approach Brașov (p124). You'll know you've arrived when you see a Hollywood-style sign spelling out the old Saxon town's name in big white letters atop Mt Tâmpa. Brașov's bulky concrete terminal dates from the 1960s – the only hint it gives of the town's charm are the watercolour-style murals hanging above the upper level of the ticket hall.

Brașov's Old Town, 4km southwest of the station, is surrounded by a curtain of high mountains on all sides that lend the main square, Piața Sfatului, a snug, cosy feel. Teutonic knights established a town here in 1211 and Brașov grew into a German colony named Kronstadt. The

Alba Iulia — 83km — **Mediaș** — 39km — **Sighișoara** — 127km

Visit the birthplace of the inspiration for Bram Stoker's Dracula

Saxons built ornate churches and townhouses, protected by a massive medieval wall, sections of which remain in place. Stay here a couple of days, especially if you plan to visit nearby Bran Castle (p125).

Predeal

Stand by for some gorgeous scenery as you travel south out of Braşov and into the pine tree–clad Prahova Valley as it cuts through the Bucegi Mountains. The train goes uphill to Predeal, at 1054m above sea level. The impressive station, dating to 1964, has an angular, saddle-shaped roof topping a fully glazed facade. Alight here to access hiking trails and the popular and well-equipped **Predeal Ski Resort** *(predeal.ro)*.

Buşteni

It's downhill into the Prahova Valley to reach Buşteni. Get off here to visit **Cantacuzino Castle** *(Castelul Cantacuzino; cantacuzino castle.com; adult/child 75/40 lei; 10am-7pm Mon-Thu, 10am-8pm Fri-Sun),* which you will see clearly uphill left of the station. The grand, early-20th-century summer residence of the noble Cantacuzino family doubles as Nevermore Academy in the Netflix *Addams Family* spin-off *Wednesday.* Tour the lavish interiors and have lunch at **Canta Cuisine** – its terrace tables offer fabulous views of the Bucegi Mountains.

As you close in on Sinaia, gaze up to the jagged ridges of the Bucegi Mountains to see the

Continues on page 126

Along the Way We Met...

OVIDIU BOTONI Combine visiting Bran Castle with one of the region's fortified churches such as World Heritage–listed Prejmer, which is just 15km from Braşov. The church at the Prejmer Fortress *(bisericafortificataprejmer.ro)* was originally built in the 13th century, and in the 14th century, 12m-tall defensive walls were added. Strategically positioned near the Buzău Pass in the Carpathian Mountains, it was often the first line of defence against invading forces and is one of the most formidable fortified churches in Transylvania.

Ovidiu runs Boutique Romania tours (boutiqueromania.com).

OVIDIU'S TIP: *Arrive at Bran Castle when it opens at 9am or visit at the end of the day (5pm in summer, 3pm in winter) to avoid the tour bus crowds.*

Braşov — 18km — Predeal — 11km — Buşteni

Detour: The pretty Saxon fortified village of Viscri is 42km southeast of Sighişoara

Visit Bran Castle, 30km southwest of Braşov, for another tenuous link to Dracula

CITY GUIDE:
Brașov

Overlooked by Mt Tâmpa, Brașov offers a taste of Transylvania with its well-preserved Old Town that's a delight to explore. It's also not far from Bran Castle, a dramatically located fortress that somewhat milks its tenuous connections to Dracula and his inspiration, Vlad Țepeș.

HOW TO

Getting here: There are nine direct trains daily connecting Budapest to Brașov (12½ hours). If you're heading in the opposite direction from Bucharest, the trains are numerous and take between 2¼ and 3¼ hours.

Getting around: Brașov station is about 4km northeast of the Old Town. There are regular buses or you can take a taxi for about 20 lei.

Sleeping: Brașov has a good range of accommodation. Our picks include the budget Secret Boutique Hostel (p126) and the more upmarket Schuster Boarding House (p126) and Bella Muzica (p126).

Tip: Walkabout Free Walking Tours *(brasov.walkaboutfreetours.com)* start daily at 10.30pm and 6.30pm from Piața Sfatului.

More info: brasovtourism.eu

Brașov is best enjoyed on foot exploring the picturesque streets that radiate off the main square, **Piața Sfatului**, which is surrounded by many good places to eat and drink including La Ceaun (p119) and Ograda (p119). In the square itself you'll find the **Council's House** (Casa Sfatului), dating from 1420 and topped by the Trumpeter's Tower, which is home to a small local **history museum** *(9am-5pm Tue-Sun)*. Nearby, search out the 16th-century **Catherine's Gate**, the early-19th-century **Schei Gate**, the handsome **Beth Israel Synagogue** just off Str Poarta Schei, and the narrow graffiti-covered **Strada Sforii** (Rope St).

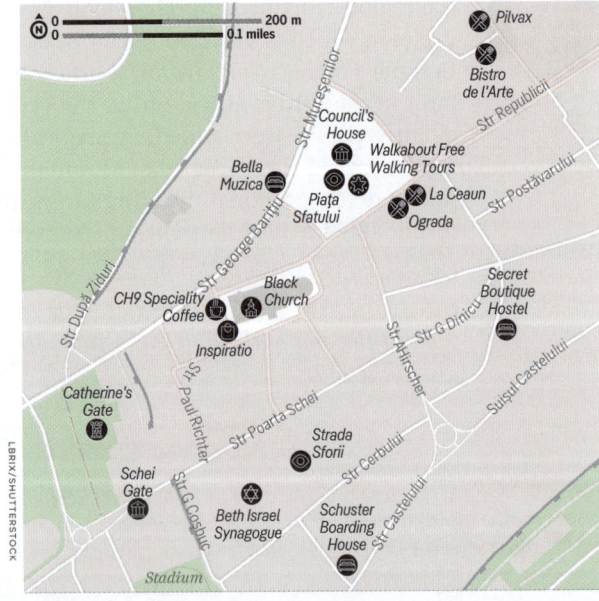

VLAD THE IMPALER

Throughout Transylvania you can't ignore the omnipresence of Dracula; from mugs and T-shirts all the way to bat- and blood-themed menus and cape-bedecked waiters. But what's really chilling is that a blueprint for the pale, shape-shifting count from literature and films actually existed, though not in a black cape and cloud of fog, but rather as a Wallachian warrior king with a predilection for extreme cruelty.

Fifteenth-century prince Vlad Ţepeş is often credited with being the inspiration for Dracula, the vampire-count originally featured in the classic Gothic horror story *Dracula* (1897). His princely father, Vlad II, was called Vlad Dracul. 'Dracula' means 'son of the house of Dracul', which itself translates as 'devil' or 'dragon'. Add to this diabolical moniker the fact that Vlad used to impale his victims – from which you get his surname: Ţepeş (Impaler) – and it's easy to see why Dracula's creator, Irishman Bram Stoker, tapped into Vlad's bloodline.

While Bran Castle has little to do with Vlad Ţepeş, the pretty Saxon citadel of Sighişoara (p122) was Vlad's birthplace.

Bran Castle

Romania's Largest Gothic Church

The 14th-century **Black Church** *(Biserica Neagră; bisericaneagra.ro; admission 25 lei; 10am-7pm Tue-Sat, noon-7pm Sun & Mon)* is so named because of its charred appearance following the Great Fire of 1689. The most notable feature of the interior is the rich collection of 16th- to 19th-century Oriental and Ottoman rugs (pictured bottom left) that are draped across the pews and hung from the balconies; these were donated by wealthy members of the congregation. Organ recitals are held here every Saturday at 6pm from May to October. Buy entry tickets from the Inspiratio giftshop opposite the church.

Learn the Real Story of Bran Castle

Some 30km southwest of Braşov, **Bran Castle** *(Castelul Bran; bran-castle.com; admission 70 lei; 9am-6pm Tue-Sun, noon-6pm Mon)* is arguably Romania's best-known tourist attraction. Towering above the town atop a rock, it certainly looks the part of a vampire's lair, though connections to the novel *Dracula* and Vlad Ţepeş are thin. For centuries the castle was controlled by Braşov's Saxons, but was given to Romania's ruling monarchy after WWI, becoming a favourite of Romania's beloved Queen Marie, who made it a cosy retreat. The restaurant in Queen Marie's old teahouse is lovely.

BEST PLACES TO EAT & DRINK

Bistro de l'Arte €€ Long-running bistro turning out some of the city's most inventive cooking. *noon-11pm*

Pilvax €€€ Upscale fusion of Transylvanian and Hungarian food in a modern setting. *noon-10pm Tue-Sat, noon-4pm Sun*

CH9 Speciality Coffee € Opposite the Black Church, this is one of the best places for a cuppa. *8am-7pm Mon-Fri, 9am-8pm Sat & Sun*

Continued from page 123

Heroes' Cross on Caraiman Peak. This 39.3m monument, completed in 1928 as a memorial to the railway workers who died while serving Romania during WWI, was an initiative of King Ferdinand and Queen Marie.

Sinaia

Sinaia's handsome station, befitting royal arrivals, dates to 1913 and replaced the original 1879 station. The station's platform was the scene of dramatic events on 29 December 1933 when Prime Minister Ion G Duca was assassinated by the Iron Guard – there's a memorial plate marking the spot.

Alight at Sinaia to visit Peleș Castle and Pelișor Castle (p128) and explore the historic and beautiful **Sinaia Monastery**. For an overnight stay, consider Hotel Smart (left) and **Villa Oblique** (hotelpaj.ro; €€€), which is about 700m west of Peleș Castle. Good spots for a meal include La

Interior, Sinaia Monastery

BEST PLACES TO SLEEP

Schuster Boarding House, Brașov €€€
In a quiet part of the Old Town, this luxuriously reconstructed townhouse is the best place to stay in Brașov. *schusterhotel.ro*

Secret Boutique Hostel, Brașov €
Budget Old Town hostel in a quiet location with spotless, well-appointed six- and eight-bed dorms. *ibe.channex.io/secrethostelbrasov*

Bella Muzica, Brașov €€
A 400-year-old Brașov building has been tastefully restored to create this antique-style hotel. *bellamuzica.ro*

Hotel Smart, Sinaia €€
Beautifully maintained property 1km from central Sinaia. Rooms have balconies. *hotelsmart.ro*

Hotel Medieval, Alba Iulia €€
Charming hotel in a former 18th-century barracks within Alba Iulia's citadel. *hotel-medieval.ro*

Teleferic (p119), Bruma GastroBar (p119) and La Tunuri (p128) at Peleș Castle.

Ploişeti Vest

By the time you reach Ploişeti Vest, a 50-minute journey southeast of Sinaia, the mountains of Transylvania are far behind and you are now travelling across the Romanian Plain. An oil field lies beneath the ground here and oil-refining has been central to Ploişeti's identity since the mid-19th century. This made the city a prime target for Allied bombers during WWII. Despite the damage sustained, Ploişeti has an attractive core, with a smattering of gracefully ageing 19th-century mansions.

Ploişeti is a jumping-off point for Wallachia's historic capitals to the west and the Dealu Mare winemaking region.

București Nord

Approaching București Nord (Bucharest North; also called Gara de Nord), the Romanian capital's principal train station, you'll pass under the Basarab Overpass, a 1.9km span that is also one of Europe's widest cable-stay bridges at 44.5m.

București Nord is a big, bustling place with some 200 trains coming and going daily. The area around the station is not unsafe, but it is far from the most attractive part of the city – opposite the station's northeast corner is an art deco former hotel that's in an advanced state of decay. Moving on is easy either by taxi or the Gara de Nord metro station, which is beneath the railway terminus.

Look beyond the station's modern food and drink outlets and you'll notice remnants of the original late-19th-century architecture. In the main entrance hall, photos of old Bucharest landmarks hang alongside evocative images celebrating the European Year of Rail 2021. A hidden gem is the Royal Salon decorated in grand Empire style; however, it is very rarely open to the public.

Along the Way We Saw...

SINAIA MONASTERY The original late-17th-century wall paintings in the tiny, cruciform Old Church at Sinaia Monastery *(manastireasinaia.ro)* are astonishing in their creativity and detail. Inside the monastery's larger mid-19th-century church, 10 Greek Orthodox monks, dressed in black robes and veils, were chanting vespers, their harmonious voices echoing off the dimly lit, gilded walls. After the service, I chatted briefly with monk Yeroteo. He tells me he's 40 and has been here for a decade. When I ask how long he will stay, he answers, 'Until I die.'

Simon Richmond

Bușteni — 8km — Sinaia — 62km — Ploişeti Vest — 59km — Bucharest

Look out for the Heroes' Cross on Caraiman Peak between Busteni and Sinaia

Bucharest Henri Coanda International Airport is 45km south of Ploiseti at Otopeni

Tour a Pair of Romanian Castles

Peleş Castle (Castelul Peleş), built for King Carol I and Queen Elizabeth, is one of Romania's grandest sights and was visited by passengers on the maiden journey of the *Orient Express*. A Disney-esque pile, it stands high on the slopes of Sinaia, next to the smaller Pelior Castle (Castelul Pelişor).

HOW TO

Getting here: Sinaia (p126) is one hour south of Braşov and 1½ hours north of Bucharest by train.

Getting around: It's an uphill walk of around 30 minutes (4km) to reach the castles from Sinaia train station. A taxi will cost around 15 lei.

Tip: La Tunuri *(8.30am-8.30pm; €)* serves drinks, freshly baked cakes and slices of pizza. Its terrace provides great views of Peleş Castle.

More info: Pre-book timed entry tickets online *(peles.ro)*. Both castles are closed Monday and Tuesday. Peleş is closed all November, Pelişor all of October.

Royal Residences

Born in 1839 in Germany, Karl Eitel Friedrich Zephyrinus Ludwig von Hohenzollern-Sigmaringen was crowned Carol I of Romania in 1881. He commissioned Peleş Castle as his summer residence. When the *Orient Express* guests arrived in 1883, the castle (really a palace) had barely been completed. Some were not impressed, with one writing that the road to Peleş was 'more suitable for mountain goats than human beings', another that its clashing styles of interior decoration were in the worst possible taste.

As Carol had no male successors, on his death in 1914 the crown went to his nephew Ferdinand, who was married to Marie, a granddaughter of both Britain's Queen Victoria and Russia's Alexander II. Pelişor Castle, completed in 1902, was built for them.

Peleş Castle

Carol's desires for Peleş to be magnificent resulted in an eye-boggling hodgepodge of architectural styles – the castle is part Gothic revival, part Italian neo-Renaissance. In the Honorary Hallway, note the Swiss and German landscapes, fashioned from inlaid wood, to remind the king of his homeland. Another showpiece is the Arms Room brimming with armour for soldiers and their horses. A succession of elaborate rooms follow, including a well-stocked library (with a secret passageway), Oriental Room, Music Room and Moorish Dining Room with

TICKETS

Admission to Peleş Castle and Pelişor Castle is by tour, either self-guided or guided. These depart at roughly hourly intervals. The guided tours last around 45 minutes, but it's easy enough to view either palace on your own as there's plenty of English information explaining each room.

Only 2000 people per day are allowed into Peleş and 1500 people per day for Pelişor. Book in advance, especially during the busy summer season. There are ticket machines at the castle, but you might turn up to find all admission slots sold out.

Left: Hall, Peleş Castle
Below: Pelişor Castle

walls inlaid with mother-of-pearl. The grounds are more soothing.

Pelişor Castle

Meaning 'little Peleş', Pelişor Castle is about 100m uphill from Peleş, close by the estate's entrance. With half-timbering on its facade, the castle looks like a giant hunting lodge. Inside, the design is principally art nouveau. Queen Marie acted as Pelişor's interior designer, filling the spaces with Viennese furniture. She died here in 1938 in the aptly named Golden Room, the walls of which are entirely gilded with a pattern of thistle leaves – a reminder of her homeland.

Orient Express dining carriage, wood engraving, Felician von Myrbach-Rheinfeld (1895)
INTERFOTO /ALAMY

 INSIGHT

Europe's Imagined East

The appeal of the Orient Express for European travellers stemmed from the allure of the imagined, unfamiliar and exotic 'Orient'.

WORDS BY **THARIK HUSSAIN**
Tharik Hussain is the author of Muslim Europe; A Journey in Search of a Fourteen Hundred Year History.

WHEN THE ORIENT Express first set off in 1883, it was more than a train ride. Building on the fascination for the 'East' that drove the Grand Tours wealthy Europeans embarked upon, and eventually linking Paris with Constantinople (now İstanbul), the Orient Express transported not just wealthy passengers in gilded carriages, but centuries of ideas, fears and fantasies about the 'East'. As the blurb of Philip Glazebrook's 1984 book, *Journey to Kars*, reminds us: 'For Victorian travellers a trip to Türkiye was a leap into the dark of Islam'. The landscapes that unfurled beyond the plush dining cars and velvet-lined sleepers of the luxury train, inside which

Europeans remained safely cocooned, were never neutral; they were projected upon, imagined and warped through a long tradition of European thought.

Edward Said, in his landmark book *Orientalism* (1978), argued that 'the Orient' was less a geographical reality than a European invention: a mirror against which the West defined itself. The Orient Express, running across borders into Muslim Ottoman lands, was a literal stage for this process. To ride it was to take part in a journey into an 'East' already mapped in the imagination as exotic, dangerous, alluring and 'other'.

From Crusade to Romantic East

Europe's imagination of the East did not emerge with the railway. Its roots are found in the Middle Ages, when the Crusades and various Reconquista narratives cast Islam as the enemy and reinforced this through legends and widely circulated myths that depicted Muslims and those of the East as barbaric and licentious, birthing stereotypes that continue to this day. Terms like 'Saracen', 'Turk' and 'Moor' became bywords for cruelty, despotism and sensual excess.

By the 18th and 19th centuries, this legacy merged with romanticism. Writers and travellers sought inspiration in lands that were newly accessible through the growing efficiency of travel and networks of colonial rule. They imagined the East as a realm of unrestrained passions, cruelty and exotic beauty. Lord Byron confessed in 1813, 'My head is full of Oriental names and scenes', and his poems *The Giaour* and *The Bride of Abydos* revelled in harems, betrayals and taboo love. The Victorian explorer Sir Richard Burton went further: his popular and highly embellished translations of *The Arabian Nights*, *The Kama Sutra* and *The Perfumed Garden* eroticised the East, and brought it into Victorian parlours, even as he sneered at Muslims as 'fanatical' and 'indolent'. The East was seen as both exotic and threatening, but always subservient to the West. The Orient Express, carrying its passengers into landscapes they associated with these tales, gave such imaginings a moving backdrop — each stop and vista layered with centuries of fantasy; an 'Asiatic-looking' Macedonian here, a hijab-wearing Bulgarian there.

Science, Race & Empire

By the late 19th century, this constructed racial hierarchy was being justified through the pseudo-science of eugenics or 'scientific racism', which became fashionable in Europe's universities, including Cambridge and University College London. After the turn of the century, eugenics societies were patronised by the great and good of the West, including Winston Churchill, an Honorary Vice President of the Eugenics Society in the 1920s. This offered a veneer of rationality to age-old prejudices, recasting the East seen through the windows of the Orient Express not only as culturally inferior but biologically so.

Dovetailing with Europe's colonial ambitions and attitudes, justifying domination over peoples deemed incapable of self-rule who 'naturally' needed European governance, the East was mapped as backward, savage and racially distinct. The Orient Express, cutting through newly industrialised landscapes of Austria-Hungary and the Ottoman Balkans with its iron tracks, served as an extension of Europe's superiority; a technological reminder of who claimed to be modern and who was labelled stagnant.

The East in Europe

Growing nationalist movements in the Balkans, much of which was part of the Muslim Ottoman Empire when the first trains of the Orient

---

> To ride [the Orient Express] was to take part in a journey into an 'East' already mapped in the imagination as exotic, dangerous, alluring and 'other'.

Express trundled through, had long framed Muslim rule as the 'Ottoman yoke', casting their struggles as liberation from an alien oppressor. This rhetoric helped to position the Balkans as Europe's borderland, which like its colonies was perceived to be a place of 'primitive, barbaric, disorderly societies' in need of external administration, as well as a place where Christian nations sought to rejoin the West after Oriental captivity.

Western writers and artists reinforced this view. Edith Durham in her 1909 book *High Albania* described Albania as 'wild and lawless'. A Western European woman, susceptible to the 'science' of eugenics, Durham claimed to be looking at the country 'through a vista of a thousand years' because 'the river of evolution had left them stranded'. Meanwhile, French artist Charlotte Anne de Lazen in her *Sketches of Turkey* in 1831 and 1832 claimed the Balkans was a place where 'the Mussulman [Muslim] lords the land with indolent grandeur, while the Christian tiller bends in silence beneath his burden', helping to construct the image of the Balkan region as a battlefield between Christian (Western European) civilisation and Muslim barbarism; an image that continues to endure to this day.

Moving from Parisian salons to Ottoman minarets, the train condensed these attitudes into lived experience. Passengers could sit and admire the picturesque spectacles of an oppressed veiled women or a bustling Balkan bazaar through the lens of a hierarchy where they sat at the very top. The journey was thus not only one through geography, but also through Europe's carefully constructed racial imagination.

Thus, for passengers gazing from the train windows, the Balkans became the symbolic threshold of Europe — a liminal zone that prepared the imagination for the true Orient of İstanbul.

The Train as Stage & Symbol

Aboard the Orient Express, these narratives became a kind of rolling theatre. In its compartments and dining cars, cosmopolitan Western elites sipped champagne while imagining the dangers that lay beyond the glass. Writers tapped into this duality (see p60) — Agatha Christie's *Murder on the Orient Express* trapped a cross-section of Europe's elite in a confined carriage, turning the eastward journey into a microcosm of suspicion and moral ambiguity. Graham Greene's *Stamboul Train* cast the same route as a stage for espionage, political tension and shifting identities, making the Orient Express a metaphor for Europe colliding with its imagined East.

> Muslim visitors described European societies with equal measures of wonder and disdain, often depicting them as provincial, unhygienic or spiritually and morally impoverished compared to their own

But even without fiction, the train performed a grand job as a symbol of this allure. Posters showed minarets against Balkan skylines and travellers stepping into Constantinople as if stepping into a dream.

Today, luxury heritage trains trade on nostalgia for the glamour of the Orient Express. Yet beneath the polished mahogany lies a deeper story. The Orient or East that the train symbolised was never simply geographic for Western Europeans; it was an imagined construct built from crusader and reconquest myths, Romantic fantasies, colonial tropes, nationalist rhetoric and racial science, the echoes of which are still felt today.

Edward Said wrote that Orientalism was 'a Western style for dominating, restructuring, and having authority over the Orient'. On the

Orient Express, that style of thought was lived out in motion through the smooth passage from Parisian salons to Ottoman skylines, carrying an entire culture's ideas about its 'other'.

Looking Both Ways

Yet the West–East gaze was not one way. From the medieval traveller Ibn Fadlan to the 17th-century Ottoman envoy Evliya Çelebi, Muslim visitors described European societies with equal measures of wonder and disdain, often depicting them as provincial, unhygienic or spiritually and morally impoverished compared to their own. Such accounts remind us that the Orient Express narrative of urbane Europeans encountering a barbaric East obscured a deeper reality: perceptions cut both ways.

For modern travellers worried about repeating the same gaze, one simple response is to look both ways. Just as Ottoman travellers once found Europe as strange and 'other' as Europeans found its Eastern reaches, modern passengers can embrace the route as a two-way street of encounters. Whether sipping coffee as dawn breaks outside Vienna or gazing at the darkened silhouette of a pencil-thin minaret in Sofia from a sleeper carriage, the train still offers a stage on which to reflect — not only on the journey east, but also on how we might imagine those travelling west.

Banya Bashi Mosque, Sofia
GREG BALFOUR EVANS ALAMY

CITY GUIDE:
Bucharest

Macca-Villacrosse Passage

Whether you're on a brief stopover or for a longer stay, Romania's capital is undeniably vibrant, with many surprises in store. From its rise to fame as 'Little Paris,' to its painful remnants of a dark, communist era, today's Bucharest is ever-growing with creative hotspots and innovative eats.

WORDS BY MONICA SUMA
Monica writes about travel and culture from her home base in Bucharest.

Arriving
Gara de Nord Inaugurated by King Carol I in 1872, Gara de Nord is Bucharest's main railway station and the largest in Romania. It was in 1883 that the *Orient Express* first pulled in here. In 1896 an opulent Royal Salon was unveiled, to greet Austrian emperor Franz Joseph I. Sadly, the salon is very rarely open to the public. In need of urgent repairs and upgrades, the station's outdated state has been the source of many redesign bids and countless delays. Expect some construction chaos, as a five-year renovation was announced by local authorities in autumn of 2025. Commercial spaces are set to be redeveloped and all adjacent sites modernised. **Luggage storage** *(per bag 12-15 lei)* is available between 6.30am and 9pm.

HOW MUCH FOR A

Beer **20 lei**

Three *mici* **15 lei**

Museum admission **15–50 lei**

Refuelling
Try a *covrig* (Romanian pretzel) from **LUCA** bakery, with sesame or poppy seeds – the quickest, best snack. **Bistro Nord** *(facebook.com/bistronord)*, beside the station's eastern exit, serves dishes such as smoked pork knuckle and lamb with *mămăligă* (polenta). The **Carrefour Express supermarket** *(6.30am-11pm)* at the western end of the main concourse is convenient for train supplies.

Getting Around
Public Transport To get to the city centre from Gara de Nord, avoid the yellow taxis right in front of the main entrance and instead head to the Gara de Nord 1 metro stop and take the M1 line to Piața Victoriei. Buses, trolleys and trams stop by as well, but they take longer.
Walking Traffic in Bucharest tends to be intense and chaotic, which is why central Bucharest is best explored on foot. Most top sights are sprinkled along Calea Victoriei, within walking distance from each other. The same goes for the pedestrian-only cobblestone streets of the Historic Centre by Universitate.
Rideshare Besides convenient metro rides, Bolt and Uber are most used for affordable, hassle-free trips.

For schedules and trip planning, go to Visit Bucharest:

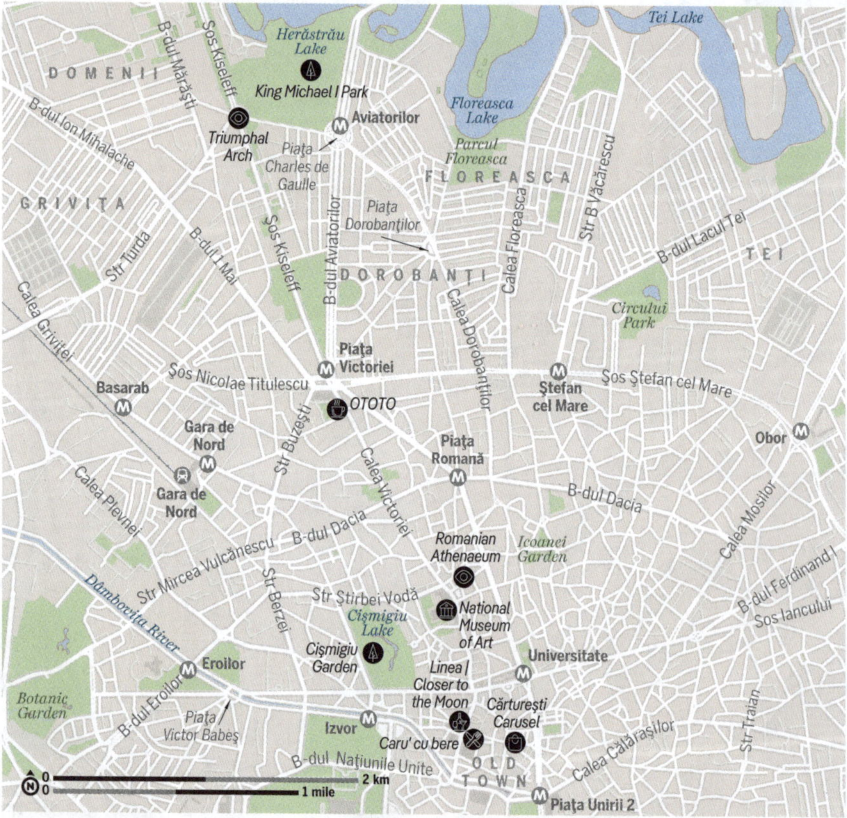

A DAY IN BUCHAREST

From Gara de Nord head straight to the city centre. After breakfast at **OTOTO** (p141), stroll along Calea Victoriei. Walk towards Piața Revoluției for an overview of Bucharest's communist-era events, as well as insight into 'Little Paris' a century ago. Stop by the **Romanian Athenaeum** (p138), the city's most cherished sight.

Explore the **National Museum of Art** (p140), the country's largest, for a memorable encounter with Romania's most celebrated painters including Nicolae Grigorescu, Theodor Aman and Nicolae Tonitza, as well as modernist masterpieces by Constantin Brâncuși. Next, walk to leafy **Cișmigiu Garden** (p141) and relax with a drink at a park cafe.

Check out gorgeous **Cărturești Carusel** (p139) for quirky souvenirs, before spending the evening in the Historic Centre. Dine at fabled brewery **Caru' cu bere** (right) or, for an unbeatable view over Bucharest's Old Town, head to **Linea | Closer to the Moon** (booklinea.me), a fashionable rooftop restaurant and cocktail bar.

Where to Stay

Hotels by the train station tend to be generic, low-budget ones – nothing special. The nicest hotels – including several heritage landmarks – are found in the city centre on Calea Victoriei, in the Old Town or Cișmigiu. Smaller boutique options reside on quaint side streets in historic districts near Piața Universității. Further north towards Floreasca and Pipera, there are new business hotels. There are also Airbnb-type stays – think full-apartment for the price of a hotel room.

BEST PLACES TO STAY

Epoque Hotel Relais & Châteaux €€€ Classy boutique hotel by Cișmigiu Garden, with discreet luxury and exquisite fine dining. *hotelepoque.ro*

InterContinental Athénée Palace €€€ Iconic art nouveau hotel once a hideout for WWII spies (pictured). *atheneepalace.intercontinental.com*

Corinthia Grand Hotel du Boulevard €€€ Revived belle époque landmark hotel. Biggest splurge on Calea Victoriei. *corinthia.com/en-gb/bucharest*

Rosetti Hotel €€ Boutique apartment-hotel grafts contemporary design onto a historic, early-20th-century villa. *rosettiaparthotel.com*

Where to Eat

Once known for cheap eats and unpretentious local fare, Bucharest's food scene has become wildly diverse and significantly pricier. Piața Amzei is great for a hip, food crawl. So is lively Victoriei, or the streets around Floreasca and Dorobanți. International foods are quick to go viral here: everything from matcha lattes to bagels mania. Craving Korean or Vietnamese instead? No problem. Fine dining devotees should sample 'New Romanian Cuisine' by Herăstrău or in historic districts.

LOCAL SPECIALITIES TO TRY

Dishes here follow a simple rule, and that is to honour agrarian customs passed through generations and farm-grown, organic produce. Typical Romanian cuisine centres on hearty meat-based stews, *ciorbă* (sour soups) and simple, yet delicious *mămăligă* with sour cream and *telemea* (a feta-like cheese). Present in several Balkan countries in different sizes, Romanian *sarmale* (pictured) are cabbage (or vine leaf) rolls stuffed with spiced meat and rice, served in most traditional restaurants. Bolder options, such as pork knuckle with sauerkraut, are best found at legendary **Caru' cu bere**, with its timeless decor and folkloric dancing – touristy, yes, but decidedly good fun.

But the star bite, and most popular street food, are *mici* or *mititei* – skinless grilled sausages made from ground meat, served with mustard and oh, so juicy. For an old-school experience (think folkloric music and cheap beer), try the sought-after *mici* at **Piața Obor** farmers market, the starting point for most chefs and the largest in the country.

BEST PLACES TO EAT & DRINK

Caru' cu bere €€ Bucharest's oldest brewery, with house beer from 1879. *carucubere.ro*

La Mița Biciclista €€ Top-notch boulangerie, cocktails and a French chef. *lamitabiciclista.ro*

Sera Eden €€ Classic garden bar in the courtyard of a historic mansion. *@seraeden.ro*

KAIAMO €€€ Experimental dishes and pioneer of 'New Romanian Cuisine' by Herăstrău. *kaiamo.com*

Visit the Romanian Athenaeum

A beloved symbol and home to the George Enescu Philharmonic Orchestra, Bucharest's most emblematic landmark is magnificent both inside and out.

HOW TO

Getting here: The closest metro stop is Piața Romană on the M2 line.

Cost: Tickets (15 lei) can be purchased at the Musicians Entrance on Str Benjamin Franklin St (cash only) or from the Box Office on Str Constantin Esarcu. For guided tours in English, schedule in advance at visit@ filarmonicaenescu.ro

More info: filarmonicaenescu.ro/ en/vizitarea-ateneului-roman

Concert tickets: filarmonicaenescu.ro

Designed by French architect Albert Galleron, the neoclassical Romanian Athenaeum, inaugurated in 1888, stands at the heart of Romania's classical-music tradition. Perhaps the finest landmark in the city, it became a symbol of Romanian unity after the 'Give a penny for the Athenaeum!' campaign helped fund the build.

Home to the **George Enescu Philharmonic Orchestra**, it's where the most celebrated Romanian composer in history debuted his *Romanian Rhapsody* masterpiece. Every two years in September, Bucharest welcomes major orchestras and soloists in tribute to George Enescu (1881–1955). The prestigious festival is a month-long feast for classical-music lovers.

The domed concert hall can be visited outside concert and rehearsal hours, with access granted via the Musicians Entrance on Str Benjamin Franklin. But if you're lucky, you can simply walk in and look around the lobby. Carrara marble, pink-hued Doric columns and four monumental staircases lead up to the Big Hall on the 1st floor, where a large 70m fresco depicting 25 scenes from Romanian history impresses.

Lobby, Romanian Athenaeum

'LITTLE PARIS'

From the late 19th century into early 20th century, Bucharest was often referred to as 'Little Paris'. It was around the time of Carol I, the first king of Romania, that neoclassical buildings and beaux-arts palaces designed by French architects started appearing in the city centre alongside grand boulevards, earning the city its long-enduring moniker. A number of today's museums stem from that period. The capital's very own **Triumphal Arch**, based on the Paris model, emerged a few years later, near sprawling **King Michael I Park** (formerly known as Herăstrău).

Calea Victoriei is the best spot to see Bucharest's most iconic landmarks, marking the city's golden era. The belle époque period also saw the rise of cafes, theatres and literary salons. Prominent figures in literature, music and politics contributed to the cultural scene, leaving a lasting impact on Bucharest's architectural legacy and identity. This is evident during summer weekends (usually from 1 May to early October), when the road welcomes a festival-like atmosphere, buzzing with artistic events and locals leisurely promenading.

Cărturești Carusel

Shop the Bookstores: Cărturești

Rocking 57 architecturally unique shops all over Romania, local darling **Cărturești** *(carturesti .ro/librarii)* brims with inspiration for book and design lovers. Don't miss one of the most beautiful bookstores in the world, thanks to social media fame, the six-floor **Cărturești Carusel** in the Old Town. It's housed in a restored, 19th-century building with a notable past in banking and retail; stock up on clever souvenirs or refuel at the bistro up top. Minutes away by Piața Universității, **Cărturești MODUL** focuses on artsy books and gifts, while **Cărturești & friends** holds one of the best selections of English-language titles about the region.

Along the Way We Saw...

LA MIȚA BICICLISTA At the forefront of Bucharest's architectural renaissance is the rebirth of La Mița Biciclista (p137) as a cultural establishment. Following 80 years of abandon, Piața Amzei's 1908 beaux-arts villa is the most photographed in town. The house of famed courtesan 'Mița the Cyclist' was once the site of lavish soirées with princes, diplomats and the literati. The Parisian-like interior now hosts exhibits, guided tours and soirées, with live music akin to the Roaring Twenties, and comes complete with a French chef. The joie de vivre continues at Mița's chic brasserie, or the cocktail garden serving signature drinks.

Monica Suma

Discover the Belle Époque

Stroll down Calea Victoriei, which links some of the most important sights between Piața Victoriei and Piața Revoluției, before continuing on to the Historic Centre.

HOW TO

Getting here: Hop on the M1 line at the Gara de Nord 1 metro stop right in front of the railway station, for a quick one-stop, into Piața Victoriei.

Ridesharing: Bolt and Uber are the most used apps for hassle-free rides, to the detriment of yellow taxis using meters, which are often tricky or require cash in the local currency.

Getting around: Traffic tends to be intense here (unless it's a quiet weekend or a pedestrian area), so walking is the best way to explore, all within reasonable distance.

Top Sights on Calea Victoriei

All along the artery, something is brewing. One of the finest monuments is Cantacuzino Palace, home to the **George Enescu National Museum** (georgeenescu.ro). The art nouveau awning gracing the sumptuous entry is a typical shell-like canopy; many historic villas have one – a clear sign of belle époque.

The **Equestrian Statue of Carol I** by the Central University Library mirrors the capital's royal past, located next to the site of events from the 1989 Revolution. The former Royal Palace houses the big **National Museum of Art** (mnar.ro) with galleries dedicated to Romanian and European art, and resplendent interiors.

Old Town Glory

Bucharest's cobblestoned Historic Centre started as a flourishing merchant quarter. The **Macca-Villacrosse Passage** connects Calea Victoriei to Str Lipscani through a statuesque portal. The **National Bank of Romania Museum** (bnr.ro) is free to visit; reserve a guided tour online two working days prior. Facing it is the **Stock Exchange Palace**, another beaux-arts beauty.

Don't miss the Byzantine-style Orthodox churches. **Stavropoleos Church** is the smallest, but most beautiful. Built in Brâncovenesc style in 1724, the ivy-covered cloisters are pure tranquillity. Steps away, Bucharest's oldest brewery Caru' cu bere (p137) reveals neo-Gothic decor and serves the same house beer from 1879, with eve-

FUEL YOUR WALK

Begin your walk with a quick detour en route to Calea Victoriei from Piața Victoriei station. **Saint Roastery** *(saint roastery.ro)* is the best cafe in the station area, both for its speciality coffee and strong community vibes. Alternatively, pick up a coffee on Calea Victoriei at **OTOTO**, a buzzing concept store selling organic, artisanal Romanian foods and drinks. For gelatos, sorbets and affogatos – plus speciality coffee – pause at **Velocità** *(velocita.ro)*, between the George Enescu National Museum and the Equestrian Statue of Carol I. The modernist restored interior oozes art deco delight.

Left: George Enescu National Museum; Below: Cișmigiu Garden

ning folkloric dancing. From its patio, the view of the beaux-arts **CEC Palace** is postcard-worthy. The grand **National History Museum of Romania** *(mnir.ro)*, in the former Post Office Palace, holds Dacian artefacts and King Carol's steel crown.

Recharge in Cișmigiu

As Str Lipscani intersects Ion Brezoianu, Cișmigiu district unfurls. Walking past heritage **Hotel Cișmigiu**, you pass by **Palatul Universul**, a former printing house turned culture hub. Wander in verdant **Cișmigiu Garden**, Bucharest's oldest public park and its most scenic.

Bucharest

On the penultimate leg of your Orient Express journey you'll cross the Danube one last time as you move from Romania to Bulgaria. On reaching Ruse on the mighty river's Bulgarian shore, there's a choice of routes to follow: either go directly to Sofia, or head east to the Black Sea resort of Varna (a stop for the original Orient Express); or chug southwest into the scenic Central Mountains to reach Veliko Tărnovo, home to the remarkable Tsarevets Fortress.

Simon Richmond

Tsarevets Fortress, Veliko Tărnovo (p155)
VALENTIN VALKOV/SHUTTERSTOCK

Sofia

490 KMS · 10½ HOURS' RIDE

THIS LEG:
- Videle
- Giurgiu
- Ruse
- Gorna Oryahovitsa
- Pleven
- Sofia Central

Riding Notes

From mid-June to mid-October there is one direct train a day from Bucharest to Sofia. At other times of the year, you'll have to change trains at Ruse, also the junction for onward travel to Varna on the Black Sea and, in the Central Mountains, Veliko Târnovo. Prepare for long journeys, as the trains go slowly.

Breaking Your Journey

If you're not in a hurry to reach Sofia, build some time into your schedule for overnight stops in both Varna and Veliko Târnovo. A night in each location is sufficient, but stay two nights and you'll be able to experience both places at a more leisurely pace.

Simon's Tips

BEST MEAL Pizza with Bulgarian-flavoured toppings at Shtastlivetsa in Veliko Târnovo. (p155)

FAVOURITE VIEW The old houses of Veliko Târnovo clinging to tumbling hillsides in a picturesque jumble. (p154)

ESSENTIAL STOP The balmy Black Sea beach resort of Varna. (p150)

TIP There are no dining facilities on this leg's trains so pack refreshments.

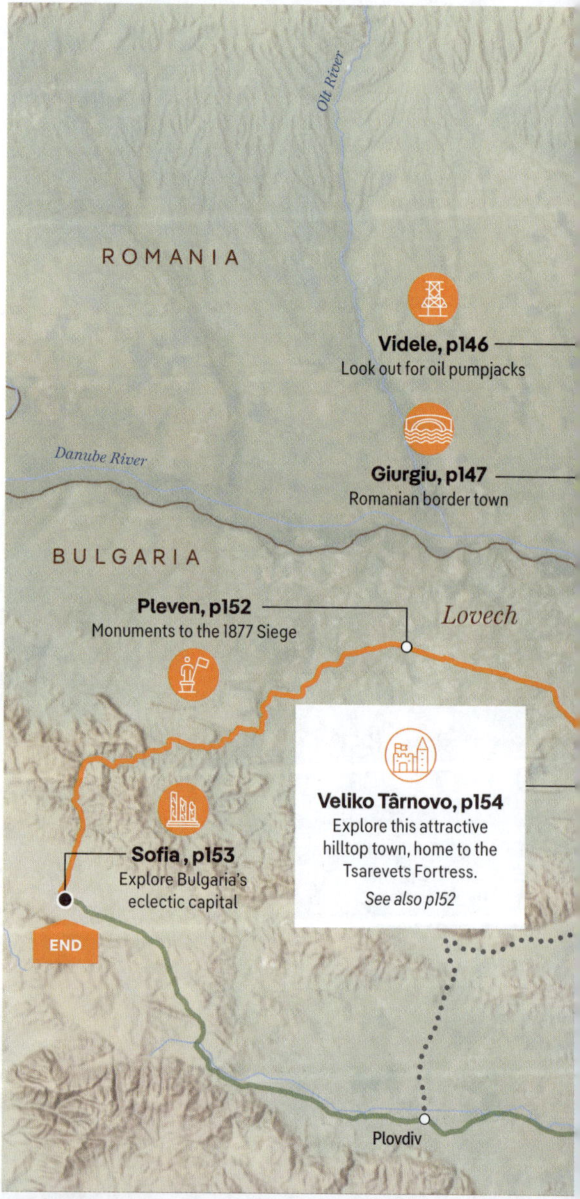

Videle, p146 — Look out for oil pumpjacks

Giurgiu, p147 — Romanian border town

Pleven, p152 — Monuments to the 1877 Siege

Veliko Târnovo, p154 — Explore this attractive hilltop town, home to the Tsarevets Fortress. See also p152

Sofia, p153 — Explore Bulgaria's eclectic capital

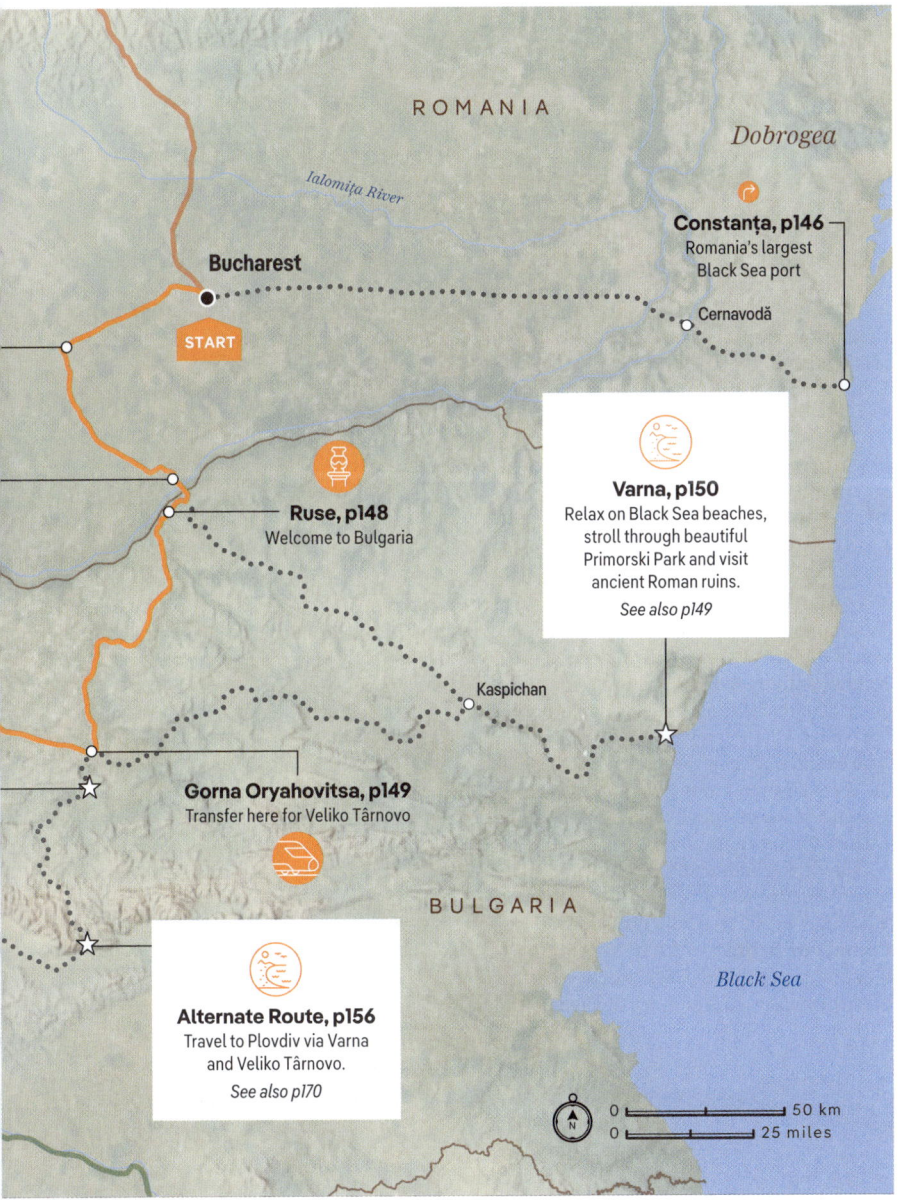

> **ONWARD TRAVEL**
>
> From mid-June to mid-October you can book a direct 2nd-class seat to Sofia, usually departing Bucharest in the morning and arriving in the Bulgarian capital around 10 hours later. This will be a Bulgarian Railways carriage (invariably plastered in graffiti) with no air-con, but with windows that open. The train travels slowly so you'll be able to enjoy the scenery en route and take photographs. In other months you will have to transfer at Ruse (p148), which also has onward services to Varna (p150) and Veliko Târnovo (p154).
>
> Also from mid-June to mid-October there is a direct Turkish couchette car from Bucharest to İstanbul. Unlike the Sofia–İstanbul Express, this train can be booked online, typically up to 90 days in advance, at bileteinternationale.cfrcalatori.ro.
>
> If you haven't already secured a ticket on the Sofia–İstanbul Express, the **International Rail Ticketing Agency** (8am-noon & 12.30-6.30pm) at Ruse Central station will be your first opportunity to do so directly with Bulgarian Railways.
>
> Check current schedules at **Romanian Railways** (cfrcalatori.ro) and **Bulgarian Railways** (bdz.bg).

DETOUR: Constanța

Two- to three-hours' ride from Bucharest

From 1895 until at least the start of WWI, Orient Express trains ran from Bucharest to the Black Sea port of Constanța, 225km to the east. This connection was made possible by the completion of the King Carol I Bridge (now called the **Anghel Saligny Bridge**) spanning one branch of the Danube between Fetești and Cernavodă. Carrying a single-track railway, the 4km-long span was, at that time, the longest in Europe and the second-longest in the world. At Constanța passengers would board a boat for the 27-hour journey to Constantinople.

Today, if you detour to Constanța (a journey of between two and three hours depending on the train you catch), you'll cross the adjacent **Cernavodă Bridge**, which opened in 1987. As Romania's largest Black Sea port and gateway to surrounding seaside resorts, Constanța is a popular destination. It has a shabby charm that rewards an overnight stay. Hints of the port's late-19th- and early-20th-century heyday can be gleaned from the once grand, but now neglected, architecture of the city centre. The beach, **Plaja Modern**, is clean, centrally located and perfectly serviceable for a day relaxing by the shore.

Videle

The tracks initially head southwest out of Bucharest towards Videle, a small countryside station where the train pauses briefly to allow passengers on and off. Along the way look out for 'nodding donkeys' – **pumpjacks** extracting oil from the Videle oil field.

After Videle the tracks make a dogleg turn southeast, running through farmlands towards the Danube river, which marks the border with Bulgaria.

Bucharest — 66km — Videle

Detour: The Black Sea port of Constanța is 461km east of Bucharest

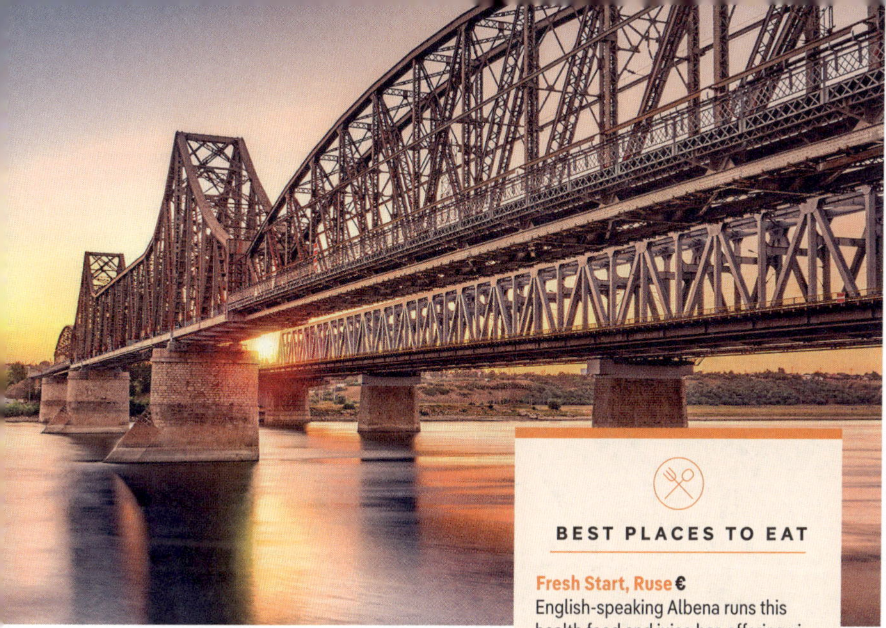

MIHAI_ANDRITOIU/SHUTTERSTOCK

Anghel Saligny Bridge, Cernavodă

Giurgiu

Shortly before you reach Giurgui, the train runs along an elevated plateau providing some far-reaching views towards the Danube's marshes and mudflats. Have your passport ready for checks on the train by Romanian border guards while there's a pause at **Giurgiu Nord**, about 4km north of the town centre. If you were to look around Giurgiu, a historical landmark is the Ottoman-era **Clock Tower** built in 1771 as a military watchtower for this strategic riverside location; it now has a cafe at its base.

On the *Orient Express*' maiden journey in 1883, and for at least the next six years, Giurgiu was a necessary stop for passengers. From here they

BEST PLACES TO EAT

Fresh Start, Ruse €
English-speaking Albena runs this health food and juice bar, offering vitamin-packed drinks and fresh salads. *7am-6pm Mon-Fri, 8.30am-6pm Sat*

Chiflika, Ruse €€
Rugs, fleeces on the walls, waiters in pantaloons and traditional Bulgarian food in the heart of Ruse. *noon-6pm Mon-Fri, noon-midnight Sat & Sun*

Bacaro, Varna €€
Contemporary bistro with an appealing menu of seasonal, international dishes. *5-11pm Tue-Sat*

Han Hadzhi Nikoli, Veliko Târnovo €€
A beautifully restored inn in Veliko Târnovo offering both Bulgarian and European cuisine. *5-11pm Tue-Fri, 10am-11pm Sat, 10am-8pm Sun*

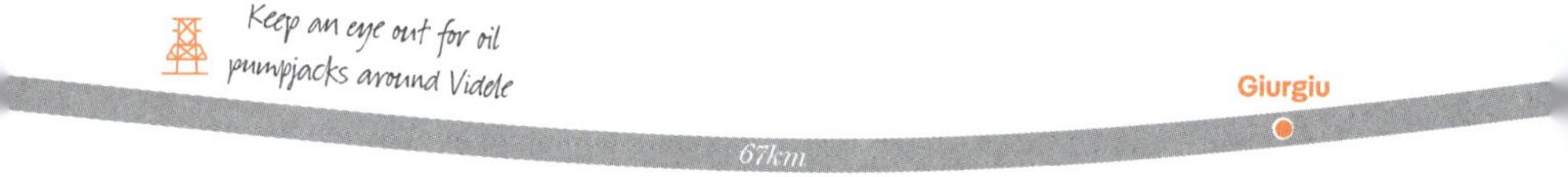
Keep an eye out for oil pumpjacks around Videle
Giurgiu
67km

Mosaics, Ruse Central train station

Ruse

Alighting at Ruse Central, you will be pleasantly surprised by this handsome station. Built at the same time as the Friendship Bridge in 1954, Ruse Central is designed in grand Stalinist style, with a two-storey central booking hall framed by soaring columns topped with Corinthian capitals, with two big chandeliers hanging from the ceiling. Locals use it as a backdrop for wedding and other celebratory photos.

Bulgaria's most important river port, Ruse's golden years were in the late 19th century when its neo-baroque and neo-rococo architecture earned it the moniker 'little Vienna'. The grey blocks of communist-era flats immediately opposite the station give little of this away. However, walk around 20 minutes north from the station towards the old part of town and you'll start to see Ruse's more attractive side. Aim for the **Regional Museum of History** *(museumruse.com; 9am-6pm)* on pl Aleksandar Battenberg, then stroll across the leafy park with fountains and statues to browse the shops along ul Alexandrovska.

Further on, close by the river, is the original 19th-century Ruse train station (Bulgaria's first), now occupied by the **National Museum of Transport and Communications** *(fan.bdz.bg; 9am-noon & 2-5.30pm Mon-Sat)*. While it's not particularly well maintained, vintage train enthusiasts will be thrilled to find locomotives from the late 19th and early 20th centuries, as well as luxe carriages that once belonged to Tsar Boris III, Tsar Ferdinand and Turkish sultan Abdul Aziz.

would have transferred to a steam boat to cross the Danube to Ruse, where another train would be waiting for onward transport.

Since 1954 trains have rattled over the river across the **Danube Bridge**. Back then this 2.2km-long steel truss span was dubbed the Friendship Bridge. As you cross, look out for cruise ships on the Danube, which is more milky-coffee coloured than blue as it nears the end of its 2857km-long run.

Detour: Leave the main route at Ruse for the alternate route to Sofia via Varna and Veliko Târnovo

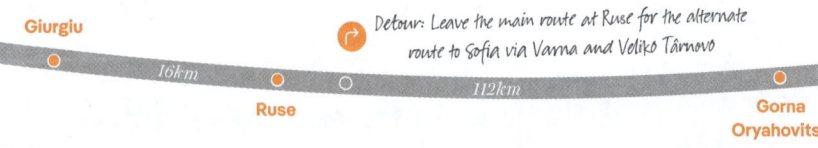

DETOUR: **Varna**
Four hours by direct train from Ruse

Seaside Varna (p150) is blessed with golden-sand beaches, lush gardens, an excellent Archaeological Museum, and plenty of attractions for the young and young-at-heart. Extend your explorations further by taking the meandering train journey from Varna to Plovdiv (p156) through mountainous landscapes and stunning scenery.

Gorna Oryahovitsa

It takes around two hours heading south from Ruse through fairly pedestrian Bulgarian countryside to arrive at the railway junction of Gorna Oryahovitsa. Alight here if you wish to detour to Veliko Târnovo, less than 20 minutes away by infrequent trains – consider catching a taxi or bus for the 9.5km journey instead.

Continues on page 152

BEST PLACES TO SLEEP

Grand Hotel Riga, Ruse €€
All modern-era amenities and some nice interior design at this high-rise hotel overlooking the Danube.
hotel-riga.com

Graffit Gallery Hotel, Varna €€€
With an art gallery and themed rooms, this modern designer hotel is one of Varna's more colourful options.
graffithotel.com

Bey House Royal Hotel, Veliko Târnovo €€€
Top-end property offering all the comforts in the residence of Veliko Târnovo's last Ottoman governor.
beyhouse.com

Hotel Mehana Gurko, Veliko Târnovo €€
Spacious and soothing rooms on a picturesque street, with blooms spilling over the balconies, great views and restaurant. *gurkohotelwg.com*

Varna beach

CITY GUIDE:

Varna

Blessed with golden sands, ruins from antiquity and a near-subtropical climate Varna makes for a very pleasant change of scene along the historic Orient Express route. When the sun gets too hot, retreat to the shade of the Black Sea resort's vast and beautifully laid-out Primorski Park.

HOW TO

Getting here: Trains connect Varna with Bucharest (two hours, 40 minutes) via Ruse (p156; four hours).

Getting around: Although it's a little hilly, Varna is very walkable with a pedestrianised town centre. A taxi from the train station to all central hotels will be around €5.

Sleeping: Book accommodation that's close to Primorski Park. Recommended places include Graffit Gallery Hotel (p149); the cosy, antique-style **Hotel Hi** (hotel-hi.com; €€); and the pirate-themed **Yo Ho Hostel** (yohohostel.com; €).

Tip: Join the free two-hour walking tour of Varna, leaving from the Tourist Information Centre at 10.30am from May to November.

More info: The **Tourist Information Centre** (visit.varna.bg; 9am-7pm May-Sep, 8.30am-5.30pm Mon-Fri Oct-Apr) has helpful multilingual staff.

Elegant and eclectic, ancient and modern, partly spruced-up and partly rundown, Varna is charmingly authentic and has everything you'd expect from an easy-going southern European city. It can get busy, but with a long sandy beach and vast maritime gardens, there are chances to escape the holidaying hordes that occupy the rest of the Bulgarian coast. The pedestrian-friendly historical core is packed with appealing dining spots such as Bacaro (p147) and is an excellent place to stretch your legs and relax after the long train journey. Here you'll also find a large Roman baths complex and some fine old churches.

BATHING IN VARNA, PAST & PRESENT

Odessos (modern-day Varna) was graced with the very best public bathing facilities, and the Roman Thermae here were a visible, powerful symbol of Roman civilisation. The baths were an integral part of civic life – a place to not only clean up and relax, but also to socialise and make business deals. All classes were allowed, though men and women were admitted at different times.

Larger baths, such as the one in Odessos, had a *palaestra*, or exercise hall, where wrestling and other athletic activities took place. Bathers would then rub themselves down with oil and sweat for a while in the *sudatorium* (a kind of sauna), before scraping it off with a *strigil*, examples of which you can see at the Archaeological Museum. A plunge in the hot water of the *caldarium* would be followed by the more bearable temperature of the *tepidarium*, then the icy *frigidarium*. The remains of these pools can be seen in the Thermae.

Public bathing in natural hot-spring water continues at a community-run open-air **thermal pool** next to beach.

Primorski Park

Seaside Park

Primorski Park is a nearly 8km-long green belt separating the beach from the city centre. The brainchild of Czech landscaper Anton Novak and established in 1878, this lush and shady space is full of promenading families, cyclers, joggers and rollerbladers. There's always something going on and the park is home to several attractions, primarily geared for children, including an **Aquarium** *(adult/child €2/1; 9am-5pm Tue-Sun Oct-May, 9am-7pm Jun-Sep)* with tanks filled with seahorses, piranhas and conger eels; and the charmingly retro **Nicolaus Copernicus Planetarium** *(astro-varna.com; adult/child €2/1)*.

Ancient Varna

Archaeologists have unearthed metal objects around Varna, including some of the world's oldest golden jewellery. These finds are displayed at the excellent **Archaeological Museum** *(museumvarna.com; adult/child €5/free; 10am-5pm daily May-Sep, Mon-Fri Oct-Apr)*, where you can also view dark-coloured Thracian pottery, Roman marbles and Hellenistic items.

Also don't miss Varna's well-preserved 2nd-century CE **Roman Thermae** *(museumvarna.com; adult/child €2.50/free; 10am-6pm daily Jun-Sep, 10am-5pm Tue-Sat Oct-May)*. These are the largest such ruins in Bulgaria and the fourth-largest of their kind in Europe.

BEST PLACES TO EAT & DRINK

Kultura € Open the elevator door to find this dimly lit, sophisticated speakeasy serving up excellent cocktails. *7pm-1am*

Ribarski Plazh € Chilled self-serve cafe-bar, great for breakfast, lunch or a drink overlooking the beach. *10am-1am*

Stariya Chinar – Port Varna €€ Upmarket Balkan soul food at its best with a great view of Varna's harbour. *10am-midnight*

Continued from page 149

DETOUR: Veliko Târnovo
9.5km from Gorna Oryahovitsa
With a spectacular hilltop location above a winding river and the impressive Tsarevets Fortress, Veliko Târnovo (p154) is a worthy detour easily accessible as a day trip from the main route or as part of the alternative route from Ruse via Varna (p156).

Pleven

Leaving Gorna Oryahovitsa, the tracks make a 90-degree turn to the west avoiding Bulgaria's Central Mountains and crossing the rural farming landscapes of the Danube Plain to reach Pleven after around an hour.

With a population of around 90,000, Pleven offers a pleasant pedestrianised core centred around a cascade of artificial waterfalls. The city is packed with memorials to the 1877 Siege, which resulted in Bulgaria regaining independence after centuries of Ottoman rule, and a few hours exploration here will be of interest to students of Balkan history.

About a 20-minute walk south of the train station is the ornate neo-byzantine **St George the Conqueror Chapel Mausoleum**, which holds the remains of the Russian and Romanian soldiers who died during the siege. About 3km south of the town centre, at the location of the siege's main battle, the **Regional Military History Museum** *(panorama-pleven.com; admission €3; 9am-6pm Apr-Oct, 9am-5pm*

Along the Way We Met...

JIWON BAEK & SODA We started in Budapest. From there we travelled by train to Timişoara, Craiova, Vidin, Sofia, Plovdiv and Veliko Târnovo. Next, we'll go to Varna. We stay for about three days in each place as Soda is eight or nine – she's a rescue dog so I'm not sure of her age – has short legs and gets hot quickly, so we need to go slowly. I brought her travel kennel with me, and I also have a doggie backpack for carrying her on the trains.

Jiwon is a former international tour leader from Incheon, South Korea, and Soda (@corgi_soda) is her corgi.

JIWON'S TIP: *It's good to travel with your dog – you'll never be lonely and people are more friendly towards you.*

Gorna Oryahovitsa

100km

Detour: Transfer at Gorna Oryahovitsa for trains to Veliko Târnovo

St George the Conqueror Chapel Mausoleum, Pleven

Nov-Mar) houses a big 360-degree panorama that puts you in the midst of the fighting.

Sofia Central

There's some spectacular scenery to come on the final section of this leg as the train partly follows the Iskar River, a tributary of the Danube and Bulgaria's longest waterway, as it flows through the Iskar Gorge between Mezdra and Novi Iskar. Soon after come the outskirts of Sofia (p158).

Opened in 1974, **Sofia Central** station replaced the original 1888 station building, which was demolished at that time. With three levels, this huge brutalist building is typical of the communist era, but inside a major 2016 refurbishment has given it a slick contemporary look with a latticed ceiling and preserved mosaic panels featuring the city's coat of arms. Also look out for a narrow-gauge heritage steam locomotive and carriage. There is a pedestrian underpass from the station to line 2 of Sofia's metro.

Pleven — *131km* — Sofia Central

Enjoy the scenery of the Iskar Gorge between Mezdra and Novi Iskar

CITY GUIDE:
Veliko Târnovo

Veliko Târnovo's spectacular location, stretched out along ridges high above the winding Yantra river, makes it a unique and unmissable destination. Come here to explore the remains of the massive Tsarevets Fortress from where Bulgaria's tsars ruled in the 13th and 14th centuries.

HOW TO

Getting here: Veliko Târnovo train station is in the valley 3km east of the town centre. There are fairly regular buses from the train station to the town centre. A taxi costs around €4.

Getting around: Walking is the best way to get around, particularly to explore the narrow streets of the town centre.

Sleeping: There's accommodation to suit all budgets, with many places in traditional buildings such as **Rooster Hostel** (facebook.com/roostervt; €) and Hotel Mehana Gurko (p149). For more luxury, try the boutique **Bridges Residence** (bridgesresidence.com; €€€) or Bey House Royal Hotel (p149).

Tip: Time your visit to coincide with the **Sound & Light Show** (soundandlight.bg) illuminating Tsarevets Fortress. They're usually held on Friday and Saturday nights, but check the website for dates and times.

More info: Tourist Information Centre (velikoturnovo.info; 9am-6pm Mon-Fri)

Veliko Târnovo's medieval majesty was cut short by the Turkish conquest, but as the Ottoman regime decayed in the late 19th century Bulgarian society recovered, endowing the city with the houses that make it so visually distinctive today. Good examples line **ul General Gurko**, its cobblestones overlooked by the jutting upper storeys of traditional-style houses; and the **Varosha Quarter**, where **Samovodska Charshiya** is lined with traditional craft shops – look for the 1858 inn Han Hadzhi Nikoli (p147). Downhill from Tsarevets lies the **Asenova Quarter**, a peaceful neighbourhood of traditional houses, churches and cobbled alleys set beside the Yantra river.

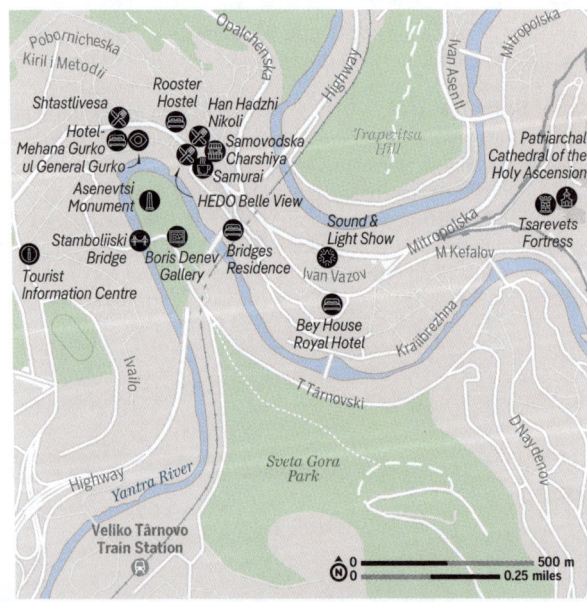

154

ARBANASI

About 15 minutes' drive north of Veliko Târnovo, occupying a ridgetop plateau, Arbanasi preserves a unique cluster of stone houses huddled behind thick stone walls. Probably founded in the 14th century, the village became home to Veliko Târnovo's richer families, retaining special privileges after Bulgaria had been swallowed up by the Ottoman Empire.

Arbanasi's spectacular churches reveal how Bulgarian Orthodox Christian culture survived under Ottoman rule. The **Church of the Nativity** is an exuberant example, its interior covered with beautifully preserved murals. With scenes from the Bible and portraits of Bulgarian tsars and saints, the painted panels add up to an illustrated account of the Orthodox Christian tradition. No less impressive is the **Church of the Archangels Michael and Gabriel**, its interior a dazzling parade of gold-haloed saintly figures.

The **Konstantsliev House** *(9am-6pm)* is preserved as it was in the early 19th century. Rooms are dominated by rug-covered divans on which guests would sit cross-legged and sip coffee under carved wooden ceilings.

Tsarevets Fortress

Stroll Around Tsarevets

The sprawling **Tsarevets Fortress** *(museum vt.com; admission €7.50; 8am-8pm)* is one of Bulgaria's most popular tourist sites. Destroyed by the Ottomans in the late 14th century, its walls and towers have been partially reconstructed to provide an idea of what it once looked like. Set aside at least a couple of hours to fully explore this hugely evocative site, which contains the remains of over 400 houses and 18 churches. At the top of the hill is the **Patriarchal Cathedral of the Holy Ascension**, inside of which are dramatic murals by Teofan Sokerov from the 1970s.

Take in the Views from Buruna

To appreciate just how dramatic Veliko Târnovo's ravine-side location actually is, head over the cast-iron **Stamboliiski Bridge** to Buruna (The Nose), a rocky promontory formed by one of the Yantra's many loops and coils. It's here you get the best views of the 19th-century quarters on the other side, their pale-hued houses seemingly tumbling down the hillside. Dominating Buruna is the dramatic **Asenevtsi Monument**, erected in 1985 and featuring a sky-piercing column surrounded by four rearing horsemen. Looming up behind is the **Boris Denev Gallery** *(admission €4; 10am-6pm)*, named after a celebrated local painter.

BEST PLACES TO EAT & DRINK

Shtastlivesa €€ Popular spot serving European-Bulgarian fare, including excellent pizzas. *11am-midnight*

HEDO Belle View €€ Classy restaurant serving a good range of local and European dishes. *4-11pm Mon, 9am-11pm Tue-Sun*

Samurai € Speciality coffees and exquisite cakes and tarts in an artsy interior, with a terrace overlooking the main strip. *7.30am-7pm*

Alternate Route: Seaside & Mountains

This alternate route to İstanbul from Ruse avoids Sofia and instead passes through the Black Sea resort of Varna (p150), a historic stop for the Orient Express. It then returns inland via Veliko Târnovo (p154) to explore the impressive Tsarevets Fortress, then cuts through the Central Balkan mountains to reach Plovdiv (p170) where you can rejoin the main route.

HOW TO

Getting here: There are three trains daily from Bucharest to Ruse, from where there are three daily direct trains to Varna (three hours). See **CFR Călători** *(cfrcalatori.ro)* and **BDZ** *(bdz.bg)* for schedules.

When to go: The **Varna Music Festival** *(varnasummerfest.org)* is held between June and mid-September.

Tip: During rose harvesting season, from May to mid-June, the **Enio Bonchev Distillery** *(eniobonchev.com)*, a 30-minute drive west of Kazanlâk, is open for tours.

Ruse to Varna

About 1½ hours into the 190km journey from Ruse to Varna, around the station at **Hitrino**, the rich soil farmlands of the Danubian Plain stretch to the horizon.

Beyond the railway junction of **Kaspichan**, the tracks follow the Provadiya River valley. Shortly after passing through **Provadiya** station, look to the ridge of the hills on the left side of the train to spot the 13th-century rock monastery **Shashkanite**.

As you close in on Varna, the train runs alongside **Lake Varna**.

Varna to Veliko Târnovo

The direct train from **Varna** (p150) to Gorna Oryahovitsa (four hours) will take you through **Shumen** *(visitshumen.bg)*. Visible within a 30km radius of the town is the bombastic **Monument to**

the Founders of the Bulgarian State, opened in 1981 to commemorate the First Bulgarian Empire's 1300th anniversary. The monument's futurist sculptures depict medieval rulers and the complex includes the Balkans' largest outdoor mosaic triptych.

At **Gorna Oryahovitsa** (p149) change trains to reach **Veliko Târnovo** (20 minutes; p154) – there are wonderful views of this hilltop town on the approach.

Veliko Târnovo to Plovdiv

There are wonderful views and many tunnels along the first section of the 130km trip towards

VALLEY OF THE ROSES

For centuries Kazanlâk has been the fragrant centre of Bulgaria's rose-oil production. The underground water and rich soil of the **Valley of the Roses** (Rozovata Dolina) are ideal for cultivating the flowers, and the region churns out scented soaps, moisturising balms, rose liqueurs, jams and candies.

Kazanlâk's valleys are aflame with pretty blooms from mid-May onwards – you'll certainly see them from the train. Kazanlâk's **Rose Festival** (rosefestivalkazanlak.com), held on the first weekend in June, is the highlight of the season.

Roman stone bridge, Borushtenska river

Plovdiv as you traverse the Central Balkan mountains. Shortly after leaving **Yavorovets** station, look out on the right side for a **Roman stone bridge** across the Borushtenska river.

Emerging onto the plains, you'll travel past fields of wheat and roses. Around **Kazanlâk** the distinctive silhouette of the **Buzludzha Monument** (buzludzha-monument.com), a relic of communist Bulgaria, stands out on the mountain's 1432m summit.

At **Graf Ignatievo**, about 10km outside of **Plovdiv** (p170), is a military airbase – look on the right of the train for missiles flanking the base's gate.

CITY GUIDE:

Sofia

Sofia is a wonderfully eclectic city where the Central European quaintness of tram lines and cobblestones meets Mediterranean ambience, richly spiced with socialist and Ottoman legacies. Its attractive historical core features Roman ruins, Byzantine churches, inviting cafes and restaurants.

WORDS BY **LEONID RAGOZIN**
Leonid is a journalist primarily focused on the Russo–Ukrainian conflict.

Arriving

Sofia Central Sofia's train station is a utilitarian modernist structure on the edge of the historical centre, with convenient transport connections to anywhere in the city, including Sofia Airport. There is no point lingering here – any waiting time between trains is best spent in an outdoor cafe or walking around the city centre. The left-luggage office is located downstairs from the main hall.

After getting off the train, go one level down to reach the entrance to the metro or exits to tram stops across the street. Serdika station in the heart of the city is two stops away on the M2 (blue) line. You can pay for public transport in Sofia by scanning your bank card.

HOW MUCH FOR A

Glass of wine €5

Main course €12

Museum admission €6

Refuelling

Khadzhidraganovite Kashti is the nearest decent restaurant to the train station (just a 15-minute walk), but if you ride two stops on the metro to Serdika, you'll be spoilt for choice.

Getting Around

Metro The modern and convenient Sofia metro network forms the skeleton of the city's transit system. There are three lines forming a transfer triangle in the heart of the city. Serdika station under Sofia's main square is where you transfer to the M2 (blue) line for train/bus stations or to the yellow line for the airport.

Trams The city is crisscrossed by tram lines, which are convenient for shorter trips in or around the centre. Buses usually come into the picture when you explore Mt Vitosha.

Walking Sofia's historical core is quite walkable, with Serdika station serving as an ideal starting point for any walking loop.

Car International taxi apps don't work in Sofia, so hail a metered cab in the street if you need or install the **Yellow Taxi app** *(yellow333.com)*. You can instantly find an electric car share vehicle through the **SPARK app** *(spark.bg)*.

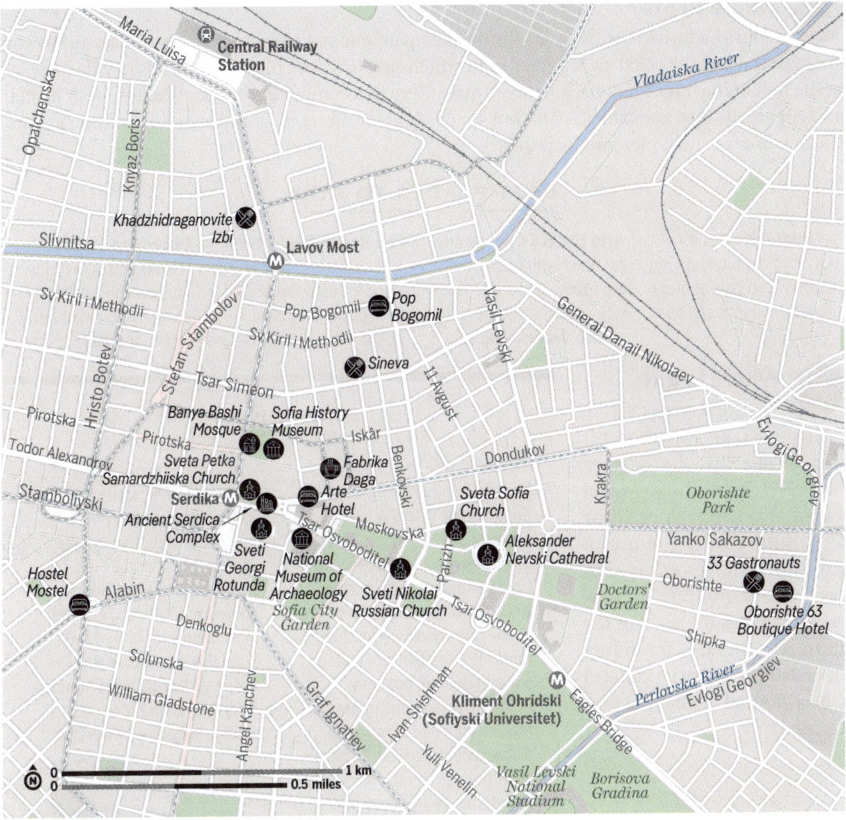

A DAY IN SOFIA

Explore the **Ancient Serdica Complex** (p161). Walk along Tsar Osvoboditel Blvd, turning at the ornate **Sveti Nikolai Russian Church** towards the Byzantine centrepiece of **Sveta Sofia Church** (p161), after which the city was named. Proceed to the vast **Aleksander Nevski Cathedral** (p161).

Spend an hour at the **National Museum of Archaeology** (naim.bg; adult/child €6/2) perusing peculiar finds from prehistoric and ancient periods. If you have the time, pay a visit to **Sofia History Museum** (visitsofia.bg; adult/child €5/1), inside the magnificent former Turkish baths, or drop into the **Banya Bashi Mosque** (visitsofia.bg) nearby.

Hit Bulgaria's main promenade, **Vitosha Boulevard**, around sunset and venture into the side lanes looking for any quirky restaurant or bar that catches your eye. End the day at **Bulgaria Square**, where some kind of festivity, performance or street market is almost inevitably underway.

Where to Stay

Sofia's historical core is by far the most convenient and pleasurable area to stay, unless you are planning to hike or ski on Mt Vitosha, in which case there are plenty of options in villa districts at the foot of the mountain. Back in the centre, there is accommodation for all tastes, from hostels and Airbnb flats to guesthouses and hotels. Leafy areas along ul Oborishte and around Doctors' Garden are the most pleasant locations.

BEST PLACES TO STAY

Hostel Mostel € A popular hostel occupying a renovated 19th-century house. *hostelmostel.com*

Arte Hotel €€ A welcoming hotel with bright, modern rooms and contemporary artworks adorning the walls. *artehotelbg.com*

Pop Bogomil €€ A hotel of 15 comfortable rooms, all individually decorated. *popbogomil.com*

Oborishte 63 Boutique Hotel €€€ A luxurious salmon-pink 1930s-era home with a cathedral view. *oborishte63.com*

Where to Eat

Two vast areas – one between Tsar Osvoboditel and Vitosha Blvds and another between Knyaginya Maria Luiza and Knyaz Aleksandr Dondukov Blvds – contain the lion's share of Sophia's best restaurants. But – as with accommodation – perhaps the most pleasant area for dining out is the leafy district along ul Oborishte and around Doctors' Garden.

URBAN HIKES

It's impossible not to notice from the moment you step off the train. **Mt Vitosha** looms over Sofia and appears in its utmost grace when observed from the namesake **Vitosha Boulevard**, which also serves as the city's main pedestrian drag. Mt Vitosha is not just a visual delight, but also Bulgaria's prime hiking destination, crisscrossed by trails and dotted with mountain lodges. Most trails at the top are easily accessible by bus from the centre and provide breezy hikes that anyone can do; climbing the mountain from its base is way more challenging though.

In winter, Vitosha is the abode of skiers with several skiing lifts operating at the top of the mountain. At the foot of the mountain, the medieval **Boyana Church** (*boyanachurch.info*) is filled with brightly coloured frescoes from the epoch of Bulgarian empires. **Dragalevtsi Monastery** (*visitsofia.bg*) is another pedigreed place of worship.

BEST PLACES TO EAT & DRINK

Fabrika Daga € A coffee roaster doubling as a breakfast and lunch spot. Many vegan and vegetarian options. *facebook.com/fabrikadag*

33 Gastronauts €€ A cosy place serving pan-Mediterranean fare in a residential area off ul Oborishte. *33gastronauts.com*

Sineva €€ This sweet garden by a sky-blue house is the place to relax over a delicious fusion meal. *facebook.com/syneva.restobar*

Khadzhidraganovite Kashti €€ Glorious Bulgarian fare amidst utmost ethnic kitsch. *izbite.com*

WHAT DID THE ROMANS DO FOR US?

Sofia is like a wedding cake – it has multiple historical layers, each of them delicious in their own way. Roman Serdica comes at the bottom. Born as a Celtic stronghold, it was conquered by Rome in 29 BCE, eventually becoming the capital of the province of Dacia Mediterranea. It was anything but a remote outpost: two Roman emperors, Aurelian and Galerius, were born here. Issued by the latter, the Edict of Serdica (also known as Edict of Toleration) was the first law legalising Christianity in the empire. This is when the 4th-century Sveti Georgi Rotunda popped up, which still stands amidst the ruins of ancient Serdica.

Emperor Constantine the Great used to say 'Serdica is my Rome' as he eyed it for the new imperial capital. Alas, he eventually opted for building Constantinople, leaving the future Sofia in the backwaters of European history.

Roman Serdica was repeatedly destroyed by invaders – the Dacians, the Goths and the Huns – but kept rising from ashes. The dawning of the Byzantine empire saw the revival of Serdica, renamed Triaditsa, with Sveta Sofia serving as the most iconic manifestation of that age.

Ancient Serdica ruins

The Site of Ancient Serdica

It's an unlikely combination – a metro station, Roman ruins and a Soviet-style government complex rising over the scene – but this is what the beating heart of Sofia is like. The ruins of **ancient Serdica** *(visitsofia.bg)* are partly incorporated into the namesake metro station, with the 16th-century **Sveta Petka Samardzhiiska Church** *(visitsofia.bg)* standing by the entrance. Above it, the **Largo Complex** contains government offices, but also hides the 4th-century **Sveti Georgi Rotunda** *(svgeorgi-rotonda.com)*, originally built as Roman baths, in one of the two vast courtyards.

Two Churches, Two Millennia

Located within a few hundred metres of each other, two of the city's major cathedrals are 14 centuries apart on Sofia's history timeline. **Sveta Sofia Church** *(hramsvetasofia.com)* is believed to have emerged in its present shape during the reign of Byzantine Emperor Justinian in the 6th century. The most fascinating part of it is the crypt, which contains a piece of Roman-era necropolis.

Looming over a square nearby, the richly decorated **Aleksander Nevski Cathedral** *(cathedral.bg)*, the city's largest, was built between 1882 and 1912 and is dedicated to Russian soldiers who died liberating Bulgaria from the Ottomans. It also comes with a crypt, which features a rich collection of icons from different epochs.

Aleksander Nevski Cathedral

Olga (left) and Kolya (right)
SIMON RICHMOND/LONELY PLANET

Brief Encounters

Simon Richmond's boyhood was filled with thrilling notions about the Orient Express. Following the legendary train's route 50 years later, there were no murders, but no shortage of fascinating characters.

WORDS BY SIMON RICHMOND
Railway enthusiast Simon has ridden trains on four continents and wrote Lonely Planet's Trans-Siberian Railway.

THE SOFIA–İSTANBUL EXPRESS was running late. It wasn't the first delayed train I encountered during my research trip for this book and it wouldn't be the last. I didn't mind – I wasn't in a hurry, and it was a chance to meet fellow passengers idling on the platform at Plovdiv.

I fell into conservation with Dimitrije and Ognjen, teenage mates from Belgrade, quizzing them on their journey so far – a slow train from Belgrade to Niš, a bus to Sofia, then a train to Plovdiv. They also brought me up to speed on the poor state of Serbia's railways. In November 2024, the collapse of the concrete canopy of Novi Sad's train station had killed 16 people. There had since been mass protests across the country about government corruption. Dimitrije and Ognjen, fluent in English at 18, were providing a masterclass on Serbian current affairs.

The train finally arrived, and I located my compartment. Next door was Nick, a fellow Brit who had travelled to Bulgaria with his girlfriend to attend a wedding. There had been an argument – she was now headed back home to Amsterdam, while he was bound for İstanbul, contemplating being newly single.

In search of some jollier company, I moved down the carriages to join a group of British travellers. Michael and his Turkish wife, Ayten, and their friends Kate and Neil were playing a trivia game. They had been following the classic Orient Express route – London, Paris, Munich, Budapest, Bucharest and Sofia. I contributed a bottle of wine to the party and we swapped travel tales and potted biographies as we fumbled to answer questions about obscure 1990s pop stars and sports events. In this merry way, time passed until 1.30am when, on arrival at Kapıkule, we all disembarked for passport and customs checks.

It's such moments of spontaneous camaraderie, connection and confession with total strangers that, for me, are the greatest pleasure of overnight train journeys – and this ultimate leg of my Paris to İstanbul Orient Express journey was delivering them in spades.

A Life on Trains

As an impressionable 11-year-old, the famous train had lodged itself in my imagination while watching the movies *Murder on the Orient Express* and *From Russia with Love*. Here was a journey that promised exotic locations, daredoing spies and mystery-solving detectives!

Once I was old enough to start travelling by myself, I gravitated towards trains. I went Interrailing across Europe and made a journey almost entirely by train from London to Hong Kong, via Russia, various 'Stans and China. I bunked down on the Indian Pacific, riding the rails from Sydney to Perth, and was a passenger on the routes of the Trans-Siberian Railway many times, over many years.

Of course, international trains are not just for leisure travellers, but also for locals on business trips or their daily commute. People like Andras, a journalist whom I met earlier on my journey, on the way from Salzburg to Budapest. Andras, a specialist on Eastern European affairs, and I struck up a fascinating conversation about regional issues, which culminated with an invitation to his home in Szentendre on the Danube.

On the leg from Ruse to Varna, the only other people sharing my carriage were Olga and Kolya, a retired Ukrainian couple. Olga was constantly crocheting and kindly gifted me some bracelets and a woollen circle (in blue, white and yellow) that she had made. She proudly showed me a card that identified her as a 'mother heroine' of Ukraine, signifying that she had raised five or more children. As she scrolled through photos on her phone of her extended family, I thought of the war that kept Olga and Kolya separated from their loved ones.

Memories of these brief encounters occupied my thoughts as I enjoyed a delicious lunch of meze in the Orient Express restaurant at Sirkeci station. A month later such a pleasant arrival in İstanbul would have been impossible due to the shuttering of the historic station prior to its transformation into museums and event spaces.

Before returning by train to the UK, I caught up again with Dimitrije and Ognjen. On a ferry along the Haliç (Golden Horn) to Eyüpsultan, we talked more about travel, their plans for university and hopes for the future of Serbia. Their youthful aspirations and desire to see the world for themselves reminded me of how I was at 18. I was happy for them – they have years of train adventures ahead of them.

Sofia

You will most likely be travelling aboard the sleeper train to İstanbul for this final leg of the journey. There will be passport and custom checks as you cross the border from Bulgaria to Türkiye in the wee small hours of the morning. Understandably, your emotions may be mixed – excitement for your arrival in the old Ottoman capital, with all its storied sights and sensuous delights, but also sadness that your Orient Express adventure is drawing to a close.

Simon Richmond

Crocuses, Rila Mountains
PETAR BOGDANOV/SHUTTERSTOCK

İstanbul

654 KMS – 15¼ HOURS' RIDE

THIS LEG:
- Kostenets
- Plovdiv
- Dimitrovgrad
- Svilengrad
- Edirne Garı
- Edirne
- Çerkezköy
- Halkalı
- Kazlıçeşme
- Sirkeci, İstanbul

Riding Notes

The Sofia–İstanbul Express (15 hours) runs all year offering both sleeping cars and couchettes. You can connect to this train in Plovdiv (p168) or Dimitrovgrad (p168). There are 10 direct trains daily from Sofia to Plovdiv, the fastest taking two hours and 40 minutes. Many of these continue on to Dimitrovgrad (one hour) and Svilengrad (one more hour). Unlike the Sofia–İstanbul Express, it's possible to either book these trains in advance online or simply turn up and buy tickets on the day.

Breaking Your Journey

Aim to spend at least one night in Plovdiv, a friendly city offering excellent accommodation and places to eat. For a taste of old Ottoman Türkiye, break your journey in Edirne (p172).

Simon's Tips

BEST MEAL Farm-fresh ingredients washed down with quaffable local wines at Pavazh. (p169)

FAVOURITE VIEW Sunset from atop Plovdiv's Old Town hill and archaeological site, Nebet Tepe. (p171)

ESSENTIAL STOP The historically multi-layered city of Plovdiv. (p170)

TIP Bring your own food and drink for the sleeper train as there's no restaurant or buffet car.

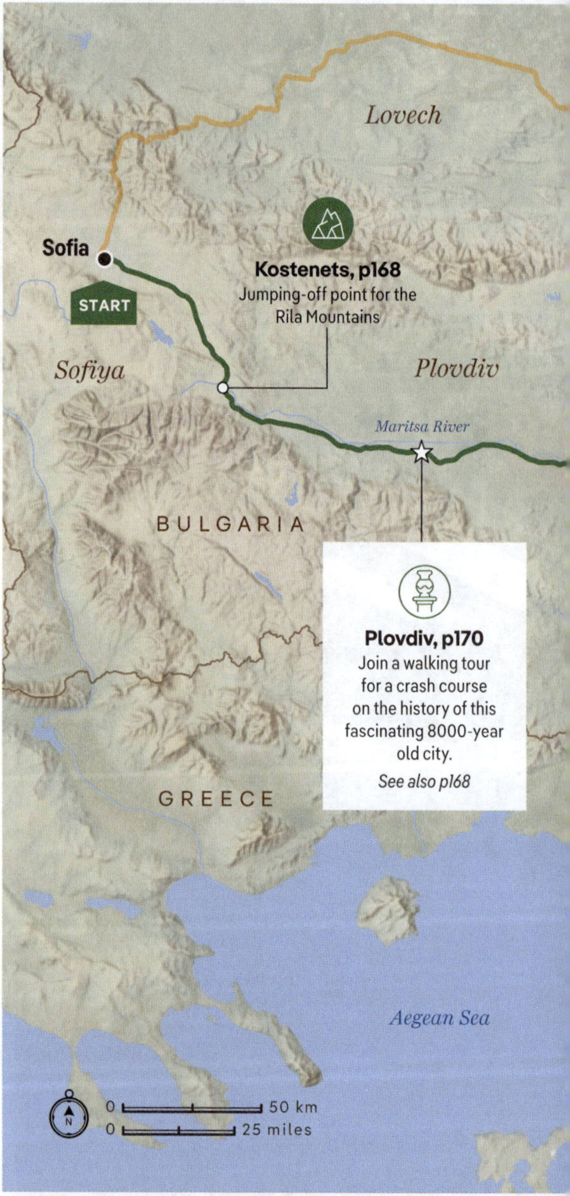
Lovech
Sofia
START
Kostenets, p168
Jumping-off point for the Rila Mountains
Sofiya
Plovdiv
Maritsa River
BULGARIA
Plovdiv, p170
Join a walking tour for a crash course on the history of this fascinating 8000-year old city.
See also p168
GREECE
Aegean Sea
0 50 km
0 25 miles
N

ONWARD TRAVEL

The daily Sofia–İstanbul Express offers a choice of either comfy sleeper carriages (two-bed compartments with a sink, fridge and pull-out table) or the simpler and cheaper couchettes, with four beds per compartment. Tickets for sleeper carriages include water, juice and a couple of snacks. Bring all other food and drink as there's no dining car.

This is a popular train, especially in summer, so booking ahead is advisable. However, at the time of research, it was not possible to book this train via bdz.bg. Instead, email bdz@bdz.bg with your booking request – if this works (and that's not guaranteed), you'll pay and pick up the tickets at the international ticket window in Sofia station.

To be sure of securing tickets for required dates, it's safer to email Andy Brabin at tickets@discoverbyrail.com. For a fee, he can arrange for tickets to be ready for you on arrival in Sofia, and also secure reservations if you are travelling on an Interrail/Eurail pass.

Alternatively you can take your chances and book directly at the international ticket window in Sofia, Ruse (p148), Plovdiv (p170) or Dimitrovgrad (below).

Kostenets

Departing Sofia you'll soon leave the city behind, as views of apartment blocks are replaced with pleasant countryside. The train passes through Kostenets, a jumping-off point for the natural hot springs and hiking routes of **Rila National Park** (rilanationalpark.bg), home to Mt Musala, at 2925m Bulgaria's highest peak.

Plovdiv

Approaching Plovdiv (p170), look out the left side of the train for **Bunardjik**, one of the seven hills that this ancient city was built on. You can't miss it as it's topped by an 11m-tall statue of a soldier (nicknamed Alyosha), a memorial to Soviet casualties during the German occupation of Bulgaria in WWII.

Plovdiv Central station, a tangerine-coloured 1908 art nouveau building, is a foretaste of what lies in store in one of Europe's oldest continuously inhabited cities. If your travel schedule allows, aim to spend at least two nights here.

Dimitrovgrad

The journey between Plovdiv and Dimitrovgrad, a model city from Bulgaria's communist era, takes between an hour and 1½ hours depending on the train you catch. The scenery along the way is mostly farmlands and woods through which flows the Maritsa river. However, if you're on the Sofia–İstanbul Express, you won't see much of the landscape as it will already be dark.

If you wish to check out Dimitrovgrad, catch an earlier daytime train from Plovdiv. Some 50,000 volunteers from across the country flocked here in 1947 to construct a modern city, which is named after Georgi Dimitrov, Bulgaria's Communist Party leader from 1933 to 1949.

Sofia — 74km — Kostenets — 96km —

Kostenets is a gateway to Rila National Park

Look out for the Alyosha monument atop Bunardjik as you pull into Plovdiv

Statue of soldier on Bunardjik, Plovdiv

Dimitrovgrad's 'Stalinist baroque' architecture, with buildings featuring decorative balconies, columns and plinths, is evident and there's lots of greenery including three big parks. The **Historical Museum** (dgmuseum.org; 9.30am-6pm) is an eight-minute walk north of the station.

Svilengrad

Svilengrad is near the point where the borders of Bulgaria, Türkiye and Greece converge. Passport checks by the Bulgarian border guards are carried out on the train while it waits at the station, which is 5km from Svilengrad town. Svilengrad's name comes from *svila*, Continues on page 172

BEST PLACES TO EAT

Pavazh, Plovdiv €€€
This pioneer of Plovdiv's Kapana dining scene serves a delicious range of dishes made with farm-fresh ingredients. *noon-11pm Tue-Sun*

Rahat Tepe, Plovdiv €€
Serves tasty traditional Bulgarian food and craft beers in the Old Town. *10am-midnight*

Kotka i Mishka, Plovdiv €
Long-running cafe-bar serving local craft beers, perfect for soaking up Kapana's buzzy atmosphere. *10am-midnight*

Meşhur Edirne Ciğercisi, Edirne €€
A standout in Edirne for the quality of its *tava ciğe* (fried beef liver) and swift service. *8am-7pm Wed-Mon*

CITY GUIDE:
Plovdiv

Originally built across seven hills, Plovdiv is visually appealing, culturally rich and very old. It mixes splendid ancient ruins and mosaics with lively arts and food scenes, and a charming Old Town where time seems to stand still.

HOW TO

Getting here: Trains connect Plovdiv with Sofia (two hours, 40 minutes; p158) and Ruse (seven to 10 hours; p148), via Veliko Târnovo (4½ hours; p156).

Getting around: The city is compact and walkable. A taxi from the train station to the city centre is around €7.

Sleeping: The business hotel **A&M Hotel** (am-hotel.bg; €€) is next to the station. Hostel Old Plovdiv (p174) and Mouse House (p174) are both great budget choices, while the stylish Villa Flavia Boutique Hotel (p174) offers more comfort, plus an on-site Roman bath.

Tip: Get your bearings on the **Free Plovdiv Tour** (freeplovdivtour.com), a by-donation walking tour lasting around 2½ hours and starting at 11am and 6pm from outside City Hall.

More info: Central Tourist Information Centre (oldpolvdiv.org; 9am-1pm & 1.30-5.30pm).

Plovdiv's Old Town is a gem, restored to its mid-19th-century appearance and packed with evocative house-museums, churches and craft shops. Here you'll find Thracian, Roman, Byzantine and Bulgarian antiquities, the most impressive being a 1st-century CE Roman amphitheatre still used for performances. The modern centre is focused around ul Knyaz Aleksandâr I, one of Europe's longest pedestrian shopping streets, under part of which lie the remains of the 250m-long Roman Stadium of Philippopolis. Rising directly above this street is Sahat Tepe, also known as Danov Hill, which is crowned with an old bell tower.

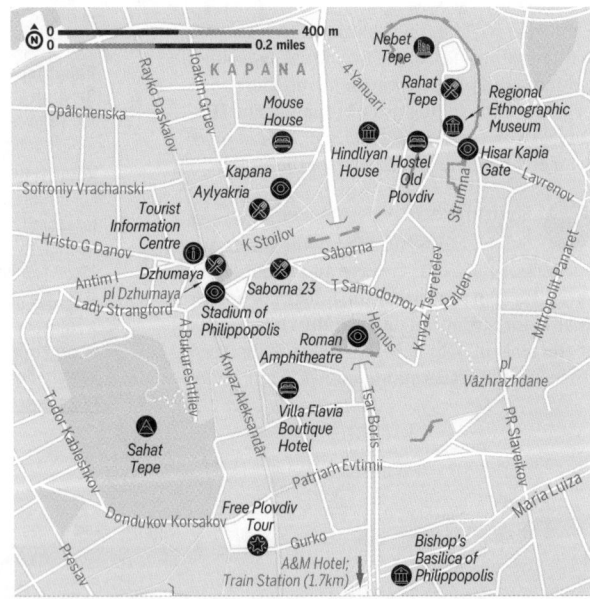

THE EVOLUTION OF KAPANA

Sandwiched between the pedestrianised mall ul Knyaz Aleksandăr I and the Old Town is **Kapana**, a lively district of bars, cafes and restaurants, plus some boutiques. Translating as 'trap', Kapana is named for its labyrinthine layout and was the original location of Plovdiv's bazaar.

In the early 21st century many of the buildings in Kapana were abandoned. A city initiative offering creatives and fledgling entrepreneurs a rent-free year kickstarted the neighbourhood's revival. The cafe-bar Kotka i Mishka (p169) and the restaurant Pavazh (p169) were pioneers, setting up in Kapana in 2015 – they are both still here and worth visiting. Kotka i Mishka has since expanded to open another bar, **Local**; a co-working space; and Mouse House (p174), a guesthouse and rental apartments for visitors. The founders, Dimitar Semkov and Ivailo Dernev, publish online guide **Lost in Plovdiv** (lostinplovdiv.com), with news on the latest up-and-coming places across the city. Pavazh also runs **5 Nat Bar**, where you can sample scores of local wines.

Hindliyan House

Walk Around the Old Town

Start at **Hindliyan House** (oldplovdiv.bg), a superb example of how a rich merchant family lived in the early 19th century. Pause at the hilltop for panoramic views from the Thracian archaeological site **Nebet Tepe**, then have lunch at nearby Rahat Tepe (p169).

Retrace your steps to the **Regional Ethnographic Museum** (ethnograph.info), where you can learn about Bulgarian traditions and explore the past in one of the Old Town's most beautiful houses. Around the corner is the well-preserved **Hisar Kapia Gate**.

Marvel at Ancient Mosaic Art

Forgotten and undisturbed for centuries underground, the mosaic floors of the 4th-century CE **Bishop's Basilica of Philippopolis** (oldplovdiv.bg) are an astonishing must-see. Built over a pagan Roman temple, the basilica was rediscovered in the 1980s. Over 2000 sq m of beautifully designed mosaic floors were restored in situ, with the museum, which opened in 2021, built over them as protection. The displays and interpretation are first rate, powerfully conveying how the largest early Christian church ever discovered in Bulgaria once looked.

BEST PLACES TO EAT & DRINK

Aylyakria €€€ Hip gastro bar in Kapana that gets its name from the word *aylyak* meaning 'to be relaxed'. *noon-11.30pm*

Saborna 23 €€ Good-value fine-dining experience in a cosy and relaxed atmosphere. *5-11pm Mon-Fri, 1-11pm Sat & Sun*

Dzhumaya € On the corner of the Dzhumaya Mosque, this authentic teahouse offers sweet Turkish treats. *8am-11pm*

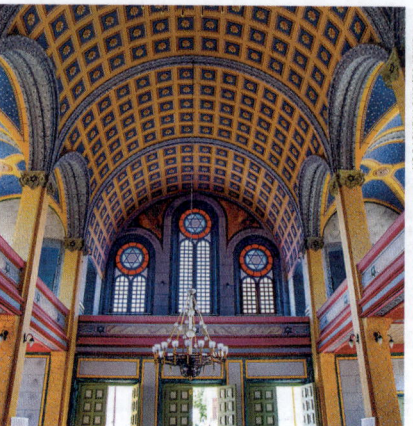

Interior, Edirne Synagogue

Continued from page 169
the local word for silk, as the town was once famous for its silk industry. A local landmark is the **Mustafa Pasha Bridge**. This elegant 300m-long stone span across the Maritsa River has 20 arches and dates to the early 16th century. Take in the view from waterside restaurants serving fresh fish dishes.

The town has also become something of a mini Las Vegas with several casinos catering to visiting Turks. Just before you cross the border, the 500-room **GoldenEye Hotel & Resort** *(goldeneye hotels.com)* comes into view on the left side, its facade a dazzling display of animated LED lights.

Edirne Garı
Your second dead-of-night station experience will be at Edirne Garı on the southeast fringes of the one-time Ottoman capital. Have your passport ready and your luggage packed as you'll need to get off the train with it to go through customs. If you're travelling in the other direction towards Bulgaria, you can leave your bags on the train.

As of August 2025, this is the processing point when crossing the border between Bulgaria and Türkiye (and vice versa), replacing Kapıkule (which is closer to the border). Border procedures might return to Kapıkule once the high-speed rail line from İstanbul is completed.

On arrival at Edirne Garı wait for your turn to disembark the train. Proceed first to the passport window for your passport to be checked and stamped. Then go to the x-ray room where your bags will be scanned. Once you're given the OK, return to the train to continue your journey to İstanbul.

That said, it is worth delaying your onward journey towards the Bosphorus to spend a night in Edirne. Don't attempt to walk into the city centre (about one hour) at this early hour of the morning – instead take a taxi (around ₺20).

Edirne
Named Hadrianopolis during Roman times, Edirne served as the Ottoman capital until the conquest of Constantinople and is home to the exquisite World Heritage–listed **Selimiye Mosque** (right). Other major sights include the **Sultan Beyazıt II Mosque Complex**, the historic houses of the **Kaleiçi district** and the grand **Edirne Synagogue**, commissioned by Sultan Abdulhamid II and opened in 1909.

A memorable place to stay is Rüstempaşa Kervansaray Hotel (p174). While here, also try the local delicacy *tava ciğe* (fried beef liver) at Meşhur Edirne Ciğercisi (p169).

Continues on page 174

Svilengrad

32km

Edirne

Unmissable on the Bulgaria-Türkiye border is the glitzy GoldenEye Hotel & Resort

Marvel at Selimiye Mosque

Dominating Edirne's skyline is World Heritage–listed Selimiye Mosque with its stunning dome and four elegant minarets, the tallest ever built in the Ottoman Empire.

HOW TO

Getting here: The mosque is around 3.7km northwest of Edirne train station. Hop on one of the reasonably frequent buses or take a taxi.

Opening hours: Mosque 8.30am-6.30pm; Edirne Turkish & Islamic Art Museum 9am-7pm Apr-Sep, 9am-5.30pm Oct-Mar

Cost: Mosque free; museum adult/child ₺7/free

More information: kulturportali.gov.tr/portal/edirneselimiyecamiivekulliyesi

Named after Sultan Selim II, the mosque was built by the Ottoman architect Mimar Sinan between 1568 and 1575. It's thought by many to be the crowning point of Sinan's work and of all classical Ottoman architecture. Its minarets, at 85.67m, are the tallest in Türkiye, and its central dome is marginally larger than the Aya Sofya's (p183).

In the interior, light cascades through hundreds of windows, bringing out the exquisite tulip-patterned tiles, intricate marble designs and delicate calligraphic inscriptions. The most striking element of the building is the Edirnekari woodwork on the *müezzin mahfili* (a raised platform), serving as a reminder of Edirne's role as an art hub for the Ottoman Empire.

Housed in the *darül Hadis* (Hadith school) in the *külliye* (mosque complex), the **Edirne Turkish & Islamic Art Museum** is filled with treasures, including masterpieces of calligraphy and an assortment of weaponry, glassware, ceramics and wooden works. Rest in the courtyard and admire the architectural details of the 16th-century structure.

Above: Dome, Selimiye Mosque
Right: Selimiye Mosque

RESUL MUSLU/SHUTTERSTOCK

BEST PLACES TO SLEEP

Hostel Old Plovdiv, Plovdiv €€
This marvellous 1868 building has been beautifully restored and is a genial place to stay in the heart of Plovdiv's Old Town. Every room features hand-picked antiques.
hosteloldplovdiv.com

Mouse House, Plovdiv €€
Stay in Plovdiv's Kapana district at these perfectly formed, contemporary-style rooms and apartments managed by Kotka i Mishka (p169).
mousehouse.bg

Rüstempaşa Kervansaray Hotel, Edirne €€€
This historic Edirne inn makes for an atmospheric and memorable place to stay. Also has a decent restaurant.
rustempasakervansaray.com.tr

Villa Flavia Boutique Hotel, Plovdiv €€€
Fantastic, family-run hotel right in the centre of Plovdiv, with remains of an ancient Roman bath on-site.
villaflaviahotel.com

Continued from page 172

When the railway reached Edirne in 1871, to save building a bridge across the Maritsa River, the station was sited in Karaağaç, 4km south of the city. This was the station that the original Orient Express would have passed through.

The 1914 version of that station, designed in Turkish neoclassical style, still stands, but is now part of Trakya University. Edirne's present train station is on the same side of the Maritsa River as the city and it's from here that, at the time of research, one daily train connects to Halkalı taking 5½ hours; for the current schedule see tcddtasimacilik.gov.tr. The high-speed line, once up and running, will cut travel times to 1½ hours.

Edirne

162km

You'll clatter through Kapıkule where Turkish border formalities used to happen pre-August 2025 and may resume in the future

Sunflower field, Çerkezköy

Çerkezköy

Unless you're travelling by the train to or from Edirne, you are not going to see much of Çerkezköy, as the Sofia–İstanbul Express pauses here either late at night or very early in the morning. The station is about 2km southeast of the town centre, and there's little reason to be lingering here, anyway.

Passengers on the historic Orient Express were not so fortunate when it came to Çerkezköy. In 1891, along this stretch of line, the train was derailed by bandits, the passengers robbed and hostages taken. A ransom was eventually paid for their release. The curse of Çerkezköy struck again in 1929 when the Orient Express was marooned in an enormous snow drift for a week. Both these incidents made international headlines, with the snow-bound train providing Agatha Christie with a plot point for her classic whodunnit *Murder on the Orient Express*.

Halkalı

You'll awake to the crop-covered fields of the **Marmara region**, where in summer there are dazzling displays of bright yellow sunflowers. Later, İstanbul's dormitory suburb of **Ispartakule** comes into view, then **Lake Küçükçekmece**, as you close in on Halkalı, the terminal for the Sofia–İstanbul Express.

About 35km west of İstanbul city centre by train, Halkalı is a modern, unlovely shed with meagre facilities. Take the escalators up from

Çerkezköy

Halkalı

92km

 Beware the Çerkezköy curse!

Sirkeci train station, İstanbul

the arrival platform to the concourse. There's an ATM just outside the station exit, on the left.

To continue into the city, first locate the **İstanbulkart** *(istanbulkart.istanbul)* machines on the concourse. Use your international bank or credit card to buy one of these pre-paid and rechargeable cards, which you will need to pay for fares on İstanbul's public transport (cash is not accepted). There is a non-refundable fee (₺165) for the card and you will also need to load it with some credit – around ₺100 (about €2) is sufficient to get into the city.

Once you have the card, you can proceed to the ticket gates and take the escalators, lift or steps down to Platforms 1 or 2 to ride the Marmaray commuter train line into İstanbul. Trains leave every 15 minutes.

Along the Way We Met...

OGNJEN JANKOVIĆ & DIMITRIJE RAJKOVIĆ Serbian trains are modern and comfortable and could go up to 200km per hour, but the tracks are so bad they go very slowly. The 250km journey from Belgrade to Niš took us 6½ hours. The countryside is nice and train enthusiasts would love it. Serbia has no international trains, so we took the bus from Niš to Sofia (two daily, four hours, €19). We were pleasantly surprised by Sofia – it's cleaner and has a lot more greenery than Belgrade.

Ognjen and Dimitrije are students from Belgrade whom we met while they were travelling from Plovdiv to İstanbul by train.

OGNJEN & DIMITRIJE'S TIP: *Sofia's National Museum of History is impressive. It has a lot of exhibits and a beautiful setting in a park.*

Halkalı   *25km*   **Kazlıçeşme**

As you pass Yeşilköy station look for Atatürk Airport

🚆 Kazlıçeşme

Now riding the Marmaray train, you'll pass **Atatürk Airport**, closed to commercial flights but still used for cargo and private jets.

If you want to arrive above ground at Sirkeci, just as Orient Express travellers of old once did – and why wouldn't you? – then **Kazlıçeşme** is the station at which you'll need to transfer to the U3 suburban train line. Go down the escalator and out the Marmaray exit gates, then tap your İstanbulkart again to go through the Kazlıçeşme-Sirkeci ticket gates and up the escalator onto the U3 platform.

Shortly after Kazlıçeşme, you'll pass through one of the main gates of the **Walls of Constantinople**. Originally built in the 4th to 5th century CE, sections of these impressive fortifications line the tracks right up to Sultanahmet.

Unmissable across the Bosphorus is the **Çamlıca Tower** *(camlicatower.com)*, soaring 587m into the sky including its steel antenna. The telecom tower's bulbous shape is modelled on a tulip that is yet to bloom.

🚆 Sirkeci

When Türkiye's first railway from Halkalı to Sirkeci was built in 1870, the Sultan gave permission for it to run through the lower garden of Topkapı Palace. It's that same route, beside the palace walls and the Sea of Marmara, that you'll travel on this ultimate leg of the journey.

Designed by German architect August Jasmund, Sirkeci opened on 3 November 1890, replacing an earlier temporary station. It ceased to be the terminus for international trains in 2013. At the time of research, as the U3 train pulled into Sirkeci, only a slender glimpse of the historic terminal's elegant European Orientalist design was visible above the hoardings, covered in tantalising and evocative images of the station in its heyday.

The station's restoration is scheduled for completion during 2026. The existing railway museum (which showcases memorabilia from the Orient Express) will be joined by a new museum highlighting Sirkeci's role in the journeys of Turkish workers to Europe in the 1960s. The revamped station will also host other galleries and cultural venues.

Immediately outside the station you're pitched into the perpetual bustle of İstanbul (p178). The fabled city, split between continents, awaits exploration – just as it has for the other passengers who arrived at Sirkeci in the last 150 years on the Orient Express. You can now count yourself among them.

Çamlıca Tower, İstanbul

SKYCUTS PRODUCTION/SHUTTERSTOCK

The ancient Walls of Constantinople appear shortly after leaving Kazlıçeşme

10km

Sirkeci

SOFIA TO ISTANBUL

CITY GUIDE:

İstanbul

İstanbul city view

When passengers on the first Orient Express arrived in this minaret-studded city in 1883, it was called Constantinople and sultan Abdul Hamid II sat on the throne. Since then, it's lost the Ottoman rulers, but retained all of its magic.

WORDS BY **VIRGINIA MAXWELL**
Virginia is a regular visitor to İstanbul and covers the city for Lonely Planet's Pocket İstanbul *and* Türkiye *guidebooks.*

Arriving
Travellers starting (or finishing) their journey in İstanbul have a number of options.
Air There are two international airports: İstanbul Airport on the European side of the city and Sabiha Gökçen Airport on the Asian side. Airport shuttle buses transfer passengers from each airport to Taksim Meydanı (Square) in Beyoğlu, close to the Old City.
Train The İstanbul–Sofya Ekspresi to/from Sofia in Bulgaria starts and terminates in the outer suburb of Halkalı (p175). From mid-June to mid-October, the sleeper-car carriages of the Bosfor Ekspresi from Bucharest in Romania are attached to the İstanbul–Sofya Ekspresi until Bulgaria, where they are uncoupled and attached to an engine that continues to Bucharest.

HOW MUCH FOR A

Glass of çay €1

Döner kebap sandwich €6

Entry to Aya Sofya €25

Getting Around
To travel on public transport you'll need an İstanbulkart (p176). Trams and the metro are operated by **Metro İstanbul** *(metro.istanbul)*. Most of the ferries are operated by **İstanbul Şehir Hatları** *(sehirhatlari.istanbul)*.
Tram Most visitors will board the T1 tram connecting Cevizlibağ and Bağcılar in the Old City with Kabataş in Beyoğlu, which has conveniently located stops at Beyazıt-Grand Bazaar, Sultanahmet, Sirkeci, Eminönü, Karaköy and Tophane. Another useful line, the T5, travels from Cibali near Eminönü along the Golden Horn to Alibeyköy.
Ferry The most enjoyable way to travel around the city is by ferry. Ferries cross between the European and Asian shores and on the Bosphorus and Golden Horn.
Metro Two metro lines are useful for visitors. The M2 connects Yenikapı with Hacıosman and has stops including Vezneciler near the Grand Bazaar; Şişhane in Beyoğlu; Taksim Sq; and Osmanbey near Bomonti. The Marmaray line connects the European and Asian sides of the city, running from Halkalı to Gebze, stopping at Sirkeci near Eminönü, at Üsküdar and at Ayrılık Çeşmesi, from where passengers can transfer to the M4 travelling to Kadıköy in one direction and Sabiha Gökçen Airport in the other.

For train and tram schedules and trip planning, go to Metro İstanbul:

A DAY IN İSTANBUL

Kick off in monument-rich **Sultanahmet Square**, the heart of the Old City. Visit venerable **Aya Sofya** (p183), the show-stopping **Blue Mosque** (p184) and the atmospheric subterranean **Basilica Cistern** (p183). Alternatively, visit **Topkapı Palace** (p182), being sure not to miss its exquisite Harem.

Head to the **Grand Bazaar** (p185), where you can grab a tasty lunch from a food stand before wandering through this historic marketplace. Then walk downhill to the **Spice Bazaar** (p185) and enjoy a Turkish coffee at **Kuru Kahveci** (p185), the cafe of famous coffee merchant Kurukahveci Mehmet Efendi.

Cross the Galata Bridge to sample the nightlife in **Beyoğlu**. Have a pre-dinner drink at the summer-only rooftop bar at **Mikla** (right) then kick on to a *meyhane* (Turkish tavern) for a meze-laden feast, or an *ocakbaşı* (grill house) for a some succulent kebaps.

Where to Stay

The big-hitting historical monuments are located in or near Sultanahmet, which has the largest concentration of hotels, *pansiyons* (pensions) and hostels. The downside is the lack of nightlife, including decent eating and drinking options. For that reason, savvy visitors tend to stay in Beyoğlu, which is the epicentre of eating, drinking and culture and has accommodation options for every budget. It's also an easy walk, tram ride or metro trip from the Old City.

BEST PLACES TO STAY

Archeo € Well-run hostel and cafe with a great Beyoğlu location. *archeopol.com*

Marmara Guesthouse €€ Friendly, family-run *pansiyon* in Sultanahmet known for its delicious breakfasts. *marmaraguesthouse.com*

Hotel Ibrahim Pasha €€€ Classy and exceptionally well run boutique hotel in Sultanahmet. *ibrahimpasha.com*

TomTom Suites €€€ Refurbished Franciscan convent in Tophane with luxe rooms and a rooftop restaurant. *tomtomsuitesistanbul.com*

Where to Eat

Though it's possible to source excellent street food around the Grand Bazaar and in Eminönü, the best food in the city is found in Beyoğlu. Most of the cafes, lunchtime *lokantas* (eateries serving ready-made dishes from bain-maries), *meyhanes*, *ocakbaşıs* and fine-dining restaurants serve Turkish cuisine, but it's also possible to source global eats.

SWEET TREATS

İstanbullus love an afternoon sugar hit, especially when it is accompanied by a glass of strong *çay* (tea; pictured below left). And two local treats fit this bill perfectly: baklava and *lokum* (Turkish delight).

Made with a gel of starch and sugar, *lokum* is generally flavoured with ingredients including *cevizli* (walnut), *fıstıklı* (pistachio) and *roze* (rose water). Although its origin is unclear (Iran and Türkiye both claim it), there is no dispute that **Ali Muhiddin Hacı Bekir** (*hacibekir.com*), a company established in İstanbul in 1777 and still selling its products from its original shop in Eminönü, was one of the first to manufacture it commercially.

Baklava's origin is just as contested, but one thing is certain – when well made, this dessert of layered filo pastry sweetened with syrup and filled with nuts (pictured below) is delectable. To sample the best baklava in the city, head to **Karaköy Güllüoğlu** (*karakoygulluoglu.com*).

BEST PLACES TO EAT & DRINK

Geyik €€ Popular neighbourhood bar in Cihangir. Great cocktails. *geyikdukkan.com*

Mıkla €€€ Swish summer-only bar with a spectacular panoramic view. *miklarestaurant.com*

Antiochia €€ Beyoğlu *ocakbaşı* serving the best kebaps in the city. *antiochiaconcept.com*

Aheste €€€ Stylish Beyoğlu restaurant serving Modern Turkish cuisine. *ahesterestaurant.com*

Explore Topkapı Palace

Libidinous sultans, ambitious courtiers and beautiful concubines lived in this sprawling palace between the 15th and 19th centuries when it was the court of the Ottoman Empire.

HOW TO

Getting here: The palace is a short walk from Sultanahmet Sq. The closest tram stops are Gülhane and Sultanahmet.

When to go: Closed Tuesdays

Cost: ₺2400

Tip: If time allows, consider visiting the **İstanbul Archaeology Museums** *(muze.gen.tr/muze-detay/arkeoloji)*, a complex located in the lower garden of the palace, just above Gülhane Park.

More info: muze.gen.tr/muze-detay/topkapi

Organised into four park-like courts, the palace comprises a multitude of opulent structures. After purchasing your ticket in the **First Court**, proceed through the Middle Gate into the **Second Court**, home to the ornate **Imperial Council Chamber** where courtiers and foreign diplomats were once received.

Also here, the sprawling **Harem**, where the sultans and their families lived, is the undoubted highlight of any visit. The Harem has dormitories, reception halls, hamams, courtyards, and a series of salons decorated with frescoes and magnificent İznik and Kütahya tilework.

The **Third Court**, originally the Sultan's private domain, has a series of pavilions set in its garden, including the 18th-century **Library of Ahmet III** and the 16th-century **Council Chamber**. Also here is the **Imperial Treasury**, where precious art and objects are stored, and the **Sacred Safekeeping Rooms** complex, where important religious relics are kept.

The **Fourth Court**, with its whimsical pleasure pavilions and terrace overlooking the Bosphorus, is the final area to explore.

Harem, Topkapı Palace

FESTIVAL CITY

İstanbul has a long pedigree as a festival city, largely due to the excellent work of the **İstanbul Foundation for Culture and Arts** *(İKSV; iksv.org)*. This non-profit organisation curates and presents high-profile events including the İstanbul Film, Theatre, Jazz and Music festivals and the İstanbul Art and Design biennales. These major dates on the city's cultural calendar are strongly supported by locals, but also attract performers and audiences from around the globe.

The **Art Biennale**, which is staged from September to November in odd-numbered years, is of particular interest as exhibitions are staged in historic buildings that aren't open to the public at other times. These include *hans* (caravanserais), school buildings and private gardens. Other notable buildings host performances of baroque, romantic, classical and contemporary music during the **Music Festival** in June, including the jewel-like **Süreyya Opera House** in Kadıköy and the **Atatürk Cultural Centre** on Taksim Sq, a modernist masterpiece that has recently undergone a refurbishment.

To attend events, especially at the Music and Jazz festivals, book well in advance.

Aya Sofya

A Sublime Place of Worship

There are many important monuments in İstanbul, but **Aya Sofya** *(muze.gen.tr/muze-detay/ayasofya; €25)* surpasses the rest due to its innovative architectural form, rich history, religious importance and extraordinary beauty. Only Turks and worshipping foreign-national Muslims can enter the prayer hall; other visitors are restricted to the upstairs galleries, which are home to a number of Byzantine-era mosaics. From here, it's possible to look down on parts of the prayer hall and look up to see mosaics and paintings on the dome. The ticket office for non-Muslims is at the rear of the building.

Basilica Cistern

Descend to Watery Depths

The largest surviving Byzantine cistern in İstanbul, the subterranean structure known as the **Basilica Cistern** *(yerebatan.com/en/; ₺1650)* was commissioned by Emperor Justinian and built in 532. It features 336 columns, many of which were salvaged from ruined temples and feature fine carved capitals. The cistern's symmetry and sheer grandeur of conception are quite breathtaking, and its cool, cavernous depths make a great retreat on summer days.

Other Byzantine cisterns in the Old City include the **Şerefiye Cistern** *(serefiyesarnici.istanbul; ₺990)*, constructed during the reign of the Emperor Theodosius (r 379–395).

Whirling dervish

Watch the Dervishes Whirl

To witness the ancient art of the *sema* (a Mevlevi Sufi ceremony involving music, poetry and dervish whirling), head to the **Hodjapasha Cultural Centre** *(hodjapasha.com; adult/child US$41/23)*. This beautifully converted 550-year-old hamam in Sirkeci stages cultural performances including a 60-minute 'Dervish Experience' at 7pm daily. The musical and dance elements of this Sufi performance symbolise stages on the path to accessing God. Note children under seven are not admitted, wheelchairs cannot be accommodated and photography is not allowed. Bookings essential.

Çiçek Pasajı

IMPERIAL MOSQUES

After the 1453 Conquest, the Ottoman sultans put their architectural stamp on the city. Mehmet demolished the 4th-century Church of the Apostles, the burial place of Byzantine emperors, and built **Fatih Mosque** in its place. This was levelled in a 1766 earthquake and replaced with the current building, which was commissioned by Mustafa III. Mehmet also commissioned the **Eyüp Sultan Mosque**, the holiest in the city.

Mehmet's son commissioned the landmark **Beyazıt II Mosque** near the Grand Bazaar that carries his name. Upon ascending to the throne, Beyazıt's grandson Süleyman I, known as 'the Magnificent', commissioned the **Süleymaniye**, widely acknowledged as the most architecturally significant Ottoman mosque. Its grandeur is only rivalled by the **Sultanahmet Camii** (Sultanahmet Mosque), İstanbul's most photogenic building. The grand project of Sultan Ahmet I (r 1603–17), the mosque's wonderfully curvaceous exterior features a cascade of domes and six slender minarets, and the huge interior is adorned with 21,000 blue İznik tiles that give the building its unofficial but commonly used name, the **Blue Mosque**. Ahmet's *türbe* (tomb) is on the north side of the mosque, facing Sultanahmet Sq.

Saunter Down İstiklal Caddesi

Beyoğlu's premier boulevard is a perfect metaphor for 21st-century Türkiye. At its northern end is **Taksim Meydanı**, the symbolic heart of the modern city. But walk downhill (south) and plenty of grand buildings from the 19th and early 20th centuries have been preserved. Don't miss the **Çiçek Pasajı** (Flower Passage) in the 1876 **Cité de Pera building** or the historic **Balık Pazarı** (Fish Market) next to it. Other splendid buildings include **Mısır Apartmanı** (Egyptian Apartment) at number 163, built in 1910 and now home to commercial art galleries, and **360** *(360istanbul.com)*, a rooftop bar with panoramic view.

Shop the Bazaars

The colourful and chaotic Kapalıçarşı (Covered Market, aka Grand Bazaar) and its Bazaar District bookend, the Mısır Çarşısı (Egyptian Market, aka Spice Bazaar), are two of the Old City's greatest drawcards.

HOW TO

Getting here: The closest tram stops to the Grand Bazaar are Beyazıt-Grand Bazaar and Çemberlitaş; the Vezneciler metro station is also close by. The Spice Bazaar is in Eminönü, the city's major transport hub.

When to go: Grand Bazaar Monday to Saturday; Spice Bazaar daily

Tip: Start at the Grand Bazaar then walk downhill through the vibrant Mahmutpaşa shopping district to reach the Spice Bazaar.

More info: instagram/grandbazaarofistanbul

Starting as a small vaulted *bedesten* (warehouse) built on the order of Mehmet the Conqueror in 1461, the **Grand Bazaar** grew to cover a vast area as more than 60 lanes between the *bedesten*, neighbouring shops and *hans* were roofed, and the market assumed the sprawling, labyrinthine form it retains today. When here, don't miss brightly lit **Kalpakçılar Caddesi**, a major thoroughfare lined with jewellery shops; the **İç (Inner) Bedesten**, where a number of the bazaar's antique stores are located; and atmospheric **Halıcılar Sokak**, home to rug and textile stores.

The steep thoroughfare of Mahmutpaşa Kapısı runs downhill from the bazaar to Eminönü, home to the 17th-century **Spice Bazaar**. Though it sells plenty of tourist tat these days, the bazaar also sells good-quality nuts, spices and dried fruits so it continues to be patronised by locals. On its western side is the always busy local shopping strip of **Hasırcılar Caddesi**, where you'll be able to enjoy a cup of perfectly made *Türk khave* (Turkish coffee) at the **Kuru Kahveci cafe** (mehmetefendi.com; €).

EXPERIENCE ★

Above: Traditional ceramics
Right: Spice Bazaar

Take a World-Famous Ferry Ride

Climbing aboard one of the city's famous ferries is the quintessential İstanbul experience. Cross-continent commuter ferries are hard to beat, but trips along the Bosphorus and Golden Horn are fabulous, too.

Linking the Sea of Marmara (Marmara Denizi) with the Black Sea (Karadeniz), the Bosphorus Strait is the geographical spine of the city. On one side is Europe, on the other Asia – both shores are lined with former fishing villages that have been transformed into ritzy suburbs. The water's edge is fringed with grandiose palaces that once housed sultans and their families – look out for Dolmabahçe, Çırağan and Beylerbeyi. There are also *yalıs*, mansions built by wealthy Ottomans and embassies as summer retreats. The ferry cruises up the Bosphorus for two hours before arriving at **Anadolu Kavağı** at the mouth of the Black Sea, where it pauses for 2½ hours before returning to **Eminönü** at 4.40pm.

Though the Bosphorus ferry trip is deservedly famous, not many travellers are aware of the ferry route along the length of the **Haliç** (Golden Horn). This easy and cheap journey passes city districts that are home to many historic monuments, and its ultimate stop, **Eyüpsultan**, is replete with Ottoman monuments, shrines and mosques.

HOW TO

When to go: The return Uzun Boğaz Turu (Long Bosphorus Tour) departs from Eminönü every day at 10.35am. Haliç Hattı (Haliç Ferry Line) services depart from the Asian shore hourly from 7.30am (from 10.30am on Sundays), picking up passengers in Karaköy en route.

Cost: Bosphorus Tour adult/child ₺640/free; Haliç one way ₺45

Tip: You'll need an İstanbulkart to travel on the Haliç and cross-continent ferries.

More info: sehirhatlari.istanbul

Anadolu Kavağı waterfront

BATHING IN STYLE

Locals have been succumbing to soapy scrubs and relaxing massages in the steam-filled interiors of magnificently decorated hamams (bathhouses) since Ottoman times, and many visitors to the city follow suit today. Our favourite hamams in the city include the 16th-century **Ayasofya Hürrem Sultan Hamamı** *(hurremsultanhamami.com)* near Aya Sofya; the 18th-century **Cağaloğlu Hamamı** *(cagalogluhamami.com.tr)* near the Grand Bazaar; the 16th-century **Zeyrek Çinili Hamam** *(zeyrekcinilihamam.com)* in the Old City's western districts; and two hamams in Beyoğlu: the grand 16th-century **Kılıç Ali Paşa Hamamı** *(kilicalipasahamami.com)* in Karaköy and the modest **Çukurcuma Hamamı** *(cukurcumahamami.com)*, a recently restored neighbourhood bathhouse.

Most of these hamams have dedicated bathing areas or times for males and females; the exception is the Çukurcuma Hamamı, which allows mixed bathing (swimsuits mandatory). Treatments usually last for around 45 minutes but it's always possible to continue steaming yourself afterwards.

Pera Palace

Afternoon Tea at the Pera Palace

Built to provide suitably luxurious accommodation for passengers on the newly inaugurated *Orient Express*, the **Pera Palace** *(perapalace.com)* is the most storied hotel in Türkiye. It has hosted many notable guests since its 1892 opening, including Agatha Christie, who wrote *Murder on the Orient Express* in room 411. To experience the glamour of this İstanbul institution, consider reserving a table for the hotel's daily afternoon tea (₺2500), which is offered in the Moorish-style **Kubbelli Lounge**, the largest and most elegant space in the building.

İstanbul Modern

Cutting-Edge Contemporary Art

Housed in a spectacular Renzo Piano–designed building next to the Bosphorus, **İstanbul Modern** *(istanbulmodern.org; adult/concession ₺750/470)* is home to an extensive collection of Turkish art that is showcased in a multi-roomed exhibition gallery. The museum also stages a constantly refreshed program of expertly curated exhibitions by high-profile local and international artists. Facilities include a terrace restaurant with Bosphorus views and a design shop selling quality souvenirs and gifts.

Next to the museum is the **Galataport** retail and entertainment development, which has a popular Bosphorus-side promenade.

INSIGHT

The Ghosts of the Taurus Express

Oliver Smith's first-ever Lonely Planet assignment took him to Syria, where he saw a 100-year-old poster marketing the Taurus Express, a 'three-continent' service that once connected Paris with Lebanon and Egypt. Listen carefully, and you can still hear its echoes.

WORDS BY OLIVER SMITH
Oliver is a travel journalist and the author of On This Holy Island: A Modern Pilgrimage Across Britain.

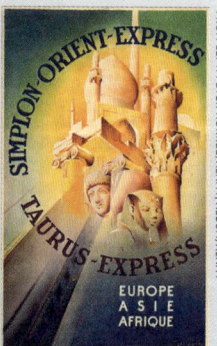

FROM LEFT: PETER HORREE/ALAMY, ALBUM/ALAMY

IN 2009, BEFORE the start of the Syrian Civil War, I found myself in the Baron Hotel in Aleppo on my first assignment for Lonely Planet. An ancient travel poster hung on the hotel's 1st-floor landing.

That poster was not far off a hundred years old, weathered and crinkled at the edges, but its ink was still vivid. It showed the Arch of Ctesiphon – part of a ruined city beside the Tigris river – rising over an ochre desert. Below were the words: 'London–Baghdad in 8 Days by Simplon-Orient-Express & Taurus-Express' and the promise 'Safety, Rapidity, Economy'. In the decades after that travel poster was published, the concept of luxury rail travel from Europe into the Middle East became impractical. Indeed, even in the decade and a half since I saw the poster, the assurance of safe and rapid transport in this region has acquired a new, cruel irony.

But – if you know where to look – there are still ghosts of the old Orient Express in the Middle East. Or, more accurately, its eastern counterpart, the Taurus Express – which waited for Orient Express trains arriving from Paris on the Bosphorus, and then shuttled passengers eastward into Asia. Though its own route culminated in İstanbul, the Orient Express marketed itself extensively on the lure of these eastern destinations – promising travel from London to the Citadel of Aleppo and the bazaars of Tehran, from Paris to the palm groves of Basra and the tombs of the Pharaohs in Egypt. It sold itself as a three-continent train, bringing together Europe, Asia and a slither of Africa. Here was the 'Orient' that had first granted the service its name.

A Brief History

The history of the Taurus Express is a short but fascinating one. The first direct Orient Express trains from Paris hauled into İstanbul in 1889 – but it took over four decades more for the Compagnie Internationale des Wagons-Lits to launch its sister, the Taurus Express, from Haydarpaşa station on the city's Asian shore in 1930. Looking rather like a French château, Haydarpaşa is one of the last places you can catch an echo of this golden age of luxury rail – to imagine the commotion of passengers and luggage arriving by water from the European shore, and the carriages of polished leather and plush upholstery that awaited them.

Long-distance services no longer depart from Haydarpaşa – but you can follow the original route of the former Taurus Express by catching a train from İstanbul's more humdrum Söğütlüçeşme station just over a mile away. From here, workaday services run southeast through Anatolia to the city of Konya – famed for its whirling dervishes – before hurrying south to the Mediterranean along a scenic stretch. Trains clatter over lofty viaducts and through dark tunnels hewn into the Taurus Mountains (the range that granted the service its name). Beyond the mustard-yellow station at Adana, however, the trail goes cold.

Trains have not operated from Türkiye across the border into Aleppo since the Civil War – but it was Syria's northern city that served as a Taurus Express hub for the Middle East, with travellers forking off east to Iraq and Iran, while others continued south to Lebanon, Palestine and Egypt. At the time of writing, Aleppo's 1912-built station was still standing, its Ottoman-era facade showing only small signs of damage from the war.

The Baron

But arguably the greatest relic of this era is a hotel. The Baron Hotel was a favoured stop-off for Orient Express and Taurus Express passengers on their comings and goings in the Middle East – used by Theodore Roosevelt and Charles de Gaulle, Kemal Atatürk and TE Lawrence. Indeed it was in Room 203 that Agatha Christie penned the first words to *Murder on the Orient Express* (which actually begins on the Taurus Express in Syria). At the time of my visit, the hotel was caught in a kind of time warp, little changed since the writer pressed the keys on her typewriter. There was a grand timber bar with weathered leather sofas, an echoing marble hallway that had reverberated with famous footfalls and, of course, those antique posters lining the walls. Here you can discover a vestige of original Orient Express glamour – despite the upheavals that followed. The hotel has also sustained war damage – but at the time of writing is still there.

> But – if you know where to look – there are still ghosts of the old Orient Express in the Middle East. Or, more accurately, its eastern counterpart, the Taurus Express

The Ghosts Live On

The decline of the Taurus Express came about gradually – conflicts in Israel, Palestine and Lebanon truncated it, while wars in Iraq and Syria sounded a death knell for international services. National networks, always limited in extent, now present a mixed picture in the Middle East – but currently the prospects for a revival of long-distance, cross-border trains is next to non-existent. Though, in one sense, the service is not entirely gone. A train with the name *Toros Express*, though currently paused, still regularly runs across the mountains from Konya to Adana in Türkiye. It is not a luxury train, nor does it range far – but in a small way, it keeps the candle burning for its long-lost, three-continent namesake.

Venice Simplon-Orient-Express

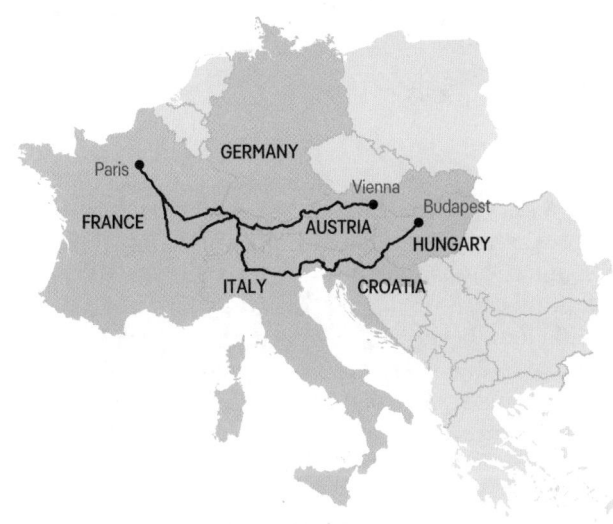

THE SIMPLON, ARLBERG & BEYOND

Paris to Constantinople via Vienna and Budapest wasn't the only route that Compagnie Internationale des Wagons-Lits trains serviced. Two equally emblematic routes – the Simplon-Orient-Express and the Arlberg Orient Express – were launched in the first decades of the 20th century. These luxurious spinoffs were the predecessors of today's ultra-glamorous revival services, some of which follow original Orient Express routes.

Paris to Venice:
The Simplon Route
p192

Venice
City Guide
p206

Venice to Budapest:
The Simplon Route
p214

Paris to Vienna:
The Arlberg Route
p226

Orient Express
Revivals
p240

Beyond the
Orient Express
p246

Paris

Imagine it's 1906 and you are about to board the first departure of the Orient Express service travelling from Paris to Italy through the newly built Simplon Tunnel under the Swiss Alps. The prospect of passing through this engineering marvel would have been thrilling, and so too would have been the greatly reduced travel time to one of Europe's most magical destinations. Emulating this journey today is just as exciting, as you'll travel on ultra-fast trains through stunning scenery and have plenty of opportunities to explore en route.

Virginia Maxwell

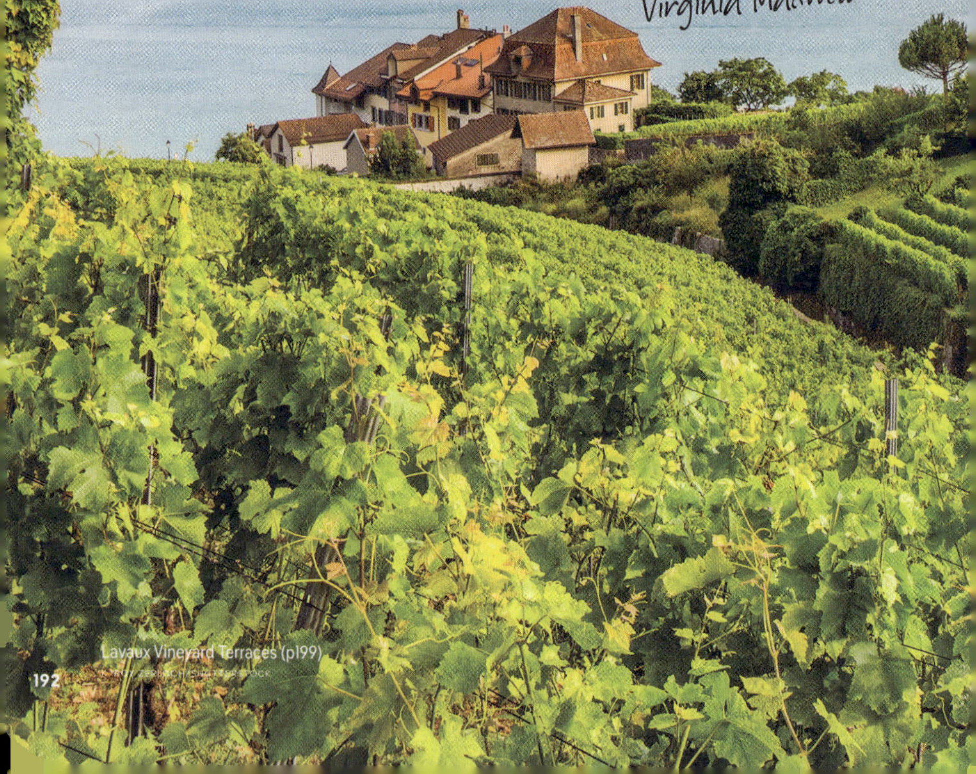

Lavaux Vineyard Terraces (p199)

ROY ZERLOCH/SHUTTERSTOCK

Venice
THE SIMPLON ROUTE

1185 KMS · 10 HOURS' RIDE

THIS LEG:

- Gare de Lyon
- Bourg-en-Bresse
- Bellegarde-sur-Valserine
- Geneva
- Lausanne
- Neuchâtel
- Zürich
- Milan
- Verona
- Vicenza
- Padua
- Venice

Riding Notes

The first stages of this journey travel between Paris Gare de Lyon and Gare de Lausanne on the ultra-fast and comfortable TGV Lyria. From Lausanne, the route heads northeast to Zürich Hauptbahnhof on a Swiss Federal Railways (SBB CFF FFS) InterCity train, then down to Milano Centrale on a Trenitalia EuroCity service. From Milan, Trenitalia trains, including high-speed Frecciarossa, head to Venezia Santa Lucia.

Breaking Your Journey
The cities of Lausanne and Milan are obvious places to pause for a few days, and there are also three enchanting cities in the northern Italian region of Veneto – Verona, Vicenza and Padua – that are well worth dedicated visits.

Virginia's Tips

BEST MEAL Start your journey at swish Le Train Bleu. (p196)

FAVOURITE VIEW Cascading down to the shore of scenic Lake Geneva, the Lavaux Vineyard Terraces are a spectacular sight. (p199)

ESSENTIAL STOP No city can match the ethereal beauty of Venice. (p206)

TIP Book well in advance to see Leonardo's *Last Supper*. (p203)

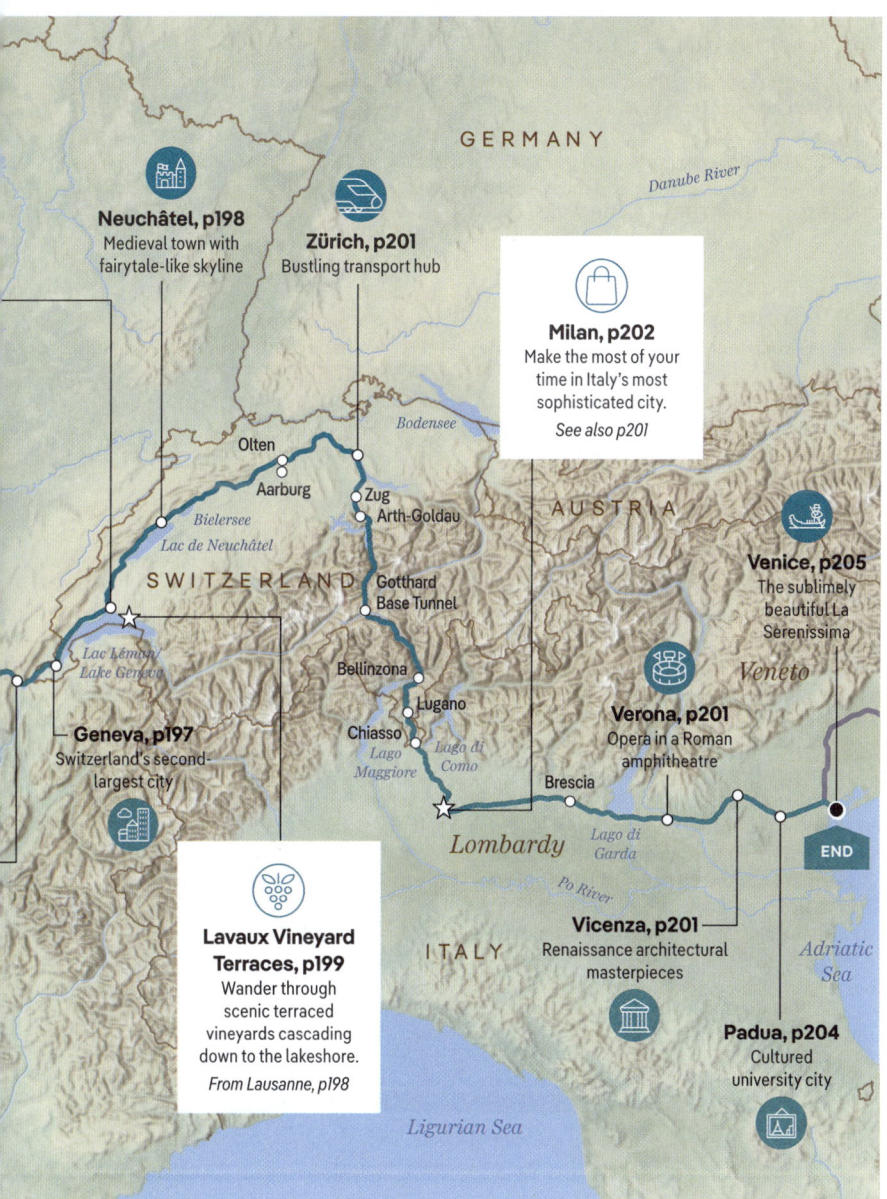

> **STARTING THE JOURNEY**
>
> Six daily double-decker TGV Lyria trains operated by **SNCF** *(sncf-connect.com)* travel between the Gare de Lyon and Lausanne. Three travel a scenic route via Bourg-en-Bresse, Bellegarde-sur-Valserine and Geneva-Coravin, which is the journey we describe here. The secondary route, via Vallorbe, Frasne, Mouchard, Dole and Dijon, takes an extra 20 minutes. When booking, try to snaffle a seat on the train's upper level as these have the best views. Services usually depart from Hall 2; scan your ticket to enter the platform. **Ticket and information offices** *(4.45am-1.30am daily)* can be found in Hall 3 (downstairs) and in the Galerie des Fresques; the Hall 3 office also has a left-luggage facility.

Gare de Lyon

As you enter the upstairs halls of Paris' second-busiest station, **Gare de Lyon** *(garedelyon.fr)*, you will find yourself in the midst of a perpetually busy ballet of suitcase-wheeling commuters moving through two huge halls with lofty iron and glass roofs. In between the halls is the delightful **Galerie des Fresques**, adorned with scenes of the cities to which passengers travelled in 1900, when the current station building was constructed and the frescoes were painted. Retail outlets here include a branch of the Parisian patisserie **Ladurée** *(laduree.fr; €)*, beloved for its delectable macarons; consider purchasing a selection to enjoy on your journey.

Allow time to begin your journey in style by dining in the magnificent **Le Train Bleu** (right), which opened as the Gare de Lyon's buffet in 1901. Its current name dates from 1963, and references the legendary train that serviced towns along the French Riviera in the 19th century. The main dining room here is a splendiferous showcase of frescoed walls and ceilings, chandeliers, carved and gilded wood, brass fittings, blue leather seating, stiffly starched white napery and elegant glassware. The menu, overseen by renowned French chef Michel Rostang, lives up to the setting, as does the impeccable service. Book well in advance to be sure of snaffling a table. The bar lounge isn't as swish, but it's a great choice if you're after a coffee or snack.

Bourg-en-Bresse

Prepare to enjoy your trip, as the TGV Lyria offers comfortable seats with power sockets, air-conditioning, a buffet car and free wi-fi that includes reading matter, TV shows and films. Flat farmland scenery unfolds after the train leaves Paris, featuring checkerboard-coloured fields of crops, wheels of hay and gold-coloured stone farmhouses with red terracotta roofs. Diminutive church spires can be spied in the distance, as can remnants of ancient aqueducts and hilltop villages. Heading towards the first stop at a cracking 320km per hour, the train passes through the **Mâcon wine region** before arriving at the first stop, Bourg-en-Bresse, located in the Auvergne-Rhône-Alpes region at the base of the Jura Mountains.

Bellegarde-sur-Valserine

Continuing east, the train slows its pace and travels along the single-track Haut-Bugey line to the mountain hamlet of Bellegarde-

---

Gare de Lyon, Paris — 365km — Bourg-en-Bresse

Look out for the vineyards of the Mâcon wine region

Le Train Bleu, Gare de Lyon, Paris

sur-Valserine, located at the confluence of the Rhône and Valserine rivers. This stretch of the journey showcases spectacular mountain scenery, climbing through forests, passing through tunnels, crossing the Ain Gorge on the **Cize-Bolozon Viaduct** and following alongside the **Lac de Nantua**, a glacial turquoise-blue lake fringed with rocky limestone massifs. Chalet-style houses start to dot the landscape, and plenty of cows appear on mountainsides.

Geneva

You'll enter the second country on this stretch of the trip 10 minutes after leaving Bellegarde-sur-Valserine and passing through

BEST PLACES TO EAT & DRINK

Le Train Bleu, Paris €€€
Operating for over a century, this magnificent belle époque–style restaurant in the Gare de Lyon is an unforgettable spot for a pre-departure meal. *le-train-bleu.com*

Camparino, Milan €€
Celebrate your arrival in Italy by sipping on a Campari-based cocktail and grazing on *aperitivo* nibbles in this historic bar in the magnificent Galleria Vittorio Emanuele II. *camparino.com*

Caffè Pedrocchi, Padua €€
Operating since 1831, this cafe in Padua's historical centre is an atmospheric stop for a coffee and pastry. *caffepedrocchi.it*

Bellegarde-sur-Valserine — 48km — *Cross the dramatic 73m-high Cize-Bolozon Viaduct* — 27km — Geneva

Beau-Rivage Palace Hotel (p200)

Lausanne

Few cities have settings as delightful as Lausanne's, making it an excellent choice for a multi-night break. The city's proximity to the Lavaux Vineyard Terraces (right), a scenic day excursion, offers an extra incentive to do this.

Your train arrives at the handsome heritage-listed **Gare de Lausanne** (sbb.ch), which has facilities including a **ticket and information office** (6.30am-8pm Mon-Fri, 7am-7.30pm Sat & Sun) that shares space with a bureau de change. There are left-luggage lockers on Platform 1. From the station, you can walk or take the metro uphill to the city centre or downhill to Ouchy on the lake's edge.

Though the Gothic Old Town and most of Lausanne's residential neighbourhoods are stacked on a hillside, **Lac Léman** is the hub of local life in fine weather, with beaches, flower-fringed promenades, outdoor activities and bars aplenty. Lausanne was a popular extended stop on the original Paris–Venice Simplon route, and Ouchy, with its luxurious belle époque Beau-Rivage Palace Hotel (p200), was where many wealthy passengers paused en route – even if you can't emulate them by booking into the hotel, consider dining in its elegant flagship restaurant or enjoying a drink at its lake-facing terrace cafe.

a long tunnel. On the Swiss side of the border, steep-sloped vineyards can be admired from the left side of the train and glimpses of Lac Léman (aka Lake Geneva) backed by mist-garlanded alps tantalise from the right-hand side. It's a relatively short distance to **Geneva-Cornavin**, where the train pauses for passengers to alight before continuing on its final, 40-minute stretch to Lausanne. Running alongside the lake's western shore, the train passes by historic hamlets, modern housing estates, small tracts of vines and the edge of the Parc Naturel Régional Jura Vaudois.

Neuchâtel

The original Paris–Venice route travelled from Lausanne to Milan via Brig in Switzerland through the newly constructed Simplon Tunnel to Domodossola in Italy. It's still possible to take this journey, but construction works mean buses are sometimes substituted for trains on

Continues on page 200

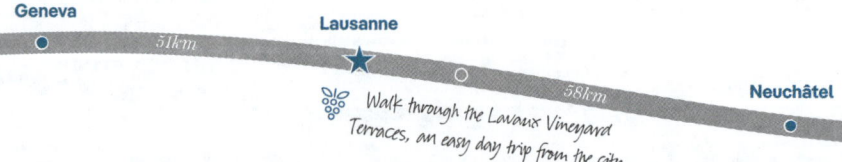

Walk Through Vineyard Terraces

Cascading down the lower slopes of mountains backdropping the northern shore of Lac Léman, the World Heritage–listed Lavaux Vineyard Terraces near Lausanne are a spectacularly scenic destination for a half-day walk.

HOW TO

Getting here: Regional train S40 or S41 (direction: Fribourg/Freiburg) from Gare de Lausanne to Grandvaux.

Tip: The lakeside village of Lutry is between Lausanne and the terraces and is a delightful spot in which to stay or eat.

More info: Tourist offices in Lausanne, Montreux and Cully stock maps showing walking trails.

Dating back to the 12th century, the vineyards are divided into neat parcels by ancient dry-stone walls that drink in the hot summer sun during the day and radiate a slow, nourishing heat at night. The proximity of Lac Léman ensures a mild, temperate climate. Crisp fruity whites crafted with Chasselas grapes represent 80% of AOC Lavaux production – the remaining 20% are fruity reds made with gamay, pinot noir and Salvagnin grapes.

The best way to explore is to take a regional train to Grandvaux then walk downhill from the station and follow the serpentine roads and vineyard paths east to St-Saphorin via Cully, Épesses and Rivaz, or west to Ouchy via Lutry. Both meandering routes are well signposted for walkers and take approximately two hours to traverse. Each village you'll encounter will have a *caveau des vignerons* (wine-growers' cellar), where you can taste local tipples, and there are plenty of picnic spots and viewpoints amid the vines. **Maison Lavaux** *(lavaux-unesco.ch)* in Grandvaux offers wine-themed exhibitions and guided walks.

EXPERIENCE ★

Above: Grapevine
Right: Lavaux Vineyard Terraces

BEST PLACES TO SLEEP

Rivage Lutry, Lavaux region €€
Charming old-world hotel in lovely Lutry near the vineyard terraces, with a bistro and rooms overlooking Lac Léman. *hotelrivagelutry.ch*

Beau-Rivage Palace Hotel, Lausanne €€€
A luxury hotel that has been hosting train passengers since the launch of the Simplon-Orient-Express route. Request a lake-facing room. *brp.ch*

Palazzo Mantua Benavides, Padua €€€
This stunning 16th-century mansion just steps from the Cappella degli Scrovegni offers eight rooms and apartments furnished with antiques. *palazzomantuabenavides.com*

Continued from page 198

legs of the journey – check **Swiss Federal Railways** *(sbb.ch)* or **Trenitalia** *(trenitalia.com)* for updates. The alternative is to take a detour to Zürich on SBB CFF FFS Train 5 (Direction: Rorschach), which travels via lakeside **Neuchâtel** in the foothills of the Jura Mountains. Approaching Neuchâtel station, the fairytale-like skyline is studded with the spires, domes and pitched roofs of its enchanting medieval Old Town. From here, the journey to Zürich passes another lake, **Bielersee**, which is fringed with terraced vineyards. Towards the end of your journey, look out for the 17th-century castle dramatically sited next to a river high above the town of Aarburg, on the approach to Olten.

Ponte Pietra, Verona

Zürich

Arriving at Zürich Hauptbahnhof (p232), it's immediately apparent that this is a major transport hub – in fact, it's the largest train station in Switzerland. There are frequent services to Milan on various types of train – the most comfortable are the EuroCity (EC) services, which take approximately 3½ hours. These have two classes, seats with power sockets (1st class only), air-conditioning, a buffet car and free onboard wi-fi. Settle back, preferably in a window seat on the right-hand side of the train, to drink in picture-perfect views of green pastures, sun-spangled lakes and majestic snow-capped mountains on the Swiss leg of your journey. After stopping at Zug and Arth-Goldau, the train enters the **Gotthard Base Tunnel**, the longest and deepest railway tunnel in the world. After 20 minutes in this Swiss-built engineering marvel, the train emerges from the base of the Alps, stopping in **Bellinzona**, the picturesque lakeside city of **Lugano**, **Chiasso** on the Swiss–Italian border and **Como S Giovanni**, where many alight to spend time in the famed lake district. From here, it's a 40-minute leg to Milan.

Milan

The second-busiest railway station in Italy (after Roma Termini), **Milano Centrale** *(milanocentrale.it)* is one of Europe's grandest stations, with massive steel-and-glass canopies enclosing the platforms and stunning art deco and liberty-style statues, carvings and mosaics adorning the interior and exterior of the building.

The **left-luggage facility** *(7am-9pm)*, **Trenitalia ticket office** *(6.15am-9.30pm)* and **Italo ticket office** *(6.15am-8.45pm)* are on the ground floor. Cafes, restaurants and fast-food stands abound. Take subway line 3 to Piazza del Duomo (seven minutes) to explore the city (p202).

Verona

A number of different trains operate on the busy Milan–Venice route; the fastest and most comfortable are the Frecciarossa services, which take 2½ hours. These are frequent and have two classes, free wi-fi and seats with power chargers. The scenery on the first leg of the journey is a letdown after the magnificence of the landscapes spotted on the journey from Zürich, but after the train's stop in **Brescia** you'll start to see a scattering of medieval settlements on hilltops and geographical features such as **Lake Garda** and the **Dolomite Mountains** appear on the left-hand side of the train. After 75 minutes, the train arrives in Verona, the city famous as the setting for Shakespeare's tale of star-crossed lovers Romeo and Juliet. A cluster of pretty piazzas in the historic centre and a majestic 1st-century **amphitheatre** that hosts **opera** in summer are the main draw here, making a half-day stop worth considering.

Vicenza

The next stop is Vicenza, a city inextricably linked with the great Renaissance architect Andrea Palladio. If architecture is your passion, alighting here to visit his masterwork, the villa known as **La Rotonda** *(villalarotonda.it; tickets €12-15)*, located 2.5km outside the city centre, is highly recommended. In the centre itself are more of Palladio's creations, including two *palazzi* (palaces) on Piazza dei Signori,

Continues on page 204

Neuchâtel — Zürich 129km — 257km — Milan — 141km — Verona 45km — Vicenza

Zoom through the 57km-long Gotthard Base Tunnel

Cross Lake Lugano and snatch glimpses of Lake Como

Spot Lake Garda and the Dolomite Mountains

CITY GUIDE:
Milan

Italy's second-largest city is often described as a business hub, but it's a lot more than that. This is the epicentre of Italian fashion, design and architecture, a city that prizes art and culture as highly as its delicious local cuisine.

HOW TO

Getting around: The city centre can be explored on foot; to venture further afield there are five convenient metro lines. Tickets covering 90 minutes' travel can be purchased from machines at metro stations.

Sleeping: Bargains are hard to come by when it comes to centrally located sleeping options. Recommended options include hostel **Casa Base** (base.milano.it; €) in the Tortona district near Navigli, and the undeniably faded but clean and welcoming **Hotel Teco** (hotelteco.com; €) near Milano Centrale.

Tip: If you're keen to visit the roof terraces at the Duomo and avoid the ubiquitous queues, book a 'Fast Track' pass well in advance.

More info: The city's official **tourism info point** (yesmilano.it; 10am-6pm) is located at Piazza del Duomo 14, in the Palazzo Reale.

Position yourself in the centre of Piazza del Duomo: this is the heart of Milan, the visual representation of its long-held wealth and power, and the place where every traveller should kick off their city visit. As well as the Gothic facade of the **Duomo** (duomomilano.it; tickets €10-36), you'll spot the Galleria Vittorio Emanuele II, the neoclassical **Palazzo Reale** (Royal Palace; palazzorealemilano.it; adult/student €15/10) and the **Museo del Novecento** (museodelnovecento.org; adult/student €5/3). Worth a visit are historic **Giacomo Caffè** (giacomomilano.com; €€) in Palazzo Reale, and Pasticceria Marchesi 1824 (p203) and Camparino (p197) in the Galleria.

SHOPPING CITY

Milanese have spent centuries perfecting the art of shopping, and their city has the reputation as being home to Italy's most sophisticated retail scene. To see the truth of this, head to the **Galleria Vittorio Emanuele II**, often described as the world's most beautiful shopping arcade. Opened in 1877, the building has always been home to shops specialising in luxury goods, a tradition that continues today. The most famous tenant is local fashion powerhouse **Prada**, which operates two boutiques, a gallery and elegant Pasticceria Marchese 1824 here.

More luxury shopping can be found a short distance northeast of the Galleria, in the **Quadrilatero d'Oro** (Golden Quadrilateral). Framed by four streets – Via Montenapoleone, Via della Spiga, Via Sant'Andrea and Via A Manzoni – the area's charming cobblestone streets are home to boutiques showcasing long-established and up-and-coming designers. During the **Milano Fashion Weeks** *(milanofashionweek.cameramoda.it)* in February/March and September/October, the streets of the Quadrilatero are awash with fashion-forward folk.

Naviglio Grande Canal

Enjoy an Aperitivo with Locals

Enjoying an *aperitivo* (pre-dinner drink) at a bar alongside the pretty canals of Milan's **Naviglio** neighbourhood is a much-loved local tradition, but it can be a challenge to identify a good venue amidst the growing number of tourist-trap businesses now operating here. Follow the local lead and head to long-standing favourites **MAG Cafe** *(farmily.webflow.io)*, **Pinch** *(pinchmilano.com)*, **Rita** *(ritacocktails.com)* or **Ugo** *(ugobar.it)*. To get here, take the M2 metro (Green line) to Porta Genova.

Opt for Full Art & Design Immersion

Great artworks are in plentiful supply in Milan, with galleries showcasing everything from Renaissance frescoes to cutting-edge contemporary works. The major attraction is, of course, Leonardo's **The Last Supper** *(cenacolovinciano.org; adult/student €15/2)*, but many art aficionados rate the **Pinacoteca di Brera** *(pinacotecabrera.org; adult/student €15/10)* even more highly. Its small but select collection includes masterpieces by Raphael, Mantegna and Piero della Francesca. For contemporary art, head to the **Fondazione Prada** *(fondazioneprada.org; adult/student €15/12)*.

BEST PLACES TO EAT & DRINK

Pasticceria Marchesi 1824 €€€
Book on opentable.com to enjoy a *molto elegante* lunch in this Prada-owned gem. *marchesi1824.com*

Trattoria Masuelli S Marco €€€
Does this trattoria serve the best risotto *alla milanese* in town? We say yes. *masuellitrattoria.com*

Ratanà €€€ Savour refined modern Milanese cuisine in a converted railway building with outdoor terrace. *ratana.it*

Continued from page 201

the nearby **Palazzo Chiericati** *(museicivici vicenza.it; adult/student €8/6)* and the exquisite **Teatro Olimpico** *(teatrolimpicovicenza.it; adult/student €12/9)*, the architect's final creation. If, after all the architectural viewing, you feel an overnight stay is a sensible idea, **B&B Portico Rosso** *(porticorosso.it; €)* is a friendly, 600-year-old Vicentine house decorated with colour and flair. Breakfasting in its beautiful garden is a highlight.

Padua

After indulging in architecture, those who also love art may also choose to alight at the next stop, the delightful university city of Padova (Padua). The trip from Vicenza takes a mere 17 minutes, passing through the built-up outskirts of Vicenza and then through a landscape where small tracts of farmland sit beside an ever-growing number of factories and small industrial estates.

Padua is home to home to one of the great artistic achievements of the Italian Renaissance, Giotto's early-14th-century fresco cycle in the **Cappella degli Scrovegni** *(cappelladegli scrovegni.it; tickets €16, advance booking essential)*. If you decide to alight and visit this city, consider staying overnight in the sumptuous Palazzo Mantua Benavides (p200) is a real treat, as is enjoying a coffee at historic Caffè Pedrocchi (p197), where you can add your name to a client list that has included literary luminaries such as Stendhal, Goethe and Lord Byron.

Along the Way We Met...

NOAH BROCKMANN & CLARA SCHMIDTKE We're on our gap-year trip before starting university. We worked for six months to save money and are now travelling through Europe by train using Interrail passes. So far we've been to the Netherlands, France and Italy – French and Italian trains are much better than German trains! Walking in the Calanques near Cassis in the south of France has been the highlight so far. We're tired but really happy. After Venice we're heading to Croatia, Austria and Switzerland.

Noah and Clara are students from Hamburg in Germany.

CLARA & NOAH'S TIP: *Pay extra to travel in 1st class. For students, it's not much more money but it's far more comfortable.*

Vicenza

30km

Teatro Olimpico, Vicenza

Venice

Prepare yourself for a scenic approach to the famed floating city of Venice. After leaving the industrial town of **Venezia-Mestre**, the train proceeds along the 3.85km-long **Ponte della Libertà** (Liberty Bridge) over the calm blue-green waters of the **Venetian Lagoon**, before arriving at **Stazione Venezia Santa Lucia** *(venezia santalucia.it)*. This distinctive modernist building was designed and constructed during the fascist era and has a low, elongated facade that evocatively references the sleek design of 20th-century trains. After exiting, you'll be confronted with the world's most spectacularly beautiful waterway – the Grand Canal (p210).

WINES OF NORTHEAST ITALY

Two famous wine-growing areas, the Valpolicella Region and the Prosecco Hills (Le Colline del Prosecco), are located in this green corner of Italy. Valpolicella's fame as a wine region predates the Roman Empire, and today it produces four flagship types of red wine: Amarone, Valpolicella Classico Superiore, Valpolicella Superiore Ripasso and sweet Recioto della Valpolicella. Amarone, which has a rich and concentrated flavour, is considered the flagship product. The sparkling wine called Prosecco Superiore produced in the foothills of the Dolomites north of Venice is equally prized. Consider trying these as you travel through the region.

Padua — 34km — **Venice**

⚠ *Warning! Do not alight at Venezia-Mestre; continue to Venezia Santa Lucia*

CITY GUIDE:
Venice

Canal, Santa Croce

Known for centuries as the Most Serene Republic of Venice and still fondly known as La Serenissima, this fragile settlement floating in the Venetian Lagoon is one of the world's most beautiful and romantic cities. Exploring its narrow *calli* (streets) and cruising its canals will be a journey highlight.

WORDS BY VIRGINIA MAXWELL
Virginia has researched multiple Italian cities for Lonely Planet; Venice is her favourite of them all.

Arriving

Venezia Santa Lucia All trains arrive at Venezia Santa Lucia station, which is located on the Grand Canal. It's a relatively small station with a few shops, fast-food stands, a bureau de change and a left-luggage facility (next to Platform 1). The **Trenitalia** *(6am-9pm)* and **Italo ticket offices** *(6.30am-8.30pm)* are in front of Platforms 12 and 13.

From the station, cross the Ponte degli Scalzi bridge to access the Santa Croce and San Polo neighbourhoods. For Dorsoduro, San Marco, Castello and other neighbourhoods, a *vaporetto* (water bus) is your best bet. There are five *vaporetto* stops in front of the station – to reach Rialto or San Marco, take *vaporetto* number 1. There's a water taxi station in front of the train station, close to the bridge.

HOW MUCH FOR A

Spritz €6

Seafood pasta €20

30-minute gondola ride €90

Getting Around

The best way to explore is on foot. The only transport available are forms of watercraft.
Vaporetto Most visitors will board one of the city's famed *vaporetti* operated by **Actv** *(actv.avmspa.it)* at least once. These traverse the city's canals and lagoon and offer a convenient and scenic way to explore. Single-trip tickets are pricey, but the one-/two-/three- or seven-day passes offer better value. *Vaporetti* travel to the major *sestieri* (districts), to Mestre on the mainland and to the islands (Lido, Murano, Burano and Torcello). Children under the age of six travel free. Tickets and passes can be purchased at many of the city's main *vaporetto* stops. Tickets must be validated before boarding. Stops along the routes are easily identified by yellow signs clearly displaying the stop name.
Motoscafo *Motoscafi* (water taxis) are a popular but expensive way to sightsee or get from point A to point B. They can be found at designated stands around the city or booked with **Radio Taxi Venezia** *(+39 041 5964; radiotaxivenezia.com)*. Surcharges apply at night.
Gondola Gondolas are only used by tourists, who pay a considerable amount to be propelled along canals on a fixed-price journey. Gondola stations are found throughout the city; look for 'Servizio Gondole' signs.

For vaporetto schedules and trip planning, go to Actv:

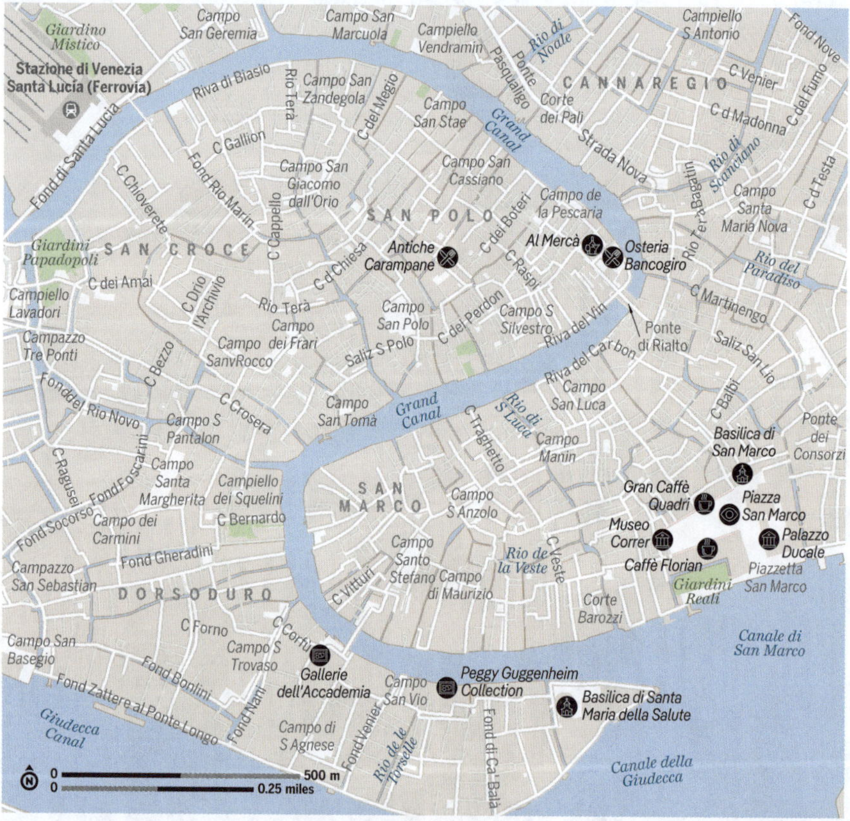

A DAY IN VENICE

Morning: Get your city bearings by boarding the number 1 *vaporetto* in front of the railway station and enjoying a scenic journey along the length of the **Grand Canal** (p210). Alight at Vallaresso and Giardinetti near **Piazza San Marco** (p212) to explore this monument-rich plaza, which is the symbolic heart of the city.

Afternoon: After a coffee and snack at San Marco's venerable **Caffè Florian** (p212) or at the more-affordable espresso bar at **Gran Caffè Quadri** opposite, walk to **Dorsoduro**, home to top-drawer attractions including the **Gallerie dell'Accademia** (p213), **Peggy Guggenheim Collection** (p213) and landmark **Basilica di Santa Maria della Salute**.

Evening: From Salute, board the number 1 again, this time heading to **Rialto**. Enjoy a drink and some *cicheti* (small tapas-style snacks) standing at the bar at **Al Mercà** or sitting at a canalside table at nearby **Osteria Bancogiro**. Then kick on to a seafood-focused dinner at Venice's beloved trattoria **Antiche Carampane** (right).

Where to Stay

San Marco is the tourist hub and can be unpleasantly crowded and noisy. As a general rule it's better to stay in one of the other *sestieri* – San Polo, Santa Croce, Dorsoduro, Cannaregio and Castello are all central and offer plenty of places to eat and drink. To save money and avoid the crowds, local areas such as Sant'Elena, Giudecca and the Lido are worth considering. Remember, though, that the latter two can only be accessed via *vaporetto*.

BEST PLACES TO STAY

Combo Venezia € Well-run hostel occupying a grand convent building in Cannaregio. thisiscombo.com

Le Terese € Simple accommodation in a converted 18th-century granary in Dorsoduro. leterese.com

Oltre Il Giardino €€ Gorgeous San Polo garden villa offering double rooms and suites. oltreilgiardino-venezia.com

Novecento €€ Family-run and super-stylish San Marco boutique hotel. novecento.biz

Where to Eat

It can be difficult to source good meals here, as too many businesses serve over-priced and underwhelming tourist-focused fare. Look for *bàcari* (small local taverns) and *enoteche* (wine bars) serving *cicheti*, and for *osterie* (casual eateries) and restaurants serving local seafood dishes.

VENETIAN CHICHETI

While wandering along the city's narrow streets, keep a lookout for small bars or taverns. These much-loved local institutions, known as *bàcari*, serve drinks including *ombre* (small glasses of wine) and a range of bite-sized snacks that are collectively referred to as *chicheti* (pictured bottom right). Invariably displayed in a glass case near the bar, *chicheti* range from small filled panini or *tramezzini* (triangular sandwiches), to crostini topped with Venetian specialities including *sarde in saor* (fresh sardine fillets in a sweet and sour sauce) and *baccalà mantecato* (whipped salted cod).

The range of *chiceti* on offer varies according to the *bàcaro* – for delicious choices, head to **All'Arco** *(€)* near the Rialto, which makes excellent use of local produce such as fresh plump shrimps from the lagoon, white Bassano del Grappa asparagus and violet Sant'Erasmo artichoke; or **Cantine del Vino già Schiavi** *(€)* in Dorsoduro, which does magical things with local cheeses and meats.

BEST PLACES TO EAT & DRINK

Rosa Salva € Institution serving pastries since 1879; cafes in San Marco and Castello. rosasalva.it

Vino Vero € Canalside wine bar in Cannaregio with good *chicheti*. vinovero.wine/luoghi/venezia

Vini da Gigio €€ Delightful traditional trattoria in Cannaregio. vinidagigio.com

Antiche Carampane €€€ Many locals and regular visitors consider this Venice's best restaurant. antichecarampane.com

Cruise the Grand Canal

The city's number-one tourism attraction is lined with over 50 *palazzi* (palaces) that form a multicoloured and marvellous showcase of Venetian architecture over the centuries. Cruising its length is a showstopper of an experience, one that every visitor should embark upon.

HOW TO

Route: Vaporetto No 1 travels from Piazzale Roma along the length of the Grand Canal, pausing to drop off and take on passengers at 16 stops including Stazione Venezia Santa Lucia, Rialto, Accademia and San Marco before continuing across the lagoon to the Lido (Beach). The entire trip takes one hour, or 45 minutes from the train station to San Marco.

Cost: A 75-minute ticket costs €9.50, but the 24-hour pass (€25) offers better value.

Tip: Head to the front of the *vaporetto* straight after boarding to snaffle a prime seat on the outdoor deck.

More info: avm.avmspa.it

Beginning your journey at **1 Piazzale Roma** is a good idea, as this will maximise your chance of securing a seat with a good view.

After leaving the dock, the *vaporetto* passes under one of the few modern structures you'll see on this trip – the glass and steel **2 Ponte della Costituzione** (aka Ponte di Calatrava). Ahead, after the railway station, you'll pass a progression of *palazzi*, many now operating as hotels. Look out for the handsome 13th-century **3 Fontego dei Turchi**, now the city's Museum of Natural History; the ornate **4 Palazzo Vendramin Calergi**, home to the city's casino; and **5 Ca' Pesaro**, now the Gallery of Modern Art.

A little way on is the exquisite **6 Ca' d'Oro**, a 15th-century filigreed confection in the Venetian Gothic style. Past this is the Rialto precinct with its Pescaria (fish market), fresh-produce stalls and landmark **7 Ponte di Rialto**, the Grand Canal's major crossing point. After the bridge, a profusion of multicoloured *palazzi* line both sides of the canal – one of the prettiest is the Venetian baroque-style

8 Ca' Rezzonico, now a museum of 18th-century Venetian culture.

After this you'll pass the timber **9 Ponte dell'Accademia** (Accademia Bridge); look out for **10 Palazzo Cavalli-Franchetti** on the San Marco side of the canal here.

VENETIAN GOTHIC

A unique blend of Italian, Byzantine and Islamic styles, Venetian Gothic architecture reflects the long and lucrative trading heritage of the Serene Republic. This trade brought local architects into contact with a rich array of building materials, engineering innovations and aesthetic ideals, which in turn led to them devising a distinctive new style in the 13th century that featured loggias of closely spaced small columns, elegantly tapered, Moorish-influenced arches and coloured patterning on wall surfaces. Ca d'Oro and the Palazzo Ducale are particularly wonderful examples of the style.

Ponte di Rialto and the Grand Canal

A bit further on, stone lions flank the water entrance to the **11 Peggy Guggenheim Collection**; look out for Marino Marini's cheeky *The Angel of the City* sculpture on its terrace.

Shortly after, you'll pass the **12 Basilica di Santa Maria della Salute** with its eye-catching dome and, on the other side of the canal, the campanile (bell tower) and massive Palazzo Ducale on **13 Piazza San Marco**. To the *palazzo*'s right (east) is the famed **14 Ponte dei Sospiri** (Bridge of Sighs).

Basilica di San Marco

Symbol of the City

A magnificent representation of the city's past glory, **Piazza San Marco** is lined by some of the city's most important institutions, chief among these being the **Basilica di San Marco** *(basilicasanmarco.it; tickets €10-30)*. Founded in the 9th century, the cathedral's interior is nearly as impressive as its dome- and mosaic-adorned facade. Next to the basilica is the massive Gothic-style **Palazzo Ducale** *(Doge's Palace; palazzoducale.visitmuve.it; tickets €25-30)*. On the main square, grand arcaded buildings including the **Museo Correr** *(correr.visitmuve.it; tickets €25-30)* possess the wow factor in spades.

CHURCH TREASURES

The lambent light and extraordinary physical beauty of Venice has stoked the imaginations of artists over centuries. A number of the great names of Renaissance art were born in the Veneto and spent their entire careers working here, becoming members of what would become known as the Venetian School – Titian, Tintoretto, Paolo Veronese, Giovanni Bellini, Giorgione, Canaletto and Carpaccio are the best known of these lauded local sons.

The Gallerie dell'Accademia (right) has a number of major Venetian School works in its collection, but many of the most important paintings can be admired in the city's churches. Particularly notable works include Titian's transcendent *Assunta* (Assumption) altarpiece and Bellini's *Madonna with Child* in the **Basilica di Santa Maria Gloriosa dei Frari** *(basilicadeifrari.it; adult/student €5/2)*; Tintoretto's *Presentation of the Virgin in the Temple* and *Last Judgement* in the **Chiesa della Madonna dell'Orto** *(chorusvenezia.org; adult/student €3.50/2.50)*; and Veronese's cycle in the **Chiesa di San Sebastiano** *(chorusvenezia.org; adult/student €3.50/2.50)*.

Sundae, Caffè Florian

Sip Coffee in Style

After visiting Piazza San Marco's monuments, it's time to investigate the square's historic cafes. Chief among these is **Caffè Florian** *(caffeflorian.com)*, which has been serving customers since 1720. **Gran Caffè Quadri** *(alajmo.it/pages/homepage-grancaffe-quadri)*, on the opposite side of the piazza, first opened its doors in 1775 and, like Florian, boasts exquisitely decorated salons and a terrace where patrons are serenaded by a small orchestra in warm weather. Both are *molto* expensive – for a more-affordable experience, Quadri's small espresso bar (mainly standing room) is a good option, as is the Correr Museum's 1st-floor cafe, which offers views over the square.

View Venice's Extraordinary Art

The city is blessed with many museums housed in *palazzi* and other historic buildings, which showcase extraordinary art and architecture.

HOW TO

When to go: Note that the Fondazione Querini Stampalia is closed on Mondays; the Accademia is closed on Monday afternoons; and the Peggy Guggenheim Collection, Palazzo Grassi and Punta della Dogana are closed on Tuesdays.

Tip: The most exciting time for art lovers to visit Venice is during the famed **Venice Art Biennale** (labiennale.org/en/art), which is held in even-numbered years.

Start your arty peregrination in Dorsoduro. The city's major arts institution, the **Gallerie dell'Accademia** (gallerieaccademia.it; entry €15), traces the history of Venetian art from the 14th to 19th centuries and holds major works by artists of the Venetian School. Don't miss Giovanni Bellini's *Madonna and Child with Saints Catherine and Mary Magdalene,* Giorgione's *The Tempest* and Titian's *Presentation of the Virgin.*

Nearby, the **Peggy Guggenheim Collection** (guggenheim-venice.it; adult/student €16/9) occupies a modernist villa where the American heiress lived from 1949 to 1979. The museum showcases Guggenheim's personal collection of early- and mid-20th-century sculpture and painting, which includes works by Jackson Pollock, Constantin Brâncuși, Alexander Calder, Fernand Léger and René Magritte.

Other museums to visit include the **Fondazione Querini Stampalia** (querinistampalia.org; adult/student €15/10) in Castello, and two spaces operated by the **Pinault Foundation** (pinaultcollection.com; joint ticket adult/student €18/7): the **Palazzo Grassi** in San Marco and the **Punta della Dogana**.

Peggy Guggenheim Collection on the Grand Canal

Venice

Prepare yourself for an exciting journey from Venice to Budapest. Four countries (Italy, Slovenia, Croatia and Hungary) and at least five trains await, as does magnificent scenery that includes mountains, sea, lakes and forests. This is most memorable in Slovenia, which is rightly described as the 'green heart of Europe'. It pays to take your time, stopping off to explore the cities of Trieste, Ljubljana and Zagreb before reaching the final destination of this leg, Budapest.

Virginia Maxwell

Ljubljana (p221)
GEORGIOS TSICHLIS/SHUTTERSTOCK

Budapest
THE SIMPLON ROUTE

714 KMS · 14¼ HOURS' RIDE

THIS LEG:

- Treviso & Udine
- Trieste
- Sežana
- Postojna
- Ljubljana
- Zidani Most
- Zagreb
- Koprivnica & Siófok
- Budapest

Riding Notes

From Venezia Santa Lucia, you'll board one of the frequent Trenitalia *regionale* (regional) services to Trieste Centrale. From Trieste, one daily EuroCity (EC) service operated by ÖBB takes passengers across the border and on to Ljubljana. From there, three direct services operated by HŽ Putnički Prijevoz or ÖBB travel to Zagreb Glavni Kolodvor each day. Services from Zagreb to Budapest are few and far between; there is usually a late-afternoon direct service (IC201; six hours) that involves a change in Koprivnica. Check the ÖBB website for updates.

Breaking Your Journey
Three attractive cities with long and rich histories are located on this route: Trieste, Ljubljana and Zagreb.

Virginia's Tips

BEST MEAL Le Bistro, Zagreb. (p219)

FAVOURITE VIEW Admire the lush landscape as your train travels alongside the fast-flowing Sava River between Ljubljana and Zagreb.

ESSENTIAL STOP Overnight in charming riverside Ljubljana. (p221)

TIP Schedule your stop in Ljubljana for a Friday so as to dine at the open kitchens at its famed food festival. (p221)

Ljubljana, p221 — Delightful riverside Old Town

Udine, p218 — Gastronomic hotspot

Drava River

Treviso, p218 — Medieval walled town

Sežana, p219 — Somnolent Slovenian border town

ITALY — Monfalcone

Gulf of Trieste

Venice — START

Divača

Postojna, p221 — Spectacular cave system with underground river

Trieste's Coffee Culture, p220
Sip coffee in elegant surrounds in this neoclassical jewel on the Adriatic.
In Trieste, p218

Adriatic Sea

> **ONWARD TRAVEL**
>
> From Venezia Santa Lucia station in Venice, you'll head northeast to the historic Italian port city of Trieste before crossing the border into Slovenia. There's no need to purchase your ticket from Venice to Trieste in advance, as Trenitalia operates frequent *regionale* services between the two cities – the fastest direct services are the Lagune Line trains travelling inland from the coast via Trieste Airport (two hours) and the Regionale Veloce services (three hours) via Treviso, Udine and Gorizia. There is only one class and seat reservations are not possible. When you arrive at the station, purchase your ticket from a machine in the main hall or at the **Trenitalia ticket office** *(6am-9pm)* located in front of Platforms 12 and 13.
>
> The famous *gelaterie* (gelato shops) **Venchi** *(it.venchi.com; €)* and **Grom** *(grom.it; €)* have branches in the main hall. Consider enjoying a cup or cone while waiting for your train.

Treviso & Udine

The train glides out of the station and over the lagoon causeway bridge, stopping at Venezia-Mestre and then passing through a vineyard-laden landscape where the grapes for Italy's famous sparkling wine, Prosecco, are grown. After 30 minutes, the Regionale Veloce services stop at Treviso, a small city with canals and a *centro storico* (historical centre) surrounded by medieval walls. The train then continues into the **Friuli-Venezia Giulia region**, which shares borders with both Austria and Slovenia. Another provincial city on this route, Udine, has a well-earned reputation as the gastronomic capital of the region.

Trieste

Both direct services from Venice stop in **Monfalcone** on the Gulf of Trieste before continuing to Trieste. This final stretch of the journey is extremely scenic, with the calm blue waters of the gulf on the right and verdant forest on the left. Approaching **Trieste Centrale** *(rfi.it/en/stations/trieste-centrale.html)*, the train tracks are lined with steep slopes on which houses and apartment blocks have been built to capitalise on spectacular water views. The station's facilities include a **ticket office** *(6.30am-8.15pm)*, and **baggage storage** *(depositobagaglitrieste.it)* is available just outside the station building.

Two historic hotels – the **Grand Hotel Duchi d'Aosta** *(duchidaosta.com; €€€)* and the Hotel Savoia Excelsior Palace (p222) – are located near the seafront a short walk from the station. Both were patronised by original passengers on the Simplon-Orient-Express and the Savoia Excelsior Palace has retained many features from this time. The interior of the Duchi d'Aosta has been almost totally rebuilt.

Trieste's *centro storico* is largely unchanged from its Habsburg-era heyday, with handsome 19th-century buildings lining Piazza dell'Unità d'Italia, Piazza del Ponterosso and the streets and squares between the two. Savouring Trieste's cafe culture (p220) and joining the locals for an early-evening *passeggiata* (stroll) along the pedestrianised streets and around the Canal

Canal Grande, Trieste

Grande (Grand Canal) in this part of the city is a highlight of every visit.

Sežana

Two services travel between Trieste and the Slovenian city of Ljubljana (Lubiana in Italian). The fastest (2¾ hours) and most comfortable is the daily direct EC service operated by ÖBB. After passing through the Italian hill town of **Villa Opicina**, the train crosses the border and stops in Sežana. The large station here was built as a stop on the 19th-century Austrian Southern Railway linking Trieste with Vienna.

Continues on page 221

BEST PLACES TO EAT

Caffè Tommaseo, Trieste €€€
Evoke the grandeur of the Austro-Hungarian Empire by dining in style at elegant Caffè Tommaseo. *caffetommaseo.it*

Pritličje, Ljubljana €
LGBTIQ+-friendly terrace cafe by day and pumping bar-club by night. *pritlicje.si*

Šuklje Wine Bar, Ljubljana €
The classiest of the riverside establishments, with a terrace and excellent wine list. *winebar.suklje.com*

Odprta Kuhna, Ljubljana €
Stalls serve tasty food to crowds of locals on Fridays in the warmer months. *odprtakuhna.si*

Le Bistro, Zagreb €€
The Esplanade Hotel's bistro offers a delicious, keenly priced three-course lunch menu with wine. *lebistro.hr*

Udine — 62km — **Trieste** ★ — 9km — Sežana

Look to the right after Monfalcone for your first glimpse of the Gulf of Trieste

Explore Trieste's Coffee Culture

Home to the Illy coffee company (established 1933), Trieste is justifiably proud of its coffee and the atmospheric 19th-century cafes that serve it. Indulge in a cup or two on this walk.

HOW TO

Start: Piazza dell'Unità d'Italia
End: Caffè Tommaseo
Duration: Two to three hours
Length: 2.5km

Tip: Trieste speaks its own coffee language. Locals order *nero* (espresso), *capo* (macchiato), *caffe latte* (cappuccino) and *goccia* (espresso with a drop of frothed milk).

More info: turismofvg.it/en/trieste

Kick off your afternoon walk by enjoying an excellent coffee at the long bar in **Caffè degli Specchi** *(caffedeglispecchi.it; €€)* on the city's main square, **Piazza dell'Unità d'Italia**. Dating from 1839, Specchi was originally one of four grand cafes on the square, but is now the only one standing. Continue into Piazza della Borsa, named after the elaborately decorated 1806 **Stock Exchange Building** here. Cross Corso Italia and continue into Via Dante Alighieri, passing a raft of terrace cafes until you reach hugely popular **Pasticceria La Bomboniera** *(€),* opened in 1836. Continue east along Via Niccolò Paganini, Via delle Torri and busy Via Cesare Battisto to reach **Caffè San Marco** *(caffesanmarco.com; €),* little changed since 1914. Browse the shelves of its bookshop before backtracking to Trieste's iconic **Canal Grande**, bookended by the **Church of Sant'Antonio** and the waterfront. From here, head to elegant Caffè Tommaseo (p219), opened in 1830. Its terrace overlooking the water is a perfect place to enjoy a sunset *aperitivo* (pre-dinner drink).

Caffè San Marco

Continued from page 219

Postojna

From Sežana, the train continues through the heavily forested mountain landscape that Slovenia is so famous for. The tracks are on high terrain for parts of the journey, so you'll be able to look down on small farming settlements huddled in green valleys backdropped by majestic mountain ranges. After stopping at **Divača**, the train heads to Postojna, home to the fascinating subterranean **Postojna Cave Park** (postojnska-jama.eu; tickets from €33). It's worth stopping here to explore this extraordinary natural phenomenon with an underground river and a 24km cave system featuring passages, galleries and halls filled with massive limestone stalagmites that are up to half a million years old. Tours include a 3.5km ride on the park's underground railway and tickets include entry to the medieval **Predjama Castle**, which is marketed as the world's largest cave castle. The park is located 2km from the railway station.

Postojna Cave Park

Ljubljana

Its name may be difficult to pronounce, but enjoying your visit to Slovenia's enchanting capital is easy as pie – consider a one- or two-night stop. The **railway station** (potniski.sz.si) has a **ticket hall** (5am-10pm) and cafe-bar; left-luggage lockers are on the first platform. A short walk away is the Grand Hotel Union Eurostars (p222), built in 1905 and retaining a few traces of its original Vienna Succession-style elegance. This is where passengers on the Simplon-Orient-Express would have stayed, and it's still one of the best hotels in the city.

Start your exploration through the pedestrianised Old Town at the main square, **Prešernov trg**, which overlooks Ljubljana's iconic **Tromostovje (Triple Bridge)**. Near this is the city's open-air **Central Market** (Mon-Sat). On Fridays between March and October, locals flock to Pogačar Sq in the market precinct to eat at the **Odprta Kuhna (Open Kitchen) Food Festival** (p219), where 50-odd stalls serve a vast array of foods including Slovenia's famed Carniolan sausage. The Old Town's other attractions include **Mestni trg**, lined with historic buildings housing shops and cafes including Pritličje (p219) and **Fétiche Patisserie** (fetichepatisserie.com; €€); and the **riverside promenade**, where you'll be able to find hotels and hostels, cheap eateries and excellent wine bars such as Šuklje (p219). The city's landmark 12th-century **hilltop castle** (ljubljanskigrad.si) overlooks the Old Town and can be reached via cable car.

Sežana — 28km — Postojna — 39km — Ljubljana

Spot the historic train engines at stations along this part of the route

The world-famous Postojna Caves are a short walk from the station

Esplanade Hotel, Zagreb

BEST PLACES TO SLEEP

Hotel Savoia Excelsior Palace, Trieste €€€
On the waterfront close to the central square, with extremely comfortable and attractive rooms. *collezione.starhotels.com*

Ad Hoc Hostel, Ljubljana €
Well-situated, efficiently run hostel in a great riverside location. *info@adhoc-hostel.com*

Grand Hotel Union Eurostars, Ljubljana €€
Excellent location and comfortable rooms. *grandhotelunioneurostars.com*

Swanky Mint, Zagreb €
Happening backpackers with a garden bar, seasonal pool, Asian restaurant and variety of sleeping options. *stayswanky.com*

Esplanade Hotel, Zagreb €€€
Luxury establishment with bar, famous terrace cafe, two restaurants and well-appointed rooms. *esplanade.hr*

Zidani Most

Prepare yourself for one of the least comfortable legs of your journey as you depart Ljubljana: the trains heading to Zagreb are usually old, have only one class and lack air-conditioning. There are three direct services per day, taking between two and 2½ hours. All follow the same route, with the fastest service making only three stops. Tickets can be booked on the ÖBB website.

Ljubljana — 52km — **Zidani Most** — 69km

Enjoy views of the Sava river for most of this leg

Though this leg might be a bit uncomfortable, there's no doubt that it's extremely scenic. The train follows the course of the Sava river for the first hour or so, passing through an extremely green and attractive landscape dotted with farms, chalet-style houses and villages with steep-spired churches; the best views are from the right-hand side of the train. The first major stop, Zidani Most, is a pretty village sitting in a valley where the Sava and Savinja rivers meet.

Zagreb

You're now only 45 minutes away from **Dobova** near the Croatian border, where all trains make a quick stop before proceeding towards Zagreb's grand, heritage-listed **Glavni Kolodvor station**, built in 1890. There are fast-food stands in the station's main hall and the **ticket office** *(6am-9pm)* is on the eastern side of the building; baggage lockers are next to it.

Exiting the station, Zagreb's Old Town (p224) is straight ahead and the luxury 1925 **Esplanade Hotel** (left), built for passengers on the Simplon-Orient-Express, is to the left (west), across a small park. This is *the* hotel to stay at if you want to emulate the original passengers' experience, but there are many other options in the Lower Town, including the popular Swanky Mint hostel (left). For a memorable meal, head to the Esplanade Hotel's excellent Le Bistro (p219), which serves classic Croatian dishes such as *štrukli* (dough filled with a creamy cheese).

Moving On from Zagreb

The original Simplon-Orient-Express travelled from Zagreb to İstanbul via **Belgrade** in Serbia and **Sofia** in Bulgaria. Sadly, it's impossible to follow this route today as buses have replaced trains on both sections. To continue on the rails, you'll need to head to **Budapest** and then continue east on the Classic Orient Express route (p114). If you decide to substitute part of your route by bus, **Flixbus** *(global. flixbus.com)* operates four services between the main bus stations in Zagreb and Belgrade daily. The journey takes 5½ hours. From Belgrade, there is one daily Flixbus service to Niš, where passengers can transfer to a bus heading to Sofia. The journey from Belgrade to Sofia takes approximately 15 hours. See p164 for details of the train journey from Sofia to İstanbul.

At the time of our research, there was only one direct daily train travelling from Zagreb to Budapest: the IC (InterCity) 201 AGRAM-TÓPART late-afternoon service jointly operated by HŽ Putnički Prijevoz and MÁV. Tickets (2nd class only) for this six-hour journey can be purchased on the **MÁV website** *(jegy.mav. hu)* or at Glavni Kolodvor; they are cheapest if purchased before the day of travel. The train usually travels direct to **Koprivnica** on the Croatian–Hungarian border, where three of the five carriages are uncoupled and continue to the Croatian city of Osijek near the Serbian border – make sure you sit at the front of the train, in one of the two carriages that are going to Budapest (check with the conductor that you are in the right spot).

Koprivnica & Siófok

After leaving Zagreb, the train passes through flat farmland on its 2¼-hour leg to Koprivnica. The landscape gets greener and

Continues on page 225

Zagreb — 77km — Koprivnica — 150km — Siófok

⚠ Warning! Make sure you're on the connecting train to Budapest rather than to Osijek

Zagreb's Old Town

Good things come in small packages and that's certainly the case with Zagreb. There aren't many top-drawer attractions, but the city's compact Gornji Grad (Old Town) has plenty of charm.

HOW TO

Getting here: From the station, walk straight ahead until you reach Josipa Jelačića Sq. Then walk uphill past the flower stalls to reach the Old Town.

Tip: For those not keen on walking uphill, a funicular (closed for restoration when we visited) connects Tomićeva in the Lower Town with Lotrščak Tower in the Upper Town.

More info: infozagreb.hr

Shaded by bright red umbrellas and bustling with shoppers every morning, the street stalls at **Tržnica Dolac (Dolac Market)** display a wealth of fresh local produce. After browsing here, head right (east) to the Gothic **Zagreb Cathedral**, constructed in the 13th century but greatly changed over the centuries. The cathedral has been closed to the public since being damaged by an earthquake in 2020; restoration is ongoing. From the cathedral, walk up Kaptol, veer left close to Opatovina Park and head down the Tkalčićeva cafe strip to explore the Old Town's western sector, a storybook-like maze of cobblestone streets and squares. While wandering, look out for the shrine at **Stone Gate** and the wildly photogenic **St Mark's Church** with its colourful glazed tiled roof. These aren't the area's major tourist draw, though: that honour belongs to a modern institution, the small **Museum of Broken Relationships** *(brokenships.com; adult/student €7/5.50)*. Focusing on mementos of relationships that have ended – sometimes amicably but often acrimoniously – this unique museum experience is sometimes amusing and often extremely moving. Don't miss it.

Above: Display at Museum of Broken Relationships
Right: Tržnica Dolac

Along the Way We Met...

ALVINA ADIMOELJA & HARRY CARTER Alvina is a fan of the David Suchet *Poirot* TV series, and was keen to follow some legs of the historic Orient Express routes. We started in Italy and have travelled a loop through Switzerland and Austria. Now we're making our way through Slovenia before returning to Vienna. We've done the whole trip in 2nd class and it's been comfortable and safe. As we're only travelling for two weeks, we purchased separate tickets rather than a rail pass.

Alvina, from Indonesia, and Harry, from the UK, are PhD candidates at Stanford University in California.

HARRY & ALVINA'S TIP: *The most spectacular scenery has been around Zell am See in Austria and on the Bernina Express between Italy and Switzerland.*

Continued from page 223

passes a series of attractive villages in the latter half of the journey, but views from the train are often obscured by metal screens.

On the next stretch of the journey, the train travels alongside 78km-long **Lake Balaton**, the largest lake in Central Europe. By this point in the trip it's usually dark, so if you are keen to see the lake in daylight, consider planning an overnight stop in the village of Siófok, one of two stops on the lake's shore. This is a popular holiday destination for Hungarians, and there are multiple accommodation options to choose from.

Budapest

It's just under two hours to Budapest (p106) and its World Heritage–listed historic centre, where this leg of the journey ends. The IC201 usually arrives at **Budapest-Déli** railway station on the western side of the Danube river, although this can be subject to change. The areas where most tourists stay are reasonably close by and the city is a marvellous place to pause for a few days. However, if you're keen to continue your journey without doing this, the train to Bucharest (p134) departs from Budapest-Keleti (p105), the main international station, which is on the other side of the river.

Siófok

114km

Budapest

Enjoy views of Central Europe's largest lake – Balaton

Paris

Named for the Arlberg Tunnel in Austria, the historical Arlberg route of the Orient Express was in use from 1930 until 1962, with the exception of the wartime years. Tracing this route today takes you to a string of appealing Swiss and Austrian cities and through some marvellous landscapes, which become increasingly wild and Alpine, reaching a scenic crescendo as you ascend from the lake at Zürich to Innsbruck.

Helena Smith

Hafelekar, Innsbruck (p234)
SIMON DANNHAUER/SHUTTERSTOCK

Vienna
THE ARLBERG ROUTE

1034 KMS — 14 HOURS' RIDE

THIS LEG:

- Dijon
- Mulhouse
- Basel
- Zürich
- Arlberg Tunnel
- Innsbruck
- Salzburg
- Linz
- Vienna

Riding Notes

TGV trains depart Gare de Lyon in Paris around six times a day for Zürich: to follow the Orient Express route, make sure your train goes via Basel. From Zürich, ÖBB's Railjet Xpress runs direct to Vienna via Innsbruck around three times per day.

Breaking Your Journey
This trip is all about breaking the journey. You can hop off at Dijon for lunch and overnight at Basel or Zürich, with a possible pause en route to Basel to see the train museum at Mulhouse. Beyond that, Innsbruck, Salzburg and Linz are all great overnighters on the way to Vienna.

Helena's Tips

BEST MEAL Rösti with asparagus at Weisser Wind in Zürich. (p231)

FAVOURITE VIEW Turquoise Walensee lake, backed by the cliffs and crags of the Churfirsten mountain chain. (p232)

ESSENTIAL STOP Basel, to float down the Rhine. (p230)

TIP Don't rush! All the cities en route make worthy stops.

START Paris

Basel, p230 Float downstream on the Rhine

Mulhouse, p230 View historic Orient Express carriages

Montbard

Dijon, p230 Beautifully preserved historic core

STARTING THE JOURNEY

This journey begins at the Gare de Lyon in Paris (p196). Swish TGV Lyria services depart from Gare de Lyon six times per day – they are fully equipped with charging, free wi-fi and a decent cafe-bar. Reservations are required: upper decks have prime views. Note that these trains don't call at Chaumont, which was a stop on the original route, but instead at Dijon. Time your journey right, and you can have breakfast at classic Le Train Bleu (p196) in Gare de Lyon, get to Dijon (one hour, 35 minutes) in time for lunch, and then travel on to Basel (another one hour, 25 minutes) or Zürich (two hours, 25 minutes).

If, for the sake of completeness, you'd like to visit **Chaumont**, a town on the Marne river with an ancient basilica church and an impressive 19th-century viaduct, take a regional train from Paris Gare de l'Est (two hours, 40 minutes; p50). Rather than backtracking, travel on from Chaumont to Mulhouse (2½ hours).

Dijon

Within 15 minutes of departing Paris, the TGV starts making its beeline for Switzerland through open Burgundy countryside, with gentle hills punctuated by patches of woodland. The train flashes through Montbard, a modest hillside town sitting pretty on the banks of the Brenne river.

From the utilitarian station at Dijon it's a pleasant 10-minute walk to the pedestrianised historic core, with its regal palaces, gargoyle-hung Gothic church and ancient timbered houses. The former seat of the wealthy Duchy of Burgundy, the region's capital is still a cultural powerhouse of gastronomy, architecture and art. Synonymous with mustard, *escargots* and *oeufs en meurette* (eggs poached in wine), Dijon is also renowned as the home of gingerbread-adjacent delicacy *pain d'épices*. Pick up some for the onward journey at **Maison Mulot et Petitjean** (€), the last artisanal producer.

Mulhouse

A little way east of Dijon, the tree cover begins to increase and the fields give way to steeper pastures, dotted with villages that take on an increasingly Alpine air, with low tiled roofs and neat shutters. Just before the border with Switzerland the train stops at Mulhouse, an essential stop for train fans. Take tram 3 from Mulhouse station for the pleasant 25-minute glide through arcaded squares and leafy streets to **Cité du Train** (citedutrain.com). Housed in a brightly painted shed-like building, the museum lets you experience the muscular presence of huge steam engines up close. Plus there are late 1920s luxury sleeping cars commissioned for the Orient Express and other services, with gleaming wooden fixtures and curved doors revealing elegantly compact washing facilities.

Basel

If you've stopped at Mulhouse, consider taking a characterful regional train on to Basel,

Gare de Lyon, Paris — 260km — Dijon

Explore the pedestrianised core of Dijon

Cité du Train, Mulhouse

some of which have six-seater carriages. Look out to the left and ahead you'll see the thickly wooded Black Mountains in Germany. Soon after crossing the French–Swiss border you arrive in Basel.

The city's 1907 **station** is a sight in its own right, with its vast timbered roof supported by sage-green metal trusses giving the feel of a medieval great hall; spectacular 1920s murals depict Alpine scenes. A huge regional and international hub, the station has 1000 departures daily, and is well equipped with cafes, shops and left luggage (down the escalators in the main hall). The modern SBB Travel Centre is also in the main hall.

BEST PLACES TO EAT

Markthalle, Basel €
Large indoor market/food hall, around the corner from Basel SBB station: a popular spot for a cheap lunch on the go.

Weisser Wind, Zürich €€
This 1425 guild house has had an arty update and offers a delicious modern spin on Swiss classics. weisserwind.ch

Olive, Innsbruck €
Vegetarians and vegans are in their element at this cute bistro with vintage furniture. restaurant-olive.at

Verdi Restaurant & Einkehr, Linz €€
Traditional Austrian cuisine with a modern slant, plus a well-stocked wine cellar, just north of the city centre. verdi.at

Mulhouse — 180km — Detour to railway nerd paradise, Cité du Train — 29km — Basel

SBB train journeys past Walensee

Basel's many museums, atmospheric Old Town and vibrant nightlife make it a great place to throw anchor. On warm summer days, the right bank of the **Rhine** draws flocks of sun worshippers and swimmers to its waterline. The thing to do is float downstream with a Wickelfisch, a fish-shaped watertight bag you can buy from the tourist office and elsewhere.

Zürich

There are four or five departures per hour between Basel and Zürich: both InterCity (55 minutes) and InterRegio (1¼ hours) trains. Some 30 minutes out of Basel, the train begins a long, slow ascent past maize fields, vineyards, pine forests, apple orchards and grazing horses. Aside from a bit of industrial sprawl, this is a scenic hour-long journey.

Trains arrive into **Zürich Hauptbahnhof**, whose vast airy main hall served as a train shed when it was constructed in 1871. Here you'll find the ticket office; luggage lockers are on the lower mezzanine level. The station sits within walking distance of the major sights in this agreeable city. Long known as a savvy, hardworking financial centre, Switzerland's largest and wealthiest metropolis has emerged in the 21st century as a happening and culturally ambitious destination. Its idyllic lake provides wonderful locations for urban swims, in stylish swimming spots known as *badi* (right).

Through the Arlberg Tunnel

All aboard the ÖBB Railjet between Zürich and Innsbruck (4½ hours), the standout stage of this journey. Book a seat, aiming for the left-hand side for views of Zürichsee. A special option is the early-morning departure on EuroCity (EC) train *Transalpin*, which has a 1st-class panorama car (booking required).

Leaving Zürich, it feels like you could reach out and dip your fingers in **Zürichsee**, whizzing past beach bars, promenades, wooden jetties and volleyball games. At **Lachen** the train leaves the lake shore – you'll see high Alpine pasture and chalets with neat timber stacks. Along and beyond **Walensee** rise the forbidding Churfirsten mountains. To the left as you approach **Sargans**, look out for the medieval schloss rising sheer from its rock. At **Buchs** the train reverses.

Continues on page 235

Take a Dip in Zürich

After sedentary train journeys, stretch out in Zürich by soaking up some *badi* (bathing house) culture or relax on a lake cruise.

HOW TO

Getting here: From Zürich Hauptbahnhof you can walk to Frauenbad and Männerbad (15 minutes), Seebad Utoquai and Seebad Enge (30 minutes), and Bürkliplatz (20 minutes).

Tip: Combine your leisurely *badi* swim with a drink or snack: all have excellent cafe-bars.

From May to mid-September, official swimming areas known as **badis** open around the lake and along the rivers. Most charge Chf8 entry. There are also plenty of free, unofficial places to take a dip, but the *badi* have changing rooms, cafe-bars and other facilities. Standout *badi* include the art-nouveau pool **Frauenbad**, which is women-only during the day but opens its bar to everyone in the evening; **Männerbad**, a men-only pool on the tree-shaded Schanzengraben canal; and the historic **Seebad Utoquai** Moorish-style bathing pavilion and hip **Seebad Enge**, both on the lake.

Alternatively, it's an easy pleasure cruising across the sparkling waters of **Zürichsee** (Lake Zürich) and admiring the scenery. Between April and December **ZSG** (zsg.ch) runs a wide range of jaunts from Bürkliplatz, as well as **riverboats** *(adult/child Chf4.60/3.20)* that connect the Landesmuseum with Zürichhorn via the Limmat river. These low-slung glassed-in boats can go under the Limmat bridges, partly compromising your views, but are still a nice way to get around the city.

EXPERIENCE ★

Above: Swimming goggles, cap and towel
Right: Frauenbad *badi*

Hit the Heights in Innsbruck

Whizz from Innsbruck's stately heart to more than 2000m above sea level, up among crags where alpine choughs glide and cowbells tinkle.

HOW TO

Nearest stop: Innsbruck Hauptbahnhof

Getting here: The funicular is a 15-minute walk from the station at the Congress Centre.

Tip: Tourist information centres on Burggraben, at the Stadtturm (tower) and the Hauptbahnhof are handy first ports of call for maps, tickets, ski passes and information.

The huge mountains on Innsbruck's doorstep are so perfectly etched they almost look like a cardboard cut-out in the sharp light of winter. Zaha Hadid's space-age **funicular** wings you from the Congress Centre to the slopes in no time, stopping at **Hungerburg** (*€13*), where you switch to a cable car to **See-grube**, and then, finally, 2256m **Hafelekar** (*€52*). A 15-minute uphill trudge brings you to 2334m **Hafelekarspitze**, where alpine choughs ride the breeze, gnarly mountains rise in great waves, and Innsbruck is just a speck in the valley below. The views are riveting, reaching all the way to 3798m Grossglockner when it's clear. From these wild heights, the city feels light years away.

On the southern rim of the **Karwendel Nature Park**, the ragged Nordkette range is where the Innsbrucker comes to play. Walking trails head off from Hungerburg and Seegrube, but for more of a challenge and chance encounters with wildlife like eagles, chamois and marmots, hike the ridgetop **Goethe Trail** from Hafelekar, through meadows and pines to the **Pfeishütte** (10km; five hours).

Above: Alpine cowbell
Right: Innsbruck funicular

Continued from page 232

From Buchs you enter **Liechtenstein**, then continue into Austria, climbing away from the valley floor amidst pine-clad elevations that will make your ears pop. At points sheer rock faces enclose the train as it winds gently upwards, with sudden vistas of meadows dotted with small wooden huts, and distant rocky peaks. Between **Bludenz** and **St Anton am Arlberg** you enter the 10km **Arlberg Tunnel**, opened in 1884.

Innsbruck

Eventually the train begins to descend towards Tyrolean capital Innsbruck: five minutes before you arrive, the **Nordkette mountain range** soars on the right-hand side.

Innsbruck's long low station was rebuilt in 2004. In the main concourse you'll find the ticket office, and there are coin-operated lockers in several locations. From here it's a 10-minute walk to the centre and the sparkling 1500 Golden Roof. Ideally, set aside at least two days to explore Innsbruck and take advantage of the surrounding area, from hiking the Nordkette range to exploring the towns and landscapes of Tyrol.

Along the Inn

Continuing along the Arlberg route, the next stop is Salzburg (one hour, 50 minutes). There is at least one departure an hour from Innsbruck on ÖBB Railjet trains, whose restaurant cars feature jaunty red seating, panoramic windows and an impressively long menu including vegan and vegetarian options.

Innsbruck's outskirts quickly give way to allotments and fields, backed by forested slopes and a changing mountain panorama as the train descends into the valley of the River Inn. Vistas are less wild than on the journey to Innsbruck, with scattered towns and villages featuring onion-domed churches, and some light industry and agriculture on the valley floor. But thickly forested hills and mountains undulate along the route, often capturing wisps of cloud. At points, the train runs alongside the wide Inn itself.

Salzburg

Crossing over the Salzach river as you come into Salzburg, the Hohensalzburg fortress looms dramatically on the right-hand side.

While the exterior of **Salzburg Hauptbahnhof** is stuccoed and classical, and the entrance hall features some vivid tiled depictions of mountain views, the interior is slickly modern. The original station opened in 1860 and underwent a major renovation in the early 2000s – note the old arched train shed roof incorporated into the new roof over the platforms. The ÖBB ticket office is beneath the tracks, near the escalators up to Platform 2/3 – in the same area is the 1st-class lounge. Left-luggage lockers are beneath Platforms 6 and 7. It's a 15-minute walk into town (p236) from here.

Linz

ÖBB Railjets depart around every half-hour for the journey from Salzburg to Austria's third-largest city, Linz (one hour, 10 minutes). You pass through a pleasant pastoral landscape, with cows grazing and patches of forest. There is, though, plenty of evidence of the local timber industry.

The station at Linz is modern and unremarkable: the 1858 original was rebuilt in 1936 by

Continues on page 238

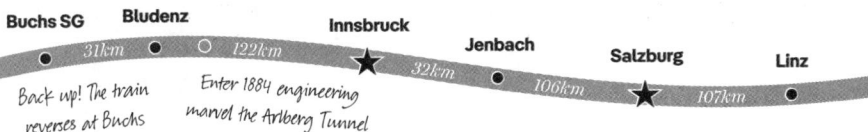

CITY GUIDE:
Salzburg

Beyond Mozart and *The Sound of Music* lies a city with a burgeoning arts scene, wonderful food, manicured parks, and side streets where classical music wafts from windows. The scenery, skyline, music and history will send your spirits soaring higher than Julie Andrews' octave-leaping vocals.

HOW TO

Getting here: Trains connect Salzburg with Vienna (two hours, 25 minutes) and Linz (one hour, 10 minutes).

Getting around: Walking is the only way to get a true feel for Salzburg's sight-packed pedestrianised backstreets.

Sleeping: YoHo *(yoho.at; €)* is a great budget choice with cheap beer and *The Sound of Music* singalongs. **Hotel & Villa Auersperg** *(auersperg.at; €€)* fuses late-19th-century flair with the contemporary, while **Arthotel Blaue Gans** *(blauegans.com; €€€)* blends avant-garde design with original vaulting, beams and floors.

Tip: Hire a bike for longer trips: this is one of Austria's most cycle-friendly cities, with a superb network of bike paths along the river.

More info: Main Tourist Office *(salzburg.info; 9am–6pm daily Apr-Sep, closed Sun Oct-Mar)*

Salzburg is at its most entrancing from above, with domes, spires and rooftops spreading out before you and the turquoise Salzach river unfurling into the mountains. One of the most memorable ways to see the city away from the masses is to get out and stride. Puff up the Nonnbergstiege to Benedictine abbey **Stift Nonnberg**, then continue your short but scenic walk along Hoher Weg and Festungsgasse to 900-year-old clifftop fortress **Festung Hohensalzburg**. The city's crowning glory has dress-circle views of the baroque **Altstadt**. Time your walk for midday to hear bells ring out across the city.

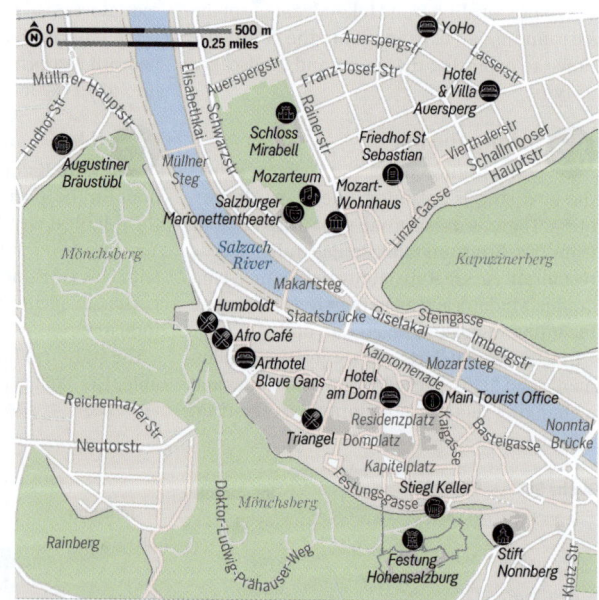

SOMETHING'S BREWING

Bavaria is but a bottle-top-pop away from Salzburg and you can feel it in the city's rollicking, stein-swinging beer halls, traditional breweries and vast beer gardens, where honeyed summer sun trickles through chestnut-tree branches. The first breweries were founded here in the late 14th century and some are still going strong today.

If you can only visit one, make it **Augustiner Bräustübl**. Since 1621 this cheery, monastery-run brewery has served potent home brews in beer steins in its vaulted hall and 1400-seat beer garden. Get your tankard filled at the foyer pump and visit the snack stands for hearty, beer-swigging grub including *Stelzen* (ham hock) and giant pretzels.

For a 365-day taste of Oktoberfest, try cavernous, Munich-style beer hall **Stiegl Keller** instead, which shares the same architect as Munich's Hofbräuhaus. Perched panoramically above the city and near Festung Hohensalzburg, it has an enormous garden above the rooftops and pairs brews with the likes of fat pork knuckles and schnitzel. Beer is cheapest from the self-service taps outside.

Mirabell Garden, Schloss Mirabell

Have a Mozart Meander

Begin at baroque **Schloss Mirabell**, where resplendent Marmorsaal (Marble Hall) is the backdrop for chamber concerts of Mozart's music. Then stroll south through fountain-dotted gardens, passing the angular **Mozarteum**, a foundation honouring Mozart, and the host of the renowned **Mozartwoche festival** in January/February. Around the corner on Makartplatz is the 17th-century **Mozart-Wohnhaus** – see how the family lived and listen to rare symphonic recordings. Amble north along Linzer Gasse to **Friedhof St Sebastian**, the arcaded cemetery where Wolfgang's father Leopold and his wife Constanze lie buried.

Experience the Music

Ever since Hollywood box-office smash *The Sound of Music* hit big screens in 1965, Salzburg has been inseparable from the world's most famous singing nun. You don't have to be a die-hard fan to belt out a few songs as you pedal between the film locations with **Fräulein Maria's Bicycle Tours** *(mariasbicycletours.com)*. Continue the musical theme at the UNESCO World Heritage–listed **Salzburger Marionettentheater** *(marionetten.at)*, where the red curtain has risen on a miniature stage since 1913. The level of detail is extraordinary and the puppeteers are incredibly talented. The repertoire star is *The Sound of Music,* with a life-sized Mother Superior.

BEST PLACES TO EAT & DRINK

Afro Café € Go for fair-trade coffees, lavish brunches and creative day specials at this Afro-chic cafe. *afrocoffee.com*

Triangel €€ Market-fresh menu at this picture-clad bistro. Gourmet salads, goulash and homemade ice cream. *triangel-salzburg.co.at*

Humboldt €€ Like a blast of nouveau alpine chic, the vibe is cool yet cosy. Season-driven menu. *humboldtstubn.at*

Continued from page 235

the Nazis, but this iteration was bombed by the Allies and replaced in the early 1950s. The ticket desk is in the main hall, where you'll find luggage lockers. Two stone lions flanking the entrance date from 1941 and were designed to decorate a bridge. You can either walk to the centre (25 minutes), or take a swish tram (10 minutes).

Built on the banks of the **Danube**, Linz has taken its industrial past and created art where there was once functionality, while holding onto its historic heart in the charming Old Town. The old industrial port-facility buildings are now one big art gallery, featuring murals that visitors can add to.

Here you can sample the world's oldest cake variety, the *Linzer Torte*, beneath the twin spires of the 17th-century **cathedral**. Head to **kuk Hofbäckerei** (€) for a taste of the oldest cake in the oldest bakery in Linz (it's been here since at least 1371). **Südbahnhofmarkt** (€) is an open-air market where fruit and veg stalls, butchers, cheese counters and flower stalls are set up next to cafes and snack bars.

Vienna

For the journey to Vienna from Linz (1¼ hours), you can travel either on an ÖBB Railjet (to Wien Hauptbahnhof or Westbahnhof), or with Westbahn to Wien Westbahnhof. Unless you are planning immediate onward travel from Wien Hauptbahnhof (p81, p96), our suggestion is to travel to Westbahnhof. It is well located for city sights, and the historic Orient Express pulled in here for more than 100 years, before heading to Budapest (p106) via Gyor. The modern iteration of the Orient Express service calls here.

Along the Way We Met...

YAO WANG I was partly inspired to come to Austria by Richard Linklater's *Before Sunrise*, where two people meet on a train and travel to Westbahnhof in Vienna. I just completed my end of semester show in Linz, and I'm using the KlimaTicket to travel round Austria for a year. I go back and forward to Vienna and Salzburg for art shows, and I'm also planning to explore the mountains. And maybe find some train romance myself!

Yao (@vonyao) is doing an MA in sculptural conceptions and ceramics at the University of Arts in Linz.

YAO'S TIP: *Go up the Schlossberg in Linz – the top of the hill is an urban getaway, with amazing city views.*

Linz	Amstetten Noe	St Poeltan	Tullnerfeld	Wien Westbahnhof
	47km	56km	29km	31km

Spot the lions outside Linz station

Sadly though, the romance of the journey itself runs out between Salzburg and Linz, as you pass through straggles of housing, nondescript fields, low hills and industrial buildings.

Wien Westbahnhof was rebuilt in the early 1950s in an angular modernist style that recalls Soviet architecture. It lost its role as an international station in 2015, but it is still well equipped with cafes and lockers, and it is on Vienna's underground system. The station sits in the **15th District**, which is brushing off its rundown atmosphere and undergoing an understated transformation with a gritty-creative edge. Walk along Mariahilfer Strasse, and it's all laid out in a tempting mantle of cafes, bars and restaurants that stretch all the way down to the Schwendermarkt local market pavilion. For more district vibes, head down to Reindorfgasse, where book, bike and eco-fashion stores jostle with old-timer institutions like **Gasthaus Quell** restaurant and **Pizzeria Mafiosi**.

To continue your journey in Vienna, see p84.

BEST PLACES TO SLEEP

Basel Youth Hostel, Basel €
Stylish modern hostel by a rushing creek, a stone's throw from the Rhine. *youthhostel.ch*

Alma, Zürich €€
Eco-aware, sustainability-focused hotel in an art nouveau townhouse. Its spa and roof terrace are for women only. *ladysfirst.ch*

Hotel Weisses Kreuz, Innsbruck €€
This 500-year-old hotel oozes history with wood-panelled parlours and a twisting staircase. *weisseskreuz.at*

Hotel am Dom, Salzburg €€
Antique meets boutique at an Altstadt hotel in an 800-year-old building. *hotelamdom.at*

Vienna streetscape

Orient Express Revivals

When the *Direct Orient Express* sleeper train departed Paris for the final time in 1977, many feared that the golden days of luxury European train travel were over. Since then, though, several initiatives to recreate its magic have been launched. These use lovingly restored CIWL rolling stock or follow original routes, helping to keep the Orient Express' rich heritage alive.

WORDS BY **VIRGINIA MAXWELL**

Luxury Train Travel

When American George Pullman came up with the idea of building luxury sleeping cars for long-distance railway travel, he kick-started a phenomenon that would revolutionise both tourism and transport. Pullman's first luxury car, the *Pioneer*, made its debut in 1865 and soon after, Georges Nagelmackers, a young Belgian banker, travelled in Pullman's carriage while on a visit to America. The rest, as they say, is history. Inspired by his experience on board the *Pioneer* and convinced that there was a market for luxury train services in Europe, Nagelmackers commissioned the construction of luxuriously outfitted railway cars and registered a name that would soon become synonymous with train travel: La Compagnie Internationale des Wagons-Lits (CIWL).

Since these beginnings, luxury train travel has had its ups and downs (see p82). The advent of affordable air travel had a deleterious impact on long-distance services such as the Orient Express, eventually making them financially unviable. Despite this, the allure of luxury travel on the rails with its associations of glamour and exclusivity remained, and entrepreneurs in Europe and America recognised this. The era of luxury train revival services was about to begin.

The Revival Process Starts

Monte Carlo, 1977. Prince Rainier and Princess Grace of Monaco, along with members of the global media, businesspeople and train enthusiasts, have congregated at Monaco's railway station for a very special auction being hosted by Sotheby's. Advertised as 'Carriages from the Great Trains of the Twenties', the lots on offer are exciting: five original CIWL Orient Express carriages. Bidding is fierce, and three buyers triumph: James Sherwood, André Paccard and Albert Glatt.

Sherwood, an American businessman and entrepreneur, paid US$104,000 for two luxury sleeping cars. He subsequently embarked on a mission to track down more original carriages, eventually spending a total of US$16 million to purchase 35 sleeper, restaurant and Pullman cars from the 1920s and '30s. In 1982, after being restored to their former splendour, these trophies from the heyday of the Orient Express took to the rails once again, travelling multiple routes including Paris to Venice under the name Venice Simplon-Orient-Express. Sherwood's hotel and luxury-travel company, which he initially named Orient Express after leasing the brand name from French national railway company SNCF, was renamed Belmond in 2014 after that lease expired. Belmond was sold to luxury company

Belmond Venice Simplon-Orient-Express

LVMH Moët Hennessy Louis Vuitton SE (LVMH) in 2019 for US$3.2 billion.

Paccard, a French interior designer, acquired two carriages for US$137,700. After his death in 1995, these were found abandoned in Belgium and were subsequently acquired by French multinational hotel group, Accor.

When he paid US$60,300 at the Sotheby's auction for a dining car, Glatt was already the owner of nine original Orient Express carriages that he operated as the Nostalgic İstanbul Orient Express service between Zürich and İstanbul. In 1983, on the 100th anniversary of the original Orient Express voyage, his company began to offer a service from Paris to İstanbul. Over the next 24 years, the Nostalgic İstanbul Orient Express added seven more original carriages to its rolling stock. The company ceased operations in 2007 and its carriages were purchased by Accor in 2018.

Today's Major Players

After being dominated by one company, Belmond, for the past four decades, luxury train travel in Europe is poised to enter a new phase, with new players offering variations on the three original Orient Express routes as well as multiple new itineraries.

Travel industry insiders offer various explanations for the renewed interest in long-distance train travel, one of which is the fact that it is more sustainable than air travel, contributing considerably fewer harmful planet-warming emissions into the environment.

Pascal Deyrolle, Area Managing Director for Trains in Continental Europe at Belmond, says the company sees luxury train travel as a growing market driven by factors including demand for slow travel: 'We physically transport guests away from their daily lives to a calmer, more mindful existence. In a world where humans are constantly striving for the next evolution, a journey on our train invites our guests to disconnect, slow down, celebrate life's pleasures and appreciate the beauty of the world we live in.'

National railway companies are capitalising on this demand, offering new services such as ÖBB's affordable **Nightjet sleeper trains** *(nightjet.com)*, but the major growth area seems to be in ultra-luxurious train travel, as evidenced by the fact that LVMH, the global leader in luxury goods, is entering the market. These services are very different to the self-directed journeys we describe elsewhere in this book, being akin to a luxury full-service cruise-ship experience. The trains are changing to meet this demand. Whereas the original Orient Express carriages didn't have full ensuite bathrooms attached to cabins, most of the new services do. Other aspects of the journey haven't changed, with luxe restaurant and bar cars being a major drawcard, along with personalised service.

Venice Simplon-Orient-Express
The Original Revival Service

Booking a cabin on one of the 40+ European journeys offered by the **Venice Simplon-Orient-Express** *(VSOE; belmond.com/trains/europe/venice-simplon-orient-express)* is the closest modern-day travellers can come to experiencing the original Orient Express at present. The company's 17-carriage train incorporates meticulously restored wagons-lits carriages that serviced Orient Express and other famous European train routes from the 1920s. Opt for Sleeping Car 3309, which operated as part of the Orient Express between 1928 and 1939 and was famously marooned in a snowdrift for a week in 1929 (the inspiration for Agatha Christie's *Murder on the Orient Express*). Or

Left: Dining service, Venice Simplon-Orient-Express; Right: Sleeping carriage, Venice Simplon-Orient-Express

Sleeping carriage, La Dolce Vita Orient Express

perhaps Sleeping Car 3425, which serviced all three original Orient Express routes and was used by King Carol of Romania when he escaped his country with his mistress aboard the train after his 1940 abdication. Meals are enjoyed in three original restaurant carriages.

Routes include a five-night Paris to İstanbul journey travelling from Paris Gare de l'Est through France, Germany, Austria, Hungary, Romania, Bulgaria and Türkiye. This trip is priced from €21,000 per passenger. Other offerings include a range of one-night Paris to Venice trips priced from €4500 per passenger; and a four-night Paris to Budapest round trip priced from €9900 per passenger.

The Orient Express
Pinnacle of Luxury

In 2019 Belmond was sold to luxury company LVMH. Then, in 2024, LVMH announced that it was partnering with Accor to jointly expand the Orient Express brand name, which Accor has co-owned with SNCF since 2017. Together, Accor and LVMH will open new hotels and launch Orient Express routes using fully restored *Nostalgic İstanbul Orient Express* and purpose-built luxury rolling stock. The new **Orient Express service** *(orient-express.com)* offers original carriages from the 1920s and '30s that have been fully restored and reimagined by French architect and furniture designer, Maxime d'Angeac. This service, the Venice Simplon-OrientExpress, and the associated La Dolce Vita Orient Express services will be the only ones able to use the 'Orient Express' name.

Above right and left: La Dolce Vita Orient Express

La Dolce Vita Orient Express
Plenty of Va-Va-Voom

In 2025 Accor-LVMH launched a new portfolio of **Italian train journeys** *(orient-express.com/la-dolce-vita)* in partnership with Italian luxury hospitality company Arsenale and the heritage arm of Italy's state railway, Ferrovie dello Stato Italiane. These journeys are made on a purpose-built train designed by Milan-based firm Dimorestudio. Rather than emulating the style of the original *Orient Express*, La Dolce Vita has nine sumptuously appointed carriages with a sleek decor inspired by the style of big-name 20th-century Italian designers such as Giò Ponti and Gae Aulenti. These journeys do not follow the original Venice Simplon-Orient-Express route; instead, the train embarks on a variety of one-, two- or three-day journeys across and between Italian regions including Tuscany, Sicily and the Veneto. Joining one of these costs between €3000 and €7000 for a single cabin.

Golden Eagle Luxury Trains
Longer Trips, Original Routes

Golden Eagle Luxury Trains *(goldeneagleluxurytrains.com)* was founded in 1989 by British rail buff Tim Littler, who was inspired by a passion for steam trains and the golden days of luxury rail travel. Today, this family-run company offers a variety of long-distance journeys on its three private trains. Some of these travel legs of the original Orient Express routes on the company's *Golden Eagle Danube Express*, which is made up of seven sleeping cars, a dining car, lounge car and bar car. The rolling stock has been sourced from across Europe, and includes luxuriously adapted and restored 1980s mail vans from the Hungarian postal service, 1985 couchette cars from German Railways and 1980s dining cars from MÁV, the Hungarian Railway Company.

James Masterson, Director of Product Development at Golden Eagle, says the company has been particularly thrilled with the success of the Paris to İstanbul offering, which launched in 2025 with four departures and increased to six departures in 2026. The majority of the passengers to date have been from North America, the UK, Australia, South America and Europe, and most have been been aged 50+. As was the case on the original Orient Express services, the journeys are expensive – a single cabin on the 11-day 'Balkan Explorer' between Venice and İstanbul costs between €31,000 and €46,000, and a single cabin on the eight-day Paris to İstanbul journey costs between €23,000 and €29,000.

What makes Golden Eagle so interesting is that it offers passengers the opportunity to travel legs of the original Orient Express routes that are not currently covered by passenger trains. For those who wish to follow as much of the original route of the Venice Simplon-Orient-Express as possible, the Balkan Explorer itinerary departs Venice travelling via Zagreb, Belgrade and Sofia en route to İstanbul, something that isn't possible if travelling on national railways. The Paris–İstanbul route travels a mash-up of the Arlberg and Venice Simplon routes, stopping in Strasbourg, Zürich, Innsbruck, Vienna, Ljubljana, Zagreb, Belgrade and Sofia.

Golden Eagle Danube Express

Beyond the Orient Express

Want to extend your journey beyond the traditional start and end points of the Orient Express? Beginning (or ending) your train travels elsewhere is easier than you might think. Here we cover some popular extensions and show you how to link back up with the Orient Express.

WORDS BY **HELENA SMITH**

Beyond Paris

Extend Your Journey West

While purists might insist Paris is the only place to begin (or end!) an Orient Express adventure, not everyone starts their journey in the City of Light. Beyond Paris lie the cosmopolitan capitals of the UK, Ireland and Belgium, from which you can easily connect with Gare du Nord in Paris.

St Pancras Station, England

London's magnificent St Pancras station is the departure point for **Eurostar** *(eurostar.com; 16 daily; 2¼ hours)* trains to Paris Gare du Nord, which pass through the Channel Tunnel. The red-brick Victorian station, built in 1868, is a showstopper: start your trip in style at **Searcys Bar & Brasserie** on the upper level. Book Eurostar tickets well in advance, particularly to snag one of the limited discounted tickets using your Interrail pass, and ensure you arrive at least 75 minutes before your train is scheduled to depart.

The adjacent King's Cross station is handily placed if you're arriving from Scotland (via Edinburgh) and other major cities on the east side of England; coming from Glasgow and the west of England a likely arrival point is Euston station, which is one stop north on the Underground or a 15-minute walk from St Pancras.

Dover, England

From the white cliffs of Dover in England, **P&O** *(poferries.com)* runs ferries to Calais, France (1½ hours), once a departure point for the Orient Express. From Calais, you can take a train direct to Gare du Nord and pick up the route from there. It takes longer than the Eurostar from London, but can be more affordable.

Dublin, Ireland

Flying direct from Dublin to Paris Charles de Gaulle Airport (one hour, 50 minutes) with Aer Lingus or Air France is the quickest way to join the start point of the Orient Express. But if you'd like to take a more leisurely and sustainable journey, travel with Irish Ferries or Stena Line across the Irish Sea to Holyhead (three hours) on the Isle of Anglesey in North Wales. From here you can take the train to Crewe, England, then change here for London's Euston station (five hours). A combined **SailRail ticket** *(tfw.wales)* is the most affordable way to make this journey.

Searcys Bar & Brasserie, St Pancras station, London

Brussels, Belgium

The Belgian capital is well positioned for the start point of the Orient Express via a journey from Brussels Midi/Zuid to Paris Gare du Nord on Eurostar (1¾ hours).

Interrailers based in Belgium can use their Interrail pass to start their trip, first reserving a discounted seat on Eurostar; from elsewhere in Belgium, you can travel to Brussels and on to Paris using an Interrail pass, providing you do so in one day.

A historic former starting point for the route was Ostend in Belgium, once accessible by ferry from the UK. If you are starting in Ostend for the sake of exploring the historic route from the Belgian coast, take the train onwards to Brussels Midi/Zuid, and from there to Paris Gare du Nord.

Exploring the Med

Trains and Ferries Await...

Partway through the Simplon route (p192), you may well feel the call of the Mediterranean. There are umpteen options for extending your trip into France and Italy – and indeed through Slovenia, Croatia and any other en-route country that takes your fancy. Unfortunately, no trains connect Greece with Orient Express stations – you'll have to take a bus from Sofia into Greece, or a ferry from Venice to reach Athens and the islands. Be aware that on French and Italian trains, Eurail/Interrail pass holders may need to pay extra for seat reservations. Note that there are no international train arrivals into Albania.

Italy

Milan (p202) is a hub for onward travel into Italy; InterCity and Frecciarossa high-speed trains make intercity travel rapid and efficient. The two major train companies in Italy are **Trenitalia** *(trenitalia.com)* and **Italo** *(italotreno.com)*. Train services crisscross Sardinia and Sicily, and you can continue to use travel passes in these destinations; the intercity train from Naples actually boards the ferry for Sicily. Services across the country tend to be regular and efficient, the stations are often magnificent and station cafes are often of an excellent standard. Be aware that in small destinations the station may be located far from the town centre.

France

France is very well served by **trains** *(sncf-connect.com)*, including the ultra-speedy TGV (Train à Grande Vitesse). Paris (p36) is the centre of a web of services that reach across the country. The French Alps and the south of France are also easily accessed from either Lausanne (p198) in Switzerland or Milan (p202) in northern Italy.

Bear in mind that TGV trains have to be reserved in advance. France also has a train equivalent to budget airlines: **Ouigo** *(ouigo.com)*, whose services are no frills, with no 1st class. Make Ouigo bookings direct, or through SNCF, Rail Europe and other companies.

Greece

Athens was once an Orient Express destination: from 1920 there was a section of the Simplon-Orient-Express that detached at Niš to go on to Thessaloniki (then Salonica) and Athens. Sadly, overland train travel to Athens is no longer possible, but there are options. It is possible to take a bus from Sofia (p158) to **Thessaloniki** *(flixbus.co.uk; 5¼ hours)*, then continue your travels through Greece by train.

Or break off from the Simplon route at Venice (p206), and travel by ferry to Patras in Greece, with onward travel by bus then train to Athens.

Left: Taormina train station, Sicily; Right: Train passes Mont Blanc in the French Alps

The Venice–Patras ferry takes up to 33 hours; boats are operated by **Superfast Ferries** *(super fast.com)* or see **Direct Ferries** *(directferries. co.uk)*. If you can't afford a cabin try to fork out for an airline-style seat, as the lounges tend to be crowded and noisy. These ferries are included in Interrail and Eurail passes: 1st-class pass holders can use the airline-style seats, 2nd-class passengers will have to use deck seating (ask a steward if you can upgrade – you may get lucky).

Note that you can also make ferry stops prior to Patras at the beautiful island of Corfu (25 hours), and at Igoumenitsa (26 hours) on the western Greek mainland.

Beyond İstanbul

Extend Your Adventures East

Doğu Ekspresi

So you want to continue your travels beyond İstanbul... While there are plenty of options for exploring Türkiye by train, international options are severely limited due to geopolitical issues. International services such as the Taurus Express (p188), which once linked İstanbul with Aleppo, Tripoli and Lebanon, are currently paused. And while you might dream of travelling from İstanbul to Moscow then taking the Trans-Siberian Railway, travel into Russia is currently impossible. So this section is for the dreamers, in the hope of safer international train travel in the future.

Türkiye

Türkiye has a good train network, with high-speed departures to Ankara, Konya and Sivas leaving from İstanbul's Söğütlüçeşme and Pendik stations. High-speed trains and night services (with comfy couchettes) need to be booked in advance at railway stations or online with **TCDD Taşımacılık** *(ebilet.tcddtasima cilik.gov.tr)*. *Doğu Ekspresi* (Eastern Express) is a spectacular Instagram-friendly ride that links Ankara with Kars on the border with Armenia, via Anatolia. There isn't a direct train service to Cappadocia, but it's possible to take the high-speed train from İstanbul to Ankara or Sivas, then change to another service to Kayseri.

Iran

Travel to Iran is currently not advised (check your government's travel advice for updates), but there is an Iranian sleeper train that runs twice weekly between Van in Eastern Türkiye and Tehran. To get to Van, you'll need to take the high-speed train (4½ hours) from Söğütlüçeşme to Ankara, then transfer to the twice-weekly *Van-gölü Ekspresi* to Tatvan, near Van (26½ hours).

Georgia & Armenia

From the border town of Kars in Türkiye, you can board a bus to Sarpi in Georgia, then continue on to Batumi, where you can take a train to the capital Tbilisi. The border between Türkiye and Armenia is currently closed, so you need to travel to Tbilisi, and then on to Yerevan in Armenia.

Toolkit

First Time
252

Money
253

On the Rails
254

Access, Attitudes & Safety
259

Where to Stay
260

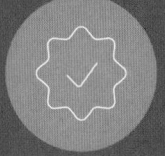
Responsible Travel
262

Language
264

Gare de l'Est
VICKY GOSSELIN/SHUTTERSTOCK

First Time

For more information on starting the journey, see **Paris** (p36) and **İstanbul** (p178).

Time Changes

Travel between Paris and İstanbul takes you across several time zones, from Central European Time (UTC/Greenwich Mean Time +1) and Central European Summer Time (UTC+2) to Eastern European Time (UTC+2) and Türkiye Time (UTC+3). Your rail planner and tickets will show arrival times in the time zone of your destination.

Health Insurance

Citizens of the EU, Switzerland, Iceland, Norway and Liechtenstein receive free or reduced-cost state-provided healthcare in European Economic Area countries, with a European Health insurance card. Australia has reciprocal health care agreements with Italy and Slovenia. In the UK, apply for a Global Health Insurance Card (GHIC).

Visas

The new European Union EU Entry/Exit System (EES) aims to digitise border crossings. Many non-EU citizens travelling to EU and Schengen Zone countries need to apply online for an ETIAS (European Travel Information and Authorisation System) authorisation; UK citizens need an ETIAS from October 2026. For this, you need a passport with at least six months' validity. Stays of longer than three months require a visa. Go to evisa.gov.tr to find out if you need a Turkish visa.

Languages

On many train services, guards and station staff speak several languages, including excellent English. If not, language translation apps are handy. Most fellow travellers in each country visited will welcome your attempts to speak their language; see p264.

Passports

Border police may board trains to do passport checks. There are full border checks when you cross into Romania, Bulgaria and Türkiye. Note that in some countries you are required to carry ID with you at all times. In case of emergencies, make two copies of all travel documents to leave with trusted people, and store documents in the Cloud.

Staying Connected

Most rail services have charging ports, but not all. There is free wi-fi on French, Swiss and Italian Frecciarossa services; otherwise check in advance with your mobile service provider to ensure you have coverage and data. Your digital rail pass will function offline.

Money

Cards & Cash

Generally speaking, you can make card or contactless payments for goods and services. But it's always a good idea to carry some cash: in onboard cafes, for example, card readers don't always function. And smaller traders often welcome cash rather than cards. The euro (€) is the currency in Austria, Bulgaria, Croatia, France, Germany, Italy and Slovenia; Hungary has the forint (Ft), Switzerland uses the Swiss franc (Chf) and Türkiye's currency is the lira (₺).

MONEY-SAVING TIPS

Travel in low season
Prices are more affordable outside of summer (June–August).

Accommodation
Staying in a hostel reduces costs. The cheapest option is a bed in a shared dorm, but you can also find good-value singles and doubles.

Pack a picnic
A picnic lunch from a deli, market or supermarket will cost less – and taste better – than a meal from a train restaurant car.

Concessions

Many museums and attractions offer discounts for young people and seniors, and sometimes also for families. Generally, concession pricing doesn't apply for non-Euro citizens. Look out for city cards in individual locations if you're planning to see more than a couple of attractions. These usually last for 24, 48 or 72 hours, and may include a city map, free transport and reductions at some shops, cafes and restaurants. See citydestinationsalliance.eu/initiatives/City-Cards-Project.

Free Attractions

You'll find excellent free attractions in all the cities featured in this guide. Just for starters, head to Notre Dame Cathedral in Paris (p45), Stavropoleos Church in Bucharest (p140) and the Blue Mosque in İstanbul (p184). Look out for free guided city tours and city walk apps and maps. In public parks you can take time out, people-watch and relax along the way without spending a cent.

HOW MUCH IS
a day on the train?

Interrail pass per day	€28
Daily seat booking	€5-30
Breakfast in a cafe	€10-15
Coffee in the station	€4
Sandwich/lunch on board	€16
Museum entry	€15-20
Drink in the bar	€5
Dinner in a restaurant	€20-40
Hostel bed	€35
Total (per day for two adults)	**€140-195**

Tipping

Across the region, tipping is much less of an expectation than in countries such as the US. If service isn't added to a restaurant bill you may choose to round up the total, or pay up to 15% for great service. For services such as tours or boat trips, tips will be generally welcomed, but are by no means required.

FROM LEFT: ANATOLIY SADOVSKIY/SHUTTERSTOCK, NEW AFRICA/SHUTTERSTOCK

On the Rails

Rail Pass or Individual Tickets?
A rail pass offers you maximum flexibility – select a trip immediately before boarding or plan in advance. But it may not be the most affordable option. On many individual journeys, seat reservations are obligatory and cost extra (€5 to €30). If you have a fixed itinerary, it may be cheaper to buy separate tickets as soon as possible from the different train operators; they advertise how far in advance tickets go on sale.

GOOD TO KNOW

While we aim to give you all the information you need for your Orient Express trip, it is only right to pay homage to the marvellous **Man in Seat 61** *(seat61.com)*. Mark Smith, a former Charing Cross station manager, shares years of European train knowledge and experience. Andy Brabin's *discoverbyrail.com* is also excellent.

Mix It Up
Consider using a combination of rail pass plus individual tickets. The daily rail pass rate is only good value in countries west of Hungary – individual train tickets in Romania, Bulgaria and Türkiye are affordable and it's unlikely you'd save any money over buying individual tickets for each of these countries. That said, if you are not on a tight budget, a rail pass might win out for ease of use and flexibility.

First Class
First class is available for many, though not all, of the trips in this guide. Benefits include more-spacious and less-crowded seating, lounge areas in a few stations, and food and drink on selected services. For example, Frecciarossa in Italy offers a complimentary refreshment and snack to passengers travelling 1st class. Travellers on Eurostar Plus (aka 1st class) get a good light meal delivered to their seats.

HOW TO

DEAL WITH DELAYS

Delays will inevitably be encountered – Germany's Deutsche Bahn is notorious for them. Rail passes make it easy to rebook services, and as long as you are within one of your planned travel days, you won't pay extra. Delays are all part of the experience and can make for a more memorable journey.

HOW TO: USE YOUR RAIL PASS

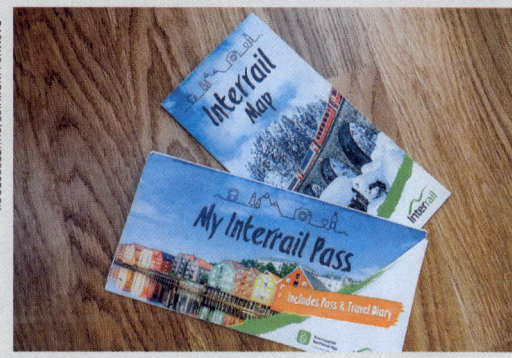

The rail pass system initially feels opaque, but once you're in the swing you'll be booking journeys like a pro.

Global rail passes allow travel across 33 European countries, and Türkiye. There are two main types of rail pass: **Interrail** *(interrail.eu)* are for European residents (including UK citizens), and **Eurail** *(eurail.com)* passes are for non-Europeans. Within these categories you can buy a flexi pass, which allows a certain number of days' travel within a given time frame, or a continuous pass, for anything between 15 days and three months of continuous journeys. There are discounts for young people and seniors.

You can buy your pass and make reservations without activating it, but you cannot travel until the pass is activated.

Your pass works in conjunction with the Rail Planner app (see right). Frustratingly, the Rail Planner app does not display all available journeys. You can add journeys manually, using the station names and relevant departure and arrival times. For a comprehensive list of trains, see **Deutsche Bahn** *(int.bahn.de/en)* or buy the print **European Rail Timetable** *(europeanrailtimetable.eu)*. *Europe by Rail* is a useful book and the website has a guide to supplementary charges *(europebyrail.eu/europe-rail-pass-supplements-and-seat-reservation-fees)*.

Be aware that conductors regularly check passes during travel, not just when you are boarding.

Seat Reservations

For journeys requiring seat reservations, Rail Planner gives you the option of booking through travel companies such as Rail Europe or Trainline, or through the relevant rail company; the latter is recommended. You'll be emailed a ticket with a QR code. You can also make reservations in person at ticket offices. For long journeys where seat reservations aren't required, consider making a booking to ensure a seat, especially at busy times. If you can't get a seat reservation for a given service, inform the train manager. You can almost always board, but you may have to stand or sit in the buffet car.

RAIL PLANNER APP

Download the Rail Planner app and add your pass, using the pass number. The app allows you to browse journeys and to make seat reservations. While not all journeys require seat reservations, you do have to add all journeys to the Rail Planner app, which generates a QR code, without which your journey is not valid.

Travellers board the Eurostar in London

RAIL TOUR AGENCIES

For help with routes and bookings, and for expert advice on all aspects of the railways, consider using a dedicated train travel agency. These include **By-way Travel** (byway.travel), **Tailor Made Rail** (tailormaderail.com), **Original Travel** (originaltravel.co.uk) and **International Rail** (internationalrail.com.au). Agencies can assist with combined train and ferry ticketing and timetables, which can be fiddly.

LEAVING OR ARRIVING IN THE UK

UK citizens can use Interrail passes for one outward and one inward journey, which can have multiple transfers but must take one day only. Book the Eurostar from London to Paris at a special discounted rate (standard/Plus €35/40) once you have your pass. These discounted tickets sell out quickly, so book well in advance.

Booking Ahead

You can do all your planning and booking in advance, but there is no need – staying flexible will make your journey more relaxing and enjoyable. Some national carrier websites do not allow you to book international tickets online, including Croatia, Slovenia, Türkiye and Bulgaria. To book the Sofia to İstanbul ticket, you'll need to front up to an actual booking office in Bulgaria – if travelling from west to east, the first one you will come to will be in Ruse (p148). Alternatively, you can book via an intermediary such as **Discover By Rail** (discoverbyrail.com) and pay a premium.

Changing Your Bookings

If you are using a rail pass and decide to change your journey time, you can simply add the new journey in the Rail Planner app. If you have already made and paid for a seat reservation, you will not get a refund unless the rail carrier has cancelled the journey. If this is the case, contact the carrier or ask at the station ticket office. If passengers need to change a non-rail-pass booking – and this is allowable according to the conditions under which it was purchased – seat selection may not be possible on the new ticket.

Eating on Board

Some but not all train services offer decent food on board, and often the on-train bar-cafe has large windows and can be a convivial place to meet fellow passengers. Our favourites include France's SNCF and the Hungarian service from Bratislava, and the menu on ÖBB's Railjet trains is impressive, catering well to vegans and vegetarians. If the train is full and you haven't got a seat, the restaurant car can be a handy refuge. Also head here if fellow passengers at your seat have the blinds down and you'd prefer to see the passing panorama.

On all trains you can bring your own food and drink, though there are some restrictions regarding BYO alcohol, so check this with individual train operators. Most city stations have good places where you can pick up food: just make sure that there is time in your schedule to do so comfortably.

FROM LEFT: AXSTOKES/SHUTTERSTOCK, SIMON RICHMOND/LONELY PLANET

Sleeper train carriage, Budapest to Stuttgart

Luggage Storage & Bikes

Throughout this book we say if a station has luggage-storage options and where to find them. If station storage is not available, download an app such as **Stasher** *(stasher.com)* to find nearby safe storage. It's almost always possible to take your bike on a given service, for a small fee. Check individual carriers' websites before you travel, and book in advance.

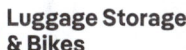

HOW TO: SLEEP ON THE TRAIN

In the spirit of the Orient Express, an authentic way to travel the routes is in a sleeper car or couchette. Sleeper cars are the most expensive and comfortable option, with private sitting areas that convert into bedrooms, usually with a sink. In couchettes, bunk beds in four- or six-person compartments are folded down at night. Austrian Railways (ÖBB) has sleeper trains linking Austria, Switzerland and Italy, while Hungarian Railways' EuroNight sleeper links both Munich and Zürich with Budapest.

The obvious downside is that you miss the views, but the upside is that you can have more time in your destination, and can (hopefully) enjoy the sensation of being rocked to sleep on the train. You may also save money on a night's accommodation, particularly if you opt for a seat rather than a pricier couchette or berth.

Another perk for travelling overnight is that rail pass days normally run from midnight to midnight. But if you board a sleeper before midnight, you only use up one day of your pass, regardless of how late in the subsequent day the service arrives. If you then board another train, you'll use up a second day of your rail pass.

PACKING PROBLEM-BUSTER

What are the train travel essentials? Aside from the obvious – passport plus phone loaded up with your tickets and/or Rail Planner app – bring a water bottle to stay hydrated and headphones to listen to podcasts, music or books en route. Tupperware is also handy for storing picnic items for a long train journey.

What about clothes? While the liveried Orient Express service may have you dressing for dinner, on the DIY version you can wear whatever you want. It's best to travel light when hopping on and off trains, so bring a small container of laundry liquid and wash clothes as you go. Bring a warm scarf or jumper for cool evenings, and a rain jacket.

How do I stay connected? Make sure you have a phone charger, adapter and a portable charger. If you are using a rail pass, your phone is also your ticket, and you need to keep it charged.

What should I bring for dorm stays? All hostels provide bedding and you can rent a towel. To save money bring a small microfibre towel. Earplugs will probably come in handy, and at some hostels you need a padlock to secure your belongings in their lockers.

Anything else? You may want to bring a camera, a Swiss army knife for picnics and bottle opening, cutlery, a keep cup and a small medical kit. And this book of course…

Access, Attitudes & Safety

Accessible Travel

Travellers with disabilities can request free assistance with getting on and off trains: check with individual train companies before you travel, and book assistance in advance. You can book a wheelchair space, and can also apply online for a complimentary caregiver's pass if you are travelling with a Eurail or Interrail pass. When planning your train travel, ensure there is enough time between trains for a comfortable transfer. If you're planning to travel with a guide dog, bring a certificate or registration. Train companies should let service dogs travel for free, but it's best to check first with individual carriers.

Women & Solo Travellers

Women and people travelling alone are not likely to encounter particular issues, but you may prefer to connect with other travellers for safety: youth hostels (which aren't exclusively for youths) are a good place to do this. If you are arriving late or early in a destination, be sure you know your onward route in advance and can confidently find your way. If you encounter any issues on particular trains, get the attention of the train guard and don't be afraid to ask for their assistance.

Family Travel

You & are likely to encounter plenty of other families travelling by train in Europe, and your kids will probably be the ultimate icebreaker. Two kids under 11 can travel for free with one adult holding a Eurail/Interrail pass; the adult does not have to be a family member. If more than two kids are travelling with one adult, additional children need a youth pass. There are also youth discounts on train passes for those aged between 12 and 27. Museums and other sights offer discounts for kids. Hostel family rooms are often the most affordable – and sociable – accommodation option.

BORDERS & RACISM

It's a sad fact that, in the current climate, people of colour are likely to be racially profiled as suspected 'illegal' immigrants. This means that your passport is far more likely to be checked at border crossings than those of white fellow travellers. Off the trains, carry ID to deflect unwanted attention from the police.

LGBTiQ+ Travellers

Most of the cities covered in this guide are progressive and open-armed places, and LGBTQI+ travellers should not encounter problems. But prejudice and discrimination do exist, and attempts by, for example, the Turkish and Hungarian governments to limit the freedoms of LGBTQI+ citizens have been retrogressive – and countered with huge resistance. In each town and city along these routes you can connect with venues, accommodation, Pride events, and support and social groups geared towards LGBTQI+ communities. For an overview of the situation on LGBTQI+ issues see the **Rainbow Map** *(rainbowmap.ilga-europe.org)*.

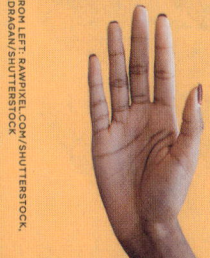

FROM LEFT: RAWPIXEL.COM/SHUTTERSTOCK, ADRAGAN/SHUTTERSTOCK

Where to Stay

HOW MUCH FOR A...

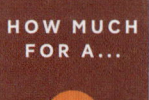

Hostel dorm bed
€35

Hostel single room €90

Hotel single room from €130

Hostels

Hostels are sociable places to stay and are the best option if you'd like to meet fellow travellers. You can stay in single-sex or mixed-sex dorms, usually with between four and 12 beds. If you opt for a single or double room in a hostel, you can enjoy the communal spaces as well as a good night's sleep. A simple breakfast is usually provided, and most hostels have game rooms and regular events.

Hostelling International *(hihostels. com)* membership is affordable and gives you discounts on accommodation and some services.

Hotels

All the locations on this route offer excellent hotel accommodation. Throughout this guide we have made suggestions for our favourite places to stay, including hotels across a range of budgets. These recommended places will set you up for a day's travel with a comfy bed and a good breakfast. Most hotels will store your luggage if you arrive before check-in time.

Camping

Camping is one of the most affordable accommodation options, and is a nature-friendly and low-impact way to stay. If you plan to bring camping gear with you, ensure it's as compact and light as possible for ease getting on and off trains. Staying in a pre-erected tent is also an option, as is glamping – spending the night in a spacious yurt or similar. If choosing the latter, everything, including bedding, is included.

HOW TO: SHARE A DORM

Find out if you have been assigned a particular bed to avoid being woken up by a roommate if you're in their spot. If you're heading out for the evening, have your toothbrush and nightwear ready to avoid late-night rustling for your stuff. Set your alarm to vibrate to avoid disturbing folk. And to sleep when those around you snore...wear earplugs!

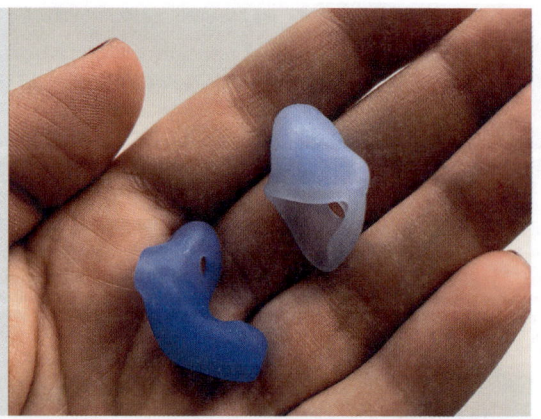

Sleeper train carriage, İstanbul to Bucharest

NIGHT TRAINS

Time was budget travellers would travel by night train, arriving early in the morning and snoozing off a long night in the station. Night-time services, having been drastically curtailed, are making a comeback. You can sleep in an upright seat and maximise on daytime adventures at your location. See p257 for more on sleeping on trains.

THE AIRBNB EFFECT

Airbnb may have revolutionised the travel market and made the search for accommodation more flexible, but the impact on local communities has been severe, reducing rental opportunities and pushing up prices. If you use Airbnb, think about renting a room in a home rather than a whole property. Or stay in a local registered B&B.

Reservations

Trains get cancelled, schedules change and suddenly your carefully planned itinerary starts to slip. It's almost inevitable if you're on the rails for a few days that things won't go entirely as planned. In high summer, though, you may struggle to find decent accommodation if you don't book in advance. So we recommend making reservations and communicating with your hotel, B&B or hostel if things change, as they may agree to alter your booking. Out of high season, it's much easier to make up an itinerary as you go, spending extra days in places that take your fancy or speeding up as the mood takes you.

Historic Accommodation

As you travel across the regions covered in this guide you'll find some richly characterful and historic places to stay. Amongst our favourites are the wonderfully wonky Hotel Schiefes Haus in Ulm (p59); the sumptuous Beau Rivage in Lausanne (p200), built to accommodate passengers on the Orient Express; Basel Youth Hostel (p239), located in a funkily converted silk ribbon factory; and Villa Flavia Boutique Hotel in Plovdiv (p174), which encompasses the ruins of a Roman bath.

Responsible Travel

Climate Change & Travel

It's impossible to ignore the impact we have when travelling; Lonely Planet urges all travellers to engage with their travel carbon footprint, which will mainly come from air travel. Travelling by train and choosing to follow in the footsteps of the Orient Express already goes a long way toward reducing your carbon footprint. In addition to being a safe, convenient and comfortable way to explore Europe, train travel is one of the most sustainable forms of travel. To further 'green' your adventures, travel slowly, tread lightly and when disembarking to explore a stop en route, consider travelling by foot, bike or local transport.

HYDRATION

Bring a water bottle – or even two – on your journey. These are essential on hot summer days. Refill at drinking water fountains or station cafes, and avoid adding to plastic waste in your destination.

The **UN Carbon Offset Calculator** shows how flying impacts a household's emissions.

The **ICAO's carbon emissions calculator** allows visitors to analyse the CO2 generated by point-to-point journeys.

Independent Historic Accommodation

Historic luxury hotels are part of the the rich Orient Express story and aren't always owned by multinationals. Reduce your impact by not having towels washed daily.

ON TRAINS

You are sure to encounter a range of people on your journey, and these interactions might end up being even more memorable than the incredible views the Orient Express offers. As well as tourists, you are likely to be sitting alongside weary commuters and seasonal workers. So while you might enjoy putting your unwashed feet up or slinging your rucksack into the neighbouring seat, be respectful.

Seating carriage, Bulgaria

SIMON RICHMOND/LONELY PLANET

FROM LEFT: FAIRBNB.COOP; MEDIA LENS KING/SHUTTERSTOCK

TOOLKIT RESPONSIBLE TRAVEL

Learn More

Using this guide you will cross a lot of borders. We've crammed as much history and culture as we could into these pages, and we've also listed some of the best experiences to help you connect, from eating farm-to-fork food in local cafes to learning more about a place in the city museum. Historically, the Orient Express was an instrument of colonial travel (see 'Europe's Imagined East', p130). But by learning a few phrases of the local language (p264), staying open and communicating with people, you can help to write a different story.

Overtourism in Venice

Of all the cities en route, it is Venice that suffers the most from overtourism, with visitor numbers vastly outweighing the resident population. There are ways to reduce your impact, though: consider a stay with **Fairbnb** *(fairbnb.coop)*, which contributes to community projects, eat at some of the city's excellent Slow Food restaurants and buy handmade local crafts rather than tourist trinkets. Even in the centre of Venice, you can take a turn up a quiet canal path and find yourself quite alone. You'll discover art treasures and marvellous architecture wherever you go, not just in the visitor hotspots.

HOW TO

HAVE A POSITIVE IMPACT ON THE ORIENT EXPRESS ROUTES

Stay local Avoid bland chain hotels and big-name accommodation booking services that impact negatively on local rental markets, and opt instead for characterful hotels, B&Bs with the personal touch, welcoming hostels and ecofriendly campsites.

Shop local Visiting neighbourhood groceries and markets to buy regional specialities and farm-to-fork food will enrich your trip and benefit small producers, whilst satisfyingly cutting out the middleman. Crafts made locally make the most special souvenirs and gifts.

Eat local Family-owned restaurants and cafes often offer a level of quality and care lacking in larger establishments. And you'll be benefitting the local economy too. Ask your waiter's advice about the local food specialities.

Speak local Try to speak some different languages on your trip. A few phrases listed on p264 will get you going, or dust off your school French or German lessons. Attempts to speak the language in any of your destinations will almost always be met with warmth, and you just might make a breakthrough that inspires further learning.

Listen local Ask around about music venues and support local musicians and establishments by attending and buying a drink or two.

Language

This chapter offers basic vocabulary to help you make your way along the Orient Express routes. Read our pronunciation guides as if they were English and you'll be understood. The stressed syllables are indicated with italics.

English	Bulgarian Note that uh is pronounced as the 'a' in 'ago' and zh as the 's' in 'pleasure'.	Croatian Note that r is rolled and that zh is pronounced as the 's' in 'pleasure'.	French French is spoken in France and Switzerland. Syllables in French words are, for the most part, equally stressed.
Hello	zdra·*vey*·te	*zdra*·vo	bon·zhoor
Goodbye	do·*veezh*·da·ne	*zbo*·gom	o·rer·vwa
Excuse me	iz·vee·*ne*·te	o·*pro*·sti·te	ek·skew·zay·mwa
Please/Thank you	*mol*·ya/bla·go·dar·*ya*	mo·lim/*hva*·la	seel voo play/mair·see
Yes/No	da/ne	da/ne	wee/non
Train	*vla*·kuht	voz	ler trun
Ticket	bee·*let*	*kar*·too	bee·yay
1st class	*purh*·vo·kla·sen	pr·vaw·*raz*·red·noo	der prem·yair klas
2nd class	*vto*·ro·kla·sen	*droo*·gaw·*raz* red noo	der se·gond klas
One way	ed·no·po·*so*·chen	*yed*·no·smyer·nu	sum·pler
Return	dvoo·po·*so*·chen	*paw*·vrat·noo	a·lay ay rer·toor
Does it stop at	*spee*·ra lee v	da lee *stai*·e oo	es·ker se trun sa·ret a
Help	*po*·mosht	*u*·po·moch	o skoor
Cheers!	na·*zdra*·ve	*zhi*·vye·li	son·tay

German	Hungarian	Italian	Romanian
The language of Germany, Austria and Liechtenstein also has official status, and is spoken in, Switzerland. Note that r is a throaty sound.	Note that aw is pronounced as in 'law', ew as 'ee' with rounded lips, and zh as the 's' in 'pleasure'. Keep in mind the r is rolled in Hungarian.	The language of Italy also has official status – and is spoken – in Switzerland. Note that r is rolled and stronger than in English.	Note that ew is pronounced as 'ee' with rounded lips, oh as the 'o' in 'note', ow as in 'how', uh as the 'a' in 'ago' and zh as the 's' in 'pleasure'.
goo·ten taak	*ser*·vus	bwon·*jor*·no	*boo*·nuh zee·wa
owf *vee*·der·zey·en	vis·lat	a·ree·ve·*der*·chee	la re·ve·*de*·re
ent·*shul*·di·gung	el·ney·zeysht *key*·rek	mee *skoo*·zee	skoo·*za*·tsee·muh
bi·te/*dang*·ke	*key*·rem/*keu*·seu·neum	per fa·*vo*·re/*gra*·tsye	vuh rog/mool·tsoo·*mesk*
yaa/nain	*i*·gen/nem	see/no	da/noo
tsook	*vaw*·not	tre·no	*tre* nool
fahr·kar·te	yej	bee·*lye*	bee·*let*
ers·ter *kla*·se	el·shēū aws·taa·yū	dee *pree*·ma kla·se	
tsvai·ter *kla*·se	*maa*·shawd·aws·taa·yū	dee se·*kon*·da *kla*·se	
ain·fa·khe	chok *aw*·do	dee so·la an·da·ta	doos
rük	*aw*·do·*vis*·so	dee an·*da*·ta e ree·*tor*·no	doos ewn·*tors*
helt es in	*meg*·aall	*kwe*·sto *tre*·no see *fer*·ma a	o·*presh*·te la
hil·fe	she·geet·sheyg	ai·*yoo*·to	a·zhoo·*tor*
prawst	e·geys·shey·ged·re	a·*loo*·te	no·rok

English	Slovak In Slovak, stress always falls on the first syllable, but it's quite light.	Slovene Note that uh is pronounced as the 'a' in 'ago', oh as the 'o' in 'note', ow as in 'how', zh as the 's' in 'pleasure', r is rolled and the apostrophe (') indicates a slight y sound.	Turkish The Turkish r is always rolled and v is pronounced a little softer than in English.
Hello	*do*·bree dyen'	*zdra*·vo	*mer*·ha·ba
Goodbye	do *vi*·dye·ni·yuh	na *svee*·den·ye	hosh·*cha*·kal
Excuse me	*pre*·pach·tye	do·vo·*lee*·te	ba·*kar* muh·suh·*nuhz*
Please/Thank you	*pro*·seem/*dyuh*·ku·yem	*pro*·seem/*hva*·la	*lewt*·fen/te·shek·*kewr* e·*de*·reem
Yes/No	*a*·no/ *ni*·ye	da/ne	e·*vet*/*ha*·yuhr
Train	vluhk	vlak	tren
Ticket	*lees*·tok	vo·*zov*·nee·tso	bee·*let*
1st class			bee·reen·*jee* mev·*kee*
2nd class			ee·keen·*jee* mev·*kee*
One way	*yed*·no·smer·nee	e·no·*smer*·no	gee·*deesh*
Return	*spyuh*·toch·nee	pov·*rat*·no	gee·deesh·der·*newsh*
Does it stop at	*sto*·yee to nuh	*a*·lee oos·*ta*·vee v	doo·*roor* moo
Help	*po*·mots	na po·*moch*	*eem*·dat
Cheers!	*nuhz*·druh·vi·ye	na *zdrav*·ye	she·re·*fe*

Index

Journey legs 000
Map pages 000

0km marker, Gare de l'Est 4, 50

accessible travel 259
accommodation 260-1, 263, *see also individual destinations*
Accor 243
activities, *see* cycling, hiking, skiing, swimming, thermal baths
Adriatic Sea 14-15
Ahmet I 184
Airbnb 261
airports 36, 178, 246
Alba Iulia 119, 122, 126
Aleppo 188-9
Alps, the 12-14
ancient Roman sites 23-4
  amphitheatre, Plovdiv 11, 23, 170
  amphitheatre, Verona 201
  Bishop's Basilica of Philippopolis, Plovdiv 171
  Les Arènes de Lutèce, Paris 44
  Roman Thermae, Varna 151
  Serdica, Sofia 161
  stone bridge, Borushtenska river 157
Anghel Saligny Bridge 146, 147
aperitivos 203
apps 255
Apuseni Mountains 120, 121
Arad 118
architecture 22-5
  art deco 36, 40, 86, 141, 201
  art nouveau 52, 53, 66, 84, 88, 91, 99, 113, 120, 129, 137, 140-1, 168, 233
  baroque 23, 66, 67, 80, 81, 88, 89, 90, 91, 96, 98, 99, 104, 122, 148, 236, 237
  belle époque 137, 139, 140-1, 196, 197, 198, 200
  Byzantine 140, 152, 161, 170, 183
  communist 99, 148, 153, 157, 168-9
  Gothic 23, 45, 51, 57, 58, 80, 88, 99, 111, 119, 120, 125, 198, 202, 224, 230
  Gothic revival 128, 140
  Moorish 23, 111, 128, 187, 233
  Ottoman 24, 147, 173, 182, 184, 186, 187
  Venetian Gothic 211, 212

Arlberg route 8, 14, 30, 226-39, **228-9**
  accommodation 236, 239
  food 231
  highlights 228-9
  route 228-9
  train services 228, 230
Arlberg Tunnel 235
Armenia 249
Attersee 80
Augsburg 55, 59
Austria
  Bludenz 235
  Innsbruck 17, 231, 234, 235, 239
  Linz 80, 231, 235, 238
  Marchegg 96
  Marchfeld 96
  Melk 80
  Salzburg 72, 79, 235, 236-7, 239
  St Anton am Arlberg 235
  St Pölten 81
  Vienna 11, 84-91, 96, 238-9, **86**
  Vöcklabruck 80

B&Bs 261
badi 233, *see also* thermal baths
Balkan Mountains 16
ballet 10, 68
Basel 230-2, 239
Bayerische Regiobahn 74
beer 20, 65, 66, 68, 137, 140, 237
Belgium 247
Bellegarde-sur-Valserine 196-7
Bellini, Giovanni 212
Bellinzona 201
Belmond 241-3
Berchtesgaden 78, 79
Bielersee 200
Black Mountains 231
Bludenz 235
boat trips 15
  Bosphorus, İstanbul 186
  Danube, Bratislava 97
  Grand Canal, Venice 210-11
  Seine, Paris 42
  Zürichsee, Switzerland 233

books 14-15, 60-1, 118, 132, 175, 187, 189, 242
border crossings
  Austria-Slovakia 96
  Bulgaria-Türkiye 169, 172
  Croatia-Hungary 223
  France-Germany 54
  France-Switzerland 197-8, 231
  Germany-Austria 78-9
  Hungary-Romania 118
  Italy-Slovenia 219
  Liechtenstein-Austria 235
  passports 252
  racial profiling 259
  Romania-Bulgaria 147
  Slovakia-Hungary 103
  Slovenia-Croatia 223
  Switzerland-Italy 201
  Switzerland-Liechtenstein 235
  Türkiye-Syria 189
Bosphorus 186
Bourg-en-Bresse 196
Braşov 122-3, 124-5, 126, **124**
Bratislava 15, 96, 97, 98-9, 100, 101, **98**
Brescia 201
breweries 68, 137, 140, 237
Brussels 247
Bucharest 127, 134-41, 146, **136**
  accommodation 137
  architecture 139, 140-1
  cafes 141
  costs 134
  entertainment 138, 139
  food 21, 134, 137, 141
  itineraries 136
  shopping 139
  sights 138, 139, 140, 141
  train station 127, 134, 146
  transport 134
Bucharest to Sofia 142-57, **144-5**, *see also* Bucharest, Classic route, Sofia
  accommodation 149, 154
  food 147, 151, 155
  highlights 144-5
  route 144-5
  train services 144, 146

Buchs 232
Budapest 11, 96, 105, 106-13, 118, 225, **108**
  accommodation 109
  architecture 24
  Budapest-Déli train station 225
  Budapest-Keleti train station 96, 105, 106, 118
  Budapest-Nyugati train station 105
  churches 110, 111
  costs 106
  culture 111
  food 21, 106, 109
  itineraries 108
  museums 110
  pálinka 109
  sights 110, 111
  synagogues 111
  thermal baths 112-13
  transport 106
Budapest to Braşov, via Oradea 120-1, **121**
Budapest to Bucharest 114-29, **116-17**, *see also* Bucharest, Budapest, Classic route
  food 119
  highlights 116-17
  route 116-17
  train services 116, 118
budgeting 253
Bulgaria
  Dimitrovgrad 168-9
  food 18
  Gorna Oryahovitsa 149, 156
  Graf Ignatievo 157
  Hitrino 156
  Kaspichan 156
  Kostenets 168
  language 264
  Pleven 152-3
  Plovdiv 11, 157, 168, 169, 170-1, 174, **170**
  Provadiya 156
  Ruse 147, 148, 149
  Sofia 153, 158-61, **159**
  Svilengrad 169, 172
  Varna 17, 147, 149, 150-1, 156-7, **150**
  Veliko Tărnovo 147, 149, 152, 154-5, 156, **154**
  Yavorovets 157

Journey legs 000
Map pages **000**

Bulgarian Railways 146
Buşteni 123, 126

cafe culture 43, 88, 141, 185, 212, 220
camping 260
carbon offset calculators 262
Carol I of Romania 128-9, 140
Carpathian Mountains 16, 121, 122-3
cash 253
castles & palaces 23
  Alba Carolina Citadel, Alba Iulia 122
  Bran Castle, Romania 125
  Bratislava Castle, Bratislava 99
  Cantacuzino Castle, Buşteni 123
  Corvin Castle, Deva 119
  Devín Castle, Bratislava 100
  Festung Hohensalzburg, Salzberg 236
  Herrenchiemsee, Chiemsee 76-7
  Hofburg Palace, Vienna 89
  Ljubljanski grad, Ljubljana 221
  Moskovits Palace, Oradea 120
  Palazzo Ducale, Venice 212
  Palazzo Reale, Milan 202
  Peleş Castle, Sinaia 128-9
  Pelişor Castle, Sinaia 129
  Predjama Castle, Postojna 221
  Residenz, Munich 67
  Royal Palace, Budapest 110
  Schloss Belvedere, Vienna 91
  Schloss Marchegg 96
  Schloss Mirabell, Salzberg 237
  Schloss Nymphenburg, Munich 66
  Schloss Schönbrunn, Vienna 90
  Topkapı Palace, İstanbul 182
  Tsarevets Fortress, Veliko Tărnovo 155
  Visegrád citadel, Visegrád 103
cathedrals, *see* churches & cathedrals
Çerkezköy 175
CFR Călători 116
Champagne houses 50, 52, 53
Charles III 122
Chaumont 230
Chiasso 201
Chiemsee 17, 74, 76-7, 78
children, travel with 259
Christie, Agatha 61, 132, 175, 187, 189, 242
Christmas markets 31, 56

churches & cathedrals 23, *see also individual destinations*
  Basilica di San Marco, Venice 212
  Cappella degli Scrovegni, Padua 204
  Cathédrale Notre Dame, Paris 45
  Cathédrale Notre-Dame, Reims 50
  Cathédrale Notre-Dame, Strasbourg 57
  Chiesa della Madonna dell'Orto, Venice 212
  Esztergom Basilica, Esztergom 24, 102
  Frauenkirche, Munich 69
  Pinacoteca di Brera, Milan 203
  Sinaia Monastery 126-7
  Stephansdom, Vienna 88
  Stift Melk, Melk 80
  Ulmer Münster, Ulm 58
Classic route 8, 14, 15-16, 30, 35, 46-177, **32**, **35**
  Bucharest to Sofia 142-57, **144-5**
  Budapest to Bucharest 114-29, **116-17**
  Munich to Vienna 70-81, **72-3**
  Paris to Munich 46-59, **48-9**
  Sofia to İstanbul 164-77, **166-7**
  Vienna to Budapest 92-105, **94-5**
climate change 262
Cluj-Napoca 120-1
coffee 5, 220, *see also* cafe culture
Cold War 29
communication 264
Como S Giovanni 201
Compagnie Internationale des Wagons-Lits 26-8, 82-3, 189
Constanţa 146
Constantine the Great 161
costs 253, 260, *see also individual destinations*
Croatia
  Koprivnica 223
  language 264
  Zagreb 219, 222, 223, 224
Curtici 118
cycling 36, 52, 56, 236, 257

da Vinci, Leonardo 203
Dachau Memorial Site 66
Danube river 14, 15-16, 55, 70, 80, 91, 92, 96, 98, 101, 103, 108, 146, 148, 238
Danube Bend 31, 94, 101-3, 104
dark tourism 79
delays 254

dervishes 184
Deutsche Bahn 74
Deva 118-19
Devínska Nová Ves 96
Dijon 230
Dimitrovgrad 168-9
disabilities, travellers with 259
discount cards 253
Divača 221
Dobova 223
Dolomite Mountains 201
Dom Pérignon 52
dorms 260
Dover 246
Dracula 125
drinks 20, *see also* beer, champagne houses, coffee, tea, water, wine
Dublin 246

E

Edirne 169, 172-4
Elisabeth of Austria 89
Enescu, George 138, 140
England 246, 256
Épernay 52
equipment 258
Esztergom 24, 102
etiquette 262
Eurail passes 29, 31, 255, 259
EuroCity services 31, 94, 201, 216, 219, 232
Eurostar 36, 246, 247, 254, 256
events, *see* festivals & events

F

Fairbnb 263
family travel 259
festivals & events 8-10
  Art Biennale, İstanbul 183
  Milano Fashion Weeks, Milan 203
  Music Festival, İstanbul 183
  Oktoberfest, Munich 68
  Open Kitchen Food Festival, Ljubljana 221
  Rose Festival, Kazanlâk 157
  Salzburg Festival 72
  Untold, Braşov 120
  Venice Art Biennale, Venice 213
films 10, 237, 238
Fleming, Ian 61
food 18-21
  baklava 181

chicheti 209
Linzer Torte 80, 238
lokum 181
mămăligă 18, 137
on trains 257
schnitzel 20, 87
Weisswurst 20, 65
France 248
  Bellegarde-sur-Valserine 196-7
  Bourg-en-Bresse 196
  Chaumont 230
  Dijon 230
  Épernay 52
  food 18
  language 264
  Metz 51, 54
  Mulhouse 230
  Nancy 52-3
  Paris 11, 36-45, 50, 194, 196, 230, **38**
  Reims 50, 51
  Strasbourg 52-3, 54, 56-7, **56**
  travel to/from France 36
Franz Joseph I of Austria 87
Fraueninsel 77, 78
Freilassing 78-9
funiculars 17, 110, 118, 224, 234
future of train travel 82-3

G

galleries, *see* museums & galleries
Geneva 197-8
George Enescu Philharmonic Orchestra 138
Georgia 249
Germany
  Augsburg 55, 59
  Berchtesgaden 78, 79
  Chiemsee 17, 74, 76-7, 78
  food 18
  Fraueninsel 77, 78
  Freilassing 78-9
  Herreninsel 76-7
  Kehl 54
  language 264
  München Ost 74
  Munich 59, 62-9, 74, **64**
  Prien am Chiemsee 74-5, 76-7
  Rosenheim 74
  Stock 76, 78
  Stuttgart 54-5
  Traunstein 75, 78
  Ulm 51, 55, 58

Giurgiu 147-8
Golden Eagle luxury trains 244-5
Gorna Oryahovitsa 149, 156
Gosset 52
Gotthard Base Tunnel 201
Graf Ignatievo 157
Great Hungarian Plain 118
Greece 248-9
Greene, Graham 60-1
Győr 96

H

Habsburg sites 86, 89, 90, 122, 218
Halkalı 175-6
hamams 187, *see also* thermal baths
Haut-Bugey line 196-7
health insurance 252
Herrenchiemsee 76-7
Herreninsel 76-7
high-speed trains 83, 194, 248
hiking
  Apuseni Mountains 121
  Berchtesgaden National Park 79
  Innsbruck 234
  Mt Vitosha 160
  Predeal 123
  Vienna Woods 91
history 23-4, 44, 45, 61
  1877 Siege 152
  1929 snowstorm 175, 242
  ancient Romans 23-4, 151, 161
  Crusades 131
  luxury train travel 240-1
  Orient Express 26-9, 54, 59, 82-3, 128-9, 134, 147-8, 174
  orientalism 130-3
  Ottoman Empire 172, 182, 184
  Taurus Express 89
  WWII 28-9, 55, 67, 69, 83, 100, 127, 137, 168
Hitler, Adolph 27, 79
Hitrino 156
hostels 260
hotels 10, 260
Houdini, Harry 110, 111
Hungary
  Arad 118
  Budapest 11, 96, 105, 106-13, 118, 225, **108**
  food 18
  Győr 96
  language 264

Hungary continued
  Lőkösháza 118
  Nagymaros 103
  Püspökladány 120
  Siófok 225
  Štúrovo 101, 102
  Szentendre 104
  Szob 103
  Szolnok 118
  Tatabánya 96
  Vác 104
  Visegrád 103

Illy 220-1
Inn (river) 235
Innsbruck 17, 231, 234, 235, 239
insurance 252
internet access 252
Interrail passes 29, 31, 255, 259
Iran 249
Ireland 246
İstanbul 11, 15, 175-7, 178-87, **180**
  accommodation 181
  architecture 24, 183, 187
  bazaars 185
  Bosphorus cruises 186
  cafes 185
  costs 178
  entertainment 184
  festivals 183
  food 21, 181, 187
  Halkalı train station 175-6
  hamams 187
  itineraries 180
  Kazlıçeşme train station 177
  mosques 183, 184
  palaces 182, 187
  shopping 185, 187
  sights 177, 183, 184
  Sirkeci train station 29, 177
  Söğütlüçeşme train station 189
  transport 176-7, 178, 189
  travel to/from 178
Italian lake district 201
Italy 248
  Brescia 201
  Como S Giovanni 201

language 264
Milan 197, 201, 202-3, **202**
Monfalcone 218
Padua (Padova) 197, 200, 204
train services 248
Treviso 218
Trieste 218-19, 220, 222
Udine 218
Venice 11, 205, 206-13, **208**, **211**
Verona 201
Vicenza 201, 204
Villa Opicina 219

Jura Mountains 196-7, 200

Karikó, Katalin 111
Karpe, Eugene 28-9
karsts 15, 221
Kaspichan 156
Kehl 54
Klimt, Gustav 80, 91
Kolodko, Mykhailo 111
Königssee 79
Koprivnica 223
Kostenets 168

La Dolce Vita Orient Express 244
Lac de Nantua 197
Lac Léman 198, 199
Lachen 232
Lake Balaton 15, 96, 225
Lake Garda 201
Lake Küçükçekmece 175
language 252, 264-6
Last Supper, the 203
Lausanne 198-9, 200
Lavaux Vineyard Terraces 17, 199
Le Train Bleu, Paris 21, 30, 40, 196, 197
LGBTQI+ travellers 259
Liechtenstein 235
Linz 80, 231, 235, 238
Lipizzaners 89
Ljubljana 219, 221, 222
Lőkösháza 118
London 246, 256
Louvre, Paris 41
Ludwig I of Bavaria 67
Ludwig II of Bavaria 77
Lugano 201

luggage storage 257
luxury train services 240-5
LVMH 241, 243, 244

Maison Ruinart 50
Man in Seat 61 254
Marchegg 96
Marchfeld 96
Maria Theresa 90
Marie of Romania 125, 128-9
marionettes 237
markets 20, 31, 56
  Grand Bazaar, İstanbul 185
  Le Marché des Enfants Rouges, Paris 43
  Marché Couvert, Metz 20, 51
  Odprta Kuhna Food Festival, Ljubljana 20
  Spice Bazaar, İstanbul 185
  Tržnica Dolac, Zagreb 224
  Viktualienmarkt, Munich 20, 65
Marmara region 175
MÁV 96, 105, 118, 223
Mediaş 122
Mehmet the Conqueror 184, 185
Melk 80
Metz 51, 54
Milan 197, 201, 202-3, **202**
Moët & Chandon 52
Monet, Claude 40
money 253
Monfalcone 218
mosques
  Aya Sofya, İstanbul 183
  Banya Bashi Mosque, Sofia 133, 159
  Beyazıt II Mosque, İstanbul 184
  Blue Mosque, İstanbul 24, 184
  Eyüp Sultan Mosque, İstanbul 184
  Fatih Mosque, İstanbul 184
  Selimiye Mosque, Edirne 173
  Süleymaniye, İstanbul 184
  Sultan Beyazıt II Mosque Complex, Edirne 172
  Sultanahmet Camii, İstanbul 184
Mozart, Wolfgang 237
Mt Vitosha 160
Mulhouse 230
mummies 104
Munich 59, 62-9, 74, **64**
  accommodation 65
  breweries & beer gardens 68

churches 66, 69
costs 62
entertainment 68
festivals 68
food 65
gardens 66
itineraries 64
markets 65
München Hauptbahnhof train station 59, 62, 74
museums 68
palaces 66, 67
sights 66, 69
transport 62
vegetarian & vegan travellers 64, 65
Munich to Vienna 70-81, **72-3**, *see also* Classic route, Munich, Vienna
  accommodation 78
  food 75
  highlights 72-3
  route 72-3
  train services 72, 74
museums & galleries, *see also individual destinations*
  Cité du Train, Mulhouse 230
  Danubiana Meulensteen Art Museum, Čunovo 100
  Deutsches Museum – Verkehrszentrum, Munich 68
  Edirne Turkish & Islamic Art Museum, Edirne 173
  Gallerie dell'Accademia, Venice 213
  İstanbul Modern, İstanbul 187
  Kunsthistorisches Museum, Vienna 88
  Lokwelt Freilassing 78-9
  Musee du Louvre, Paris 41
  Museum of Broken Relationships, Zagreb 224
  National Museum of Transport and Communications, Ruse 148
  Peggy Guggenheim Collection, Venice 211, 213

Nagelmackers, Georges 26-8, 82-3, 240
Nagymaros 103
Nancy 52-3
Napoléon Bonaparte 39, 90
national & nature parks
  Apuseni Nature Park, Romania 121
  Berchtesgaden National Park, Germany 79
  Karwendel Nature Park, Austria 234
  Rila National Park, Bulgaria 168
Neuchâtel 198, 200
night trains 29, 31, 83, 163, 164, 166, 168, 242, 257, 261, *see also* Nightjet services, Sofia-Istanbul Express
Nightjet services 31, 48, 84, 242, 257
Nordkette mountain range 235
Nové Zámky 100
Nox 83

ÖBB 79, 81, 83, 84, 96, 216, *see also* train services
  Nightjet services 31, 48, 84, 242, 257
  Railjet services 74, 84, 228, 232, 235, 238, 257
Oktoberfest 68
opera 8, 10, 68, 86, 108, 138, 183, 201
Oradea 120
orientalism 130-3
Ottoman Empire 24, 131-2, 172, 182, 184
overtourism 263

P&O ferries 246
packing 258
Padua (Padova) 197, 200, 204
palaces, *see* castles & palaces
pálinka 109
Paris 11, 36-45, 50, 194, 196, 230, **38**
  accommodation 39
  cafes 43
  churches 44, 45
  costs 36
  food 21, 39, 40, 43, 196, 197
  Gare de l'Est train station 29, 50
  Gare de Lyon train station 194, 196, 197, 230
  Gare du Nord train station 36, 246
  Gare St-Lazare train station 40
  history 44, 45
  itineraries 38
  jazz clubs 44
  markets 43
  museums 40, 41, 44
  Seine river cruises 42
  shopping 43
  sights 43, 44
  transport 36
  travel to/from Paris 36
  vegetarian & vegan travellers 43
Paris to Munich 46-59, **48-9**, *see also* Classic route, Munich, Paris
  accommodation 55, 59
  food 51, 57
  highlights 48-9
  planning 48-9
  route 48, 50
  train services 48-9
Paris to Strasbourg, via Épernay 52-3, **53**
Paris to Venice 192-205, **194-5**, *see also* Paris, Simplon route, Venice
  accommodation 200, 202
  food 197, 203, 237
  highlights 194-5
  route 194-5
  train services 194, 196, 201
Paris to Vienna 226-39, **228-9**, *see also* Paris, Vienna
  accommodation 236, 239
  food 231
  highlights 228-9
  route 228-9
  train services 228, 230
passports 252
Peleş Castle, Sinaia 128-9
Pelişor Castle, Sinaia 129
Perrier-Jouët 52
pets, travel with 152
Piano, Renzo 187
planning 8-25, 30-1, 252-61
Pleven 152-3
Ploieşti Vest 127
Plovdiv 11, 157, 168, 169, 170-1, 174, **170**
Postojna 221
Postojna Cave Park 221
Prada 203
Prandtauer, Jakob 81
Predeal 123
Prejmer 123
Prien am Chiemsee 74-5, 76-7
Primorski Park 151
Provadiya 156
Pullman, George 26, 240
Püspökladány 120

racial profiling 259
rail passes 254, 255
Rail Planner app 255
Railjet services, *see* ÖBB
Reims 50, 51

reservations 261
Residenz, Munich 67
responsible travel 130-3, 261, 262-3
revival services 240-5
Rhine 54, 232
Roman sites, *see* ancient Roman sites
Romania
  Alba Iulia 119, 122, 126
  Brașov 122-3, 124-5, 126, **124**
  Bucharest 127, 134-41, 146, **136**
  Bușteni 123, 126
  Cluj-Napoca 120-1
  Constanța 146
  Curtici 118
  Deva 118-19
  Giurgiu 147-8
  language 264
  Mediaș 122
  Oradea 120
  Ploiești Vest 127
  Predeal 123
  Prejmer 123
  Sibiu 120-1
  Sighișoara 122
  Sinaia 126-7, 128-9
  Videle 146
  Viscri 122
Romanian Athenaeum 138
Romanian Railways 146
Rosenheim 74
routes 30-1
  Arlberg route 8, 14, 30, 226-39, **228-9**
  Budapest to Brașov, via Oradea 120-1, **121**
  Classic route 8, 14, 15-16, 30, 35, 46-177, **32**, **35**
  Paris to Strasbourg, via Épernay 52-3, **53**
  Ruse to Plovdiv, via Veliko Târnovo 156-7, **157**
  Simplon route 8, 12, 14, 30, 192-225, **194-5**, **216-17**
  Vienna to Budapest, via Győr 96
Rubik's cube 111
Ruse 147, 148, 149
Ruse to Plovdiv, via Veliko Târnovo 156-7, **157**

S

safe travel 259
Said, Edward 131, 132-3
Salzburg 72, 79, 235, 236-7, 239
Sargans 232
Schengen Zone 252
schnitzel 20
seat reservations 79, 255
Seine 42
Selimiye Mosque, Edirne 173
sema 184
Semmelweis, Ignác 111
Sežana 219
Sibiu 120-1
Sighișoara 122
Simplon route 8, 12, 14, 30, 192-225, **194-5**, **216-17**
  books 61
  history 240-1
  Paris to Venice 192-205, **194-5**
  route connections 247-9
  Venice to Budapest 214-25, **216-17**
Simplon Tunnel 29, 198
Simssee 74
Sinaia 126-7, 128-9
Sinan, Mimar 173
Siófok 225
skiing 123
sleeper trains, *see* night trains
sleeping carriages 257
Slovakia
  Bratislava 15, 96, 97, 98-9, 100, 101, **98**
  Devínska Nová Ves 96
  language 266
  Nové Zámky 100
Slovenia
  Divača 221
  Dobova 223
  language 266
  Ljubljana 219, 221, 222
  Postojna 221
  Sežana 219
  Zidani Most 222-3
SNCF 83, 196, 243, 248, 257, *see also* TGV Lyria services
Sofia 153, 158-61, **159**
Sofia–İstanbul Express 146, 162-3, 166, 168, 175, 178
Sofia to İstanbul 164-77, **166-7**, *see also* Classic route, İstanbul, Sofia
  accomodation 174
  food 169, 171
  highlights 166-7
  route 166-7
  train services 146, 162-3, 166, 168, 175, 178
Sound of Music, The 237
spa towns, *see* thermal baths
St Anton am Arlberg 235
St Pölten 81
Stock 76, 78
storks 96-7
Strasbourg 52-3, 54, 56-7, **56**
Štúrovo 101, 102
Stuttgart 54-5
Süleyman I 184
sustainable travel 262-3
Svilengrad 169, 172
swimming 5, 91, 112, 232, 233
Swiss Federal Railways 194, 198, 200, 231, 232
Switzerland
  Basel 230-2, 239
  Bellinzona 201
  Buchs 232
  Chiasso 201
  food 18
  Geneva 197-8
  Lachen 232
  Lausanne 198-9, 200
  Lugano 201
  Neuchâtel 198, 200
  Sargans 232
  Zürich 15, 201, 231, 232-3, 239
synagogues
  Beth Israel Synagogue, Brașov 124
  Edirne Synagogue, Edirne 172
  Great Synagogue, Budapest 24, 111
Széchenyi 113
Szentendre 104
Szob 103
Szolnok 118

T

Taittinger 50
Tatabánya 96
Taurus Express 188-9
Taurus Mountains 189
tea 20, 178, 181
TGV Lyria services 46, 50, 194, 196, 228, 230, 248
thermal baths
  Budapest 11, 12-13
  İstanbul 187

Varna 151
Štúrovo 101
Zürich 233
tickets 254, 255
time zones 252
tipping 253
Topkapı Palace 182
tour agencies 256
train services, *see also* night trains, ÖBB
  Doğu Ekspresi 249
  EuroCity services 31, 94, 201, 216, 219, 232
  Eurostar 36, 246, 247, 254, 256
  Golden Eagle Danube Express 244-5
  La Dolce Vita Orient Express 244
  luxury services 240-5
  Orient Express revival service 243
  Sofia–İstanbul Express 146, 162-3, 166, 168, 175, 178
  TGV Lyria 46, 50, 194, 196, 228, 230, 248
  Toros Express 189
  Transalpin 232
  Vangölü Ekspresi 249
  Venice Simplon-Orient-Express 242-3
Transylvania 119-26
Traunstein 75, 78
travel agents 256
travel seasons 30-1
Travels with My Aunt 60-1
Trenitalia 194, 200, 201, 206, 216, 218, 248
Treviso 218
Trieste 218-19, 220, 222
Türkiye 249
  Çerkezköy 175
  Edirne 169, 172-4
  food 18
  Halkalı 175-6
  İstanbul 11, 15, 175-7, 178-87, **180**
  language 266
  tea 20
  train services 249
  travel to/from 178

U

Udine 218
Ulm 51, 55, 58

V

Vác 104
Valley of the Roses 157
vaporettos 206
Varna 17, 147, 149, 150-1, 156-7, **150**
vegetarian & vegan travellers 18, 257
Veliko Târnovo 147, 149, 152, 154-5, 156, **154**
Venice 11, 205, 206-13, **208**, **211**
  accommodation 209
  architecture 211
  cafes 212
  churches 211, 212
  costs 206
  festivals 213
  food 209, 212
  Grand Canal 210-11, **211**
  itineraries 208
  museums & galleries 210, 211, 213
  overtourism 263
  sights 210, 211, 212
  Stazione Venezia Santa Lucia train station 205, 206, 216, 218
  transport 206
Venice Simplon-Orient-Express revival service 242-3
Venice to Budapest 214-25, **216-17**, *see also* Budapest, Simplon route, Venice
  accommodation 222
  food 219
  highlights 216-17
  route 216-17
  train services 216, 218, 223
Verona 201
Vicenza 201, 204
Videle 146
Vienna 11, 84-91, 96, 238-9, **86**
  accommodation 87
  architecture 23, 91
  churches 88
  coffeehouses 88
  costs 84
  food 21, 84, 87
  gardens 91
  palaces 89, 90, 91
  itineraries 86
  museums 88
  transport 84
  vegetarian & vegan travellers 87

Wien Hauptbahnhof train station 81, 84, 96
Wien Westbahnhof train station 239
wine 91
Vienna to Budapest 92-105, **94-5**, *see also* Budapest, Classic route, Vienna
  accommodation 101, 222
  food 97
  highlights 94-5
  route 94-5
  train services 94, 96
Vienna to Budapest, via Győr 96
Villa Opicina 219
visas 252
Viscri 122
Visegrád 103
Vlad Ţepeş 122, 125
Vöcklabruck 80

W

Wagon-Lit 2419 27
Walensee 17, 232
Wallachia 127
Wallersee 80
water 262
Westbahn 72, 74, 238
wi-fi 252
wine 20, 50, 52, 53, 205
wine regions 91, 196, 199, 205
World Heritage-listed sites
  Castle District, Budapest 110-11
  Citadel, Sighişoara 122
  Grande Île, Strasbourg 56-7
  Lavaux Vineyard Terraces, Switzerland 199
  place Stanislas, Nancy 53
  Prejmer Fortress, Romania 123
  Salzburger Marionettentheater, Salzberg 237
  Selimiye Mosque, Edirne 173
  Stift Melk, Melk 80

Y

Yavorovets 157

Z

Zagreb 219, 222, 223, 224
Zidani Most 222-3
Zürich 15, 201, 231, 232-3, 239
Zürichsee 232, 233

THIS BOOK

Destination Editor
James Smart

Production Editor
Lauren O'Connell

Assisting Editor
Janet Austin

Image Researcher
Norma Brewer

Cartographer
Daniela Machová

Cover Illustration
Charlie Davis

Map Illustration
James Gulliver Hancock

Product Development
Anne Mason, James Smart, Marc Backwell, Katerina Pavkova

Series Development Leadership
Darren O'Connell, Piers Pickard, Chris Zeiher

Thanks
Sofie Anderson, Imogen Bannister, Daniel Bolger, Tom Hall, Sandie Kestell, Alison Killilea, Kellie Langdon, Pia Peterson, Saralinda Turner

All rights reserved. No part of this publication may be copied, stored in a retrieval system, or transmitted in any form by any means, electronic, mechanical, recording or otherwise, except brief extracts for the purpose of review, and no part of this publication may be sold or hired, without the written permission of the publisher. Lonely Planet and the Lonely Planet logo are trademarks of Lonely Planet and are registered in the US Patent and Trademark Office and in other countries. Lonely Planet does not allow its name or logo to be appropriated by commercial establishments, such as retailers, restaurants or hotels. Please let us know of any misuses: lonelyplanet.com/legal/intellectual-property.

Mapping data sources:
©Lonely Planet, ©OpenStreetMap, ©Natural Earth, ©GEBCO, ©Esri, ©NASA Earth Observatory, ©USGS-ASTER and the GIS User Community